REMBRANDT

The Human Form and Spirit

by Jacqueline and Maurice Guillaud

GUILLAUD EDITIONS / PARIS - NEW YORK
CLARKSON N. POTTER, INC. / NEW YORK
DISTRIBUTED BY CROWN PUBLISHERS, INC.

1. **The Slaughtered Ox** (detail of fig. 10)

Cover: Detail of *Isaac and Rebecca* ("The Jewish Bride").
Title page, fig. 1: Detail of *The Slaughtered Ox*.

The publication of Rembrandt's etchings in this volume has been made possible through the cooperation of the Bibliothèque Nationale, in Paris, which made available to us its extraordinary collection of prints, and enabled Gisèle Lambert to make a thorough study of them.

Assistant: Claude Le Cleach.

Translators: Suzanne Boorsch, Esther Eder, Mary Laing, Eleanor Levieux, Danièle Schnall.

Editorial manager: Margot Feely.

Editorial consultants: Mary Laing; Barbara Anderman, Ellen Shultz.

Published in the United States of America by Clarkson N. Potter, Inc., 225 Park Avenue South, New York, New York 10003 and represented in Canada by the Canadian MANDA Group

Published in France by Guillaud Editions, Paris-New York

CLARKSON N. POTTER, POTTER, and colophon are trademarks of Clarkson N. Potter, Inc.

Manufactured in Italy.

Designed by Maurice Guillaud

Library of Congress Cataloging-in-Publication Data
Guillaud, Maurice.
 Rembrandt, the human form and spirit.
 1. Rembrandt Harmenszoon van Rijn, 1606-1669 — Catalogues raisonnés. 2. Human figure in art — Catalogs. 3. Rembrandt Harmenszoon van Rijn, 1606-1669 — Criticism and interpretation. I. Guillaud, Jacqueline. II. Title.
 N6953. R4A4   1986   760'.092'4   86-12386
 ISBN 0-517-56341-X
 10 9 8 7 6 5 4 3 2 1
 First Edition

Notes from the Authors

Chronology and Groupings: As often as possible, we have attempted to present the works in chronological order. However, the need to treat certain subjects or themes has led us to place works together without regard for their dates. For example, a portrait of the artist's father appears with pictures of Biblical old men, figures 590 to 594; *Philemon and Baucis* is grouped with the pilgrims of Emmaus, figures 653 to 655. Similarly, the portraits of the artist's mother, of Saskia, and of Titus are shown in groups so that one can discern the effects of aging in their faces. Using the same rationale, and to complete this approach to Rembrandt's work, we have placed the self-portraits at the end, under the heading "Faces of a Lifetime," page 589.

Titles and References: The titles of the paintings are those adopted by Horst Gerson, *Rembrandt and His Work*, Amsterdam, 1968.
For the drawings, we have elected to use the titles in the catalogue by Otto Benesch, *The Drawings of Rembrandt*, London, 1954-1975.
The titles of the etchings have been taken from the catalogue by Charles Blanc, *Rembrandt's Complete Works*, Paris, 1859-1961.
For all other matters pertaining to the etchings, the catalogue by Christopher White and Karel G. Boon, published in 1969 and which is the most recent work on this subject, serves as a basis for our listings. The data in the chronological catalogue by George Björklund and Osbert H. Barnard, published in 1955, is also noted and is given after the White and Boon references. Where these catalogues differ in their estimations of the number of states of a particular etching, the number given by Björklund and Barnard appears in parentheses following the reference to this catalogue.
These catalogues, which have been gradually corrected and amended, make up the definitive inventory of Rembrandt's work.

Dimensions of the Etchings: The dimensions of the etchings have been taken by measuring the plate marks. The slight differences between the dimensions of the impressions given by the Bibliothèque Nationale's Department of Prints and those given in the White and Boon catalogue are the result of the restoration of the works, their being mounted on paper, and the variations in the paper and the backing. A notation has been made whenever an impression has been trimmed.

Abbreviations: The abbreviations used in the commentaries on the etchings are those used in the catalogues of Rembrandt's etchings (all of which are listed in the Bibliography), and are as follows: G. for Gersaint; B. for Bartsch; Bl. for Blanc; BB for Björklund and Barnard; W.B. for White and Boon. In the captions to the etchings, the page number listed after the title and W.B. number refers to the commentary on that etching.
In the captions to the drawings, Ben. stands for Benesch; the letter A preceding the Benesch number indicates that the work is attributed by the author to Rembrandt.
In the captions to the paintings, G. stands for Gerson.
Reproductions of works are indicated in the Index by numbers in boldface type.

Table of Contents

Unless otherwise noted, all text by Gisèle Lambert, Assistant at the Réserve du Cabinet des Estampes de la Bibliothèque Nationale, Paris

Note.
Thanks to the kindness of Mr. B. Haak, responsible for the "Rembrandt Research Project", we were able to take into account the most recent work of this Commission concerning the authenticity of Rembrandt's paintings, shortly before printing. For this reason we have marked those works eliminated by the Commission as not being authentic with a▲. Those works where some doubt still exists as to their authenticity are marked with▲▲.The publication of the "Rembrandt Research Project" takes all works into account up to 1634. The importance of this new evaluation leads us to suppose that the authenticity of some of Rembrandt's later paintings will also be questioned at a later date.

September 1986

Rembrandt: The Human Form and Spirit

And the circle tightens,
the wives and the son,
the Father and the Mother,
deeply etched on the tablet of his life,
remind us that the vast infinite of the beyond is the
    essence within — and that everything is finally
    the awareness of the Unique,
from which springs what is real in us.
— The others: portraits begun anew of himself
    rediscovered.

Portraits of oneself, endlessly repeated —
(the length of one lifetime)
each one a rendezvous with a stranger,
whom one possesses
through his own gaze in the glass.

We of the twentieth century, although we have felt
    the lightning flash
of a Picasso,
can we ever forget the hundred thousand eyes of
    that other man?
Rembrandt the Man.

But a portrait, then another, then another — this
    wasn't enough to connect him to others;
instead it imprisoned him.

All these worlds contracted
into one,
this nut-like density of human reality.
He needed to give them credibility, an objective
    life: the stories and tales of the Bible
provide the crucible
for dialogues
contained in the greater part of the work,
allowing him to create fiction — reality — to
    connect the life within and the life without.

For in all of this
there is little
faith,
the Biblical imagery is vague, the themes are
    tangled;
what we sense here of the Bible is a shiver of
    intimacy,
the overwhelming warmth generated
by these intermingled beings — men, women or
    children, rather than
prophets, demigods, or heroes.

Episode follows episode,
concentric circles converge on
Jesus The Man.

The persistent scenes reveal, like a leitmotif, the
    disquieting
reality
of a Christ who loves, proposes and suggests,

Some realms — like deep, dark forests of oak — are
    best not penetrated, unless you seek your own
    shadow there.
No spectral visions lurk; only flashes of
recognition,
pools of sunlight in the clearings,
insight upon insight,
awareness upon awareness,
in translucent paint or dense impasto,
in the blur of brush and pen,
in the stroke of the burin, harsh or suspended,
and the trace of the reed pen, sharp or dull.

Stand before a Rembrandt; it is not possible to
    escape its vibration
or elude its grip, unless you believe all otherness is
    in vain,
encounters pointless.

These figures come straight at us,
all these figures, from a Human Comedy where the
    Totality is the Unique.

We know them — recognize them — all these
    common people from the era of mendicants
that followed old wars
— Ah yes, religion —
who offered the bourgeois Rembrandt his favorite
    subjects.

As simple people fill his landscapes,
under Holland's empty sky and flat horizon
    the throngs of Jews, of doctors, of merchants,
    magistrates, and burghers inhabit
    the forty years of his works,
so diverse and contradictory
(as are the moments of a life) and yet so alike.

2. The Prodigal Son in the Tavern, c. 1636
Canvas 161 × 131 cm G. 79 Dresden, Gemäldegalerie

5

who submits and suffers, and who
endures
— So close to us (so unlike The God of Wrath) that
    he becomes familiar,
our equal.

And Rembrandt creates for him a face,
— so often the same one
that it could be
the face of someone close,
of his closest friend (figs. 3, 624 to 628).

Christ's radiance dazzles because he shows
life
as it might be
— ageless and unworn —
the eternal youth
that dwells in the heart of man.

This God
of Hope
with a human face.

In contrast, Rembrandt turns on himself the light of
    lucid reality
in his stupendous series of self-portraits.
where, year by year,
the color darkens, creases plough the skin,
the face collapses. Yet
grows stronger.
The piercing gaze
endures — intensifies —
growing wiser and wiser.

Look on time as it flows through the veins — the
    blood recharged by the full consciousness of
    inexorable change.

So many old men conceived, portrayed, conjured
    up, and remade — the father, always present —
    the shock of old age vibrates throughout the
    work. In counterpoint, images of the mother also
    recur in paintings, drawings, and etchings, at
    every stage along the one-way journey from
    youth to maturity and beyond.

The etching of 1646 (fig. 4), a powerful allegory,
    represents this inevitable progression. Although
    traditionally this work has been treated as a
    sheet of studies (called by some *Studies of Male
    Nudes,* by others *Male Nude, Seated),* its title, as
    corrected, also refers to the old woman and the
    infant. The subject — the ages of man — is one
    that was often taken on by Rembrandt's pre-
    decessors; who could forget the painting by
    Hans Baldung Grien in the Prado (fig. 5)? In Rem-
    brandt's etching the adolescent, standing, con-
    veys an air of confidence; focused in upon
    himself, he is poised for the future. At his feet, a

man is seated; it is the same figure — another
study so to speak — but he is no longer the same.
Energy is coiled within his arm and flows down
his outstretched leg to his exaggerated foot.

Joined by the gesture of their hands, the old
    woman and the infant complete the composi-
    tion. The man of forty has thrust his physical
    presence, his energy, into the foreground, while
    the oldest and the youngest — memories and
    intuition? — are cast, unreal, in the background.

In approximately the same year, two drawings
    (figs. 282, 283) show children and their mothers,
    but here there are no allegories, simply two
    instants of intense vitality, painted from life.

In the first drawing, the child is frightened by an
    overly-friendly dog; his mother tries to reassure
    him, but he puts up his little hands to protect
    himself. Higher up, at the window, another
    figure looks on with amusement. The drawing is
    accomplished with rapid strokes, emphasizing
    the main subject.

The second drawing, more elaborate but equally
    spontaneous, is not an amusing incident, but
    shows sentiments of the mother's love for her
    child. A brown ink wash both emphasizes and
    softens the child's gesture toward the mother.
    But the miracle of the family is captured here in
    this fleeting moment; the mother hurrying
    downstairs, her child in her arms.

In another drawing from the same period — same
    child? same mother? — a naughty child is being
    punished (fig. 280). A group of children and an
    elderly grandmother take part in the scene. Light
    falls harshly on the protagonist, accentuated by
    the contrasting wash on the walls. The child's
    features are distorted with fury; The mother's
    hand grabs at him; he is bare bellied, thrashing
    about in the air.

In *The Abduction of Ganymede,* an eagle carries off
    into the air another grimacing child: Ganymede,
    bare-bottomed, grasped by his shirt (fig. 7).

The bird, his wings calmly extended, seems to
    pose, as if for the camera. Only the child is in
    motion, borne along more out of rebellion than
    by the will of Jupiter. — It's not something else
    that carries you off but yourself, in combat with
    your fate. You pee from fright but you resist! The
    dark browns of the paint, and the clouds as full
    as leafy treetops give the subject reality.
Now the bird
— there are two peacocks —
is dead. Its wings, widespread and upside down,

continued on page 12

3. Christ, c. 1655
Panel 25 × 20 cm G. 323
Berlin-Dahlem, Gemäldegalerie

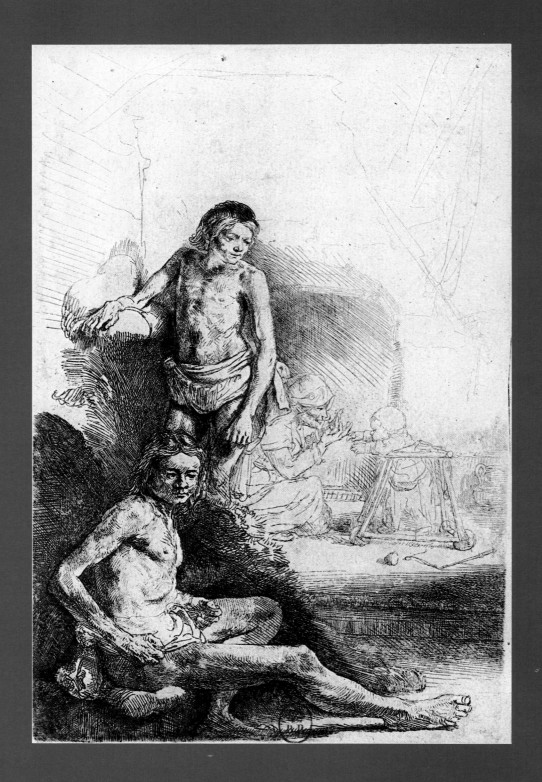

4. Nude Man Seated and Another Standing, with a Woman and Baby
Lightly Etched in the Background, W.B. 194, p. 39

5. The Ages of Life
Hans Baldung Grien
Madrid, Prado

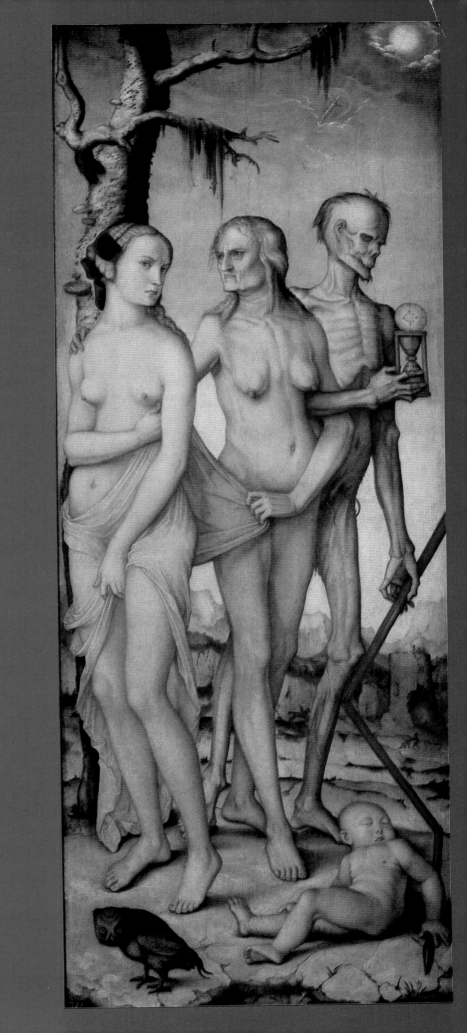

6. The Abduction of Ganymede
Pen and bistre, wash 183 × 160 mm Ben. 92
Dresden, Kupferstichkabinett

7. The Abduction of Ganymede, 1635
Canvas 171 × 130 cm G. 73
Dresden, Gemäldegalerie

continued from page 6

catch the light filtering into the shed; the child is quiet,
contemplating death — the gaping beak of the royal fowl awaiting the master's feast (fig. 8).

And now the painter, still a man of forty or so, invites us to a small and joyous party,
brightly lit,
a festive evening — is every evening so? This prodigal son (fig. 2), long identified as Rembrandt himself, with his wife Saskia, raises his glass to us. With a glance over her shoulder, his companion promises the pleasures of the flesh.
The severe stare of the peacock atop the pie calls instead for a religious feeling.
The artist's signature
is just there above the beak, shut tight with disapproval.
Velvet
billows filling the space;
drapes and clothing, ornate and rich with jewels, dilate the very air; the man
devours his life, with the sensuality of his happiness and ease.

In such circumstances, the most beautiful song of praise to his companion portrays her as the goddess Flora,
as in Leningrad (fig. 340) and London (fig. 341), where light plays on fabric in full sail around a hidden body, horn of plenty wherein unrepressed desire finds satisfaction, and highlights the decorative excess of the subject.
All of life is expressed not in the smooth round faces that quietly wait upon the master's instructions, but in a suspended pose.

Unlike these two large compositions, the little Susanna at her bath, in The Hague (fig. 608) relegates to the shadowy background the luxuriant detail
common to Rembrandt's work of this period,
to focus more clearly on the psychology of the woman surprised in her nudity. Harsh lighting allows the flesh
to stand out against the garments, and the body is offered to us, plump,
faithful to the canons of beauty of a time that knew neither dieting nor body-building.

Less youthful is the skin of his other female companion, Hendrickje, in the National Gallery of Edinburgh (figs. 390, 391, 392). The artist's treatment of his subject, too, is more mature.

Despite the several years that separate these two works, an undiminished interest in the female body is conveyed,

whether nude or richly clothed — in private
or in a stately pose, always
Rembrandt shows his boundless curiosity about woman.

The faces, often, pose an enigma that the conventions of portrait painting cannot explain
— more is suggested by the image,
than a sitter and a state of mind. Everything asks a question about existence.

So acute is the subject's gaze
that we are unsatisfied with the explanation of portraits as "paintings of character".
It is as if Rembrandt wants
to solve the mystery of life itself and explain it at all costs,
even when he paints commissioned portraits (figs. 363, 364).

What is more convincing,
than when the artist paints a person holding his hand out to his interlocutor — to us — (figs. 355, 356, 370) and by merely depicting this gesture.
or this person's gaze
achieves such an intensity that all the dialogues of the possible are inscribed there
— a compression of all discourse, past and future.

Just so, the hand of the speaker
in the *Night Watch* (figs. 373, 374) — what would this gesturing hand signify without the indefinable expression on the face?

With a mouth half open,
and a look that seems to escape the present
— like a bridge stretching beyond the visible
— the central figure is two-in-one: a man who speaks, commands, and moreover escapes from his questioner.
The paradox is made more striking by the noisy milling throng that surrounds
— observes? — these two, and of which they are the focus.
The grandeur of the scene lies in that which is beyond our understanding; the ostensible subject matter (an assembly of Captain Frans Banning Cocq's men) eludes our rational grasp, so much does it leave unexplained.
A relatively recent restoration has rescued this painting from the shadows, reestablishing the contrasts, strong sunlight, deep shadows, on this curiously ordered scene.

Other compositions, group portraits, such as the anatomy lessons (figs. 14 to 16 and 17 to 19), express an otherworldliness that persuades us to consider them symbolic or allegorical works.

8. Child with Dead Peacocks, c. 1637
Canvas 145 × 135.5 cm G. 98
Amsterdam, Rijksmuseum

9. The Carcass of an Ox, c. 1655
Panel 73.5 × 51.7 cm G. 290
Glasgow, Art Gallery and Museum

10. The Slaughtered Ox, 1655
Panel 94 × 67 cm G. 291
Paris, Musée du Louvre

From within the tradition of Dutch painting Rembrandt challenges the whole classical attitude which had constrained the Dutch figurative painters.
He brings us into a realm where the human figure expresses another dimension of existence.

The little sketch of death on horseback in Darmstadt (fig. 35) reminds us that we must keep going, come what may.

The meaty carcass hanging from a crossbar (figs. 1 and 10) arouses the curiosity of the young woman passing by the doorway.
Or is it us she is challenging?
and to what?

The answer may lie in the Glasgow version of the scene (fig. 9).
This time, the woman ignores us, she is at her chores, scrubbing the floor — bloodstained? —
but in the foreground, amid the shapeless mass of hair and hide, the dead eye of the slaughtered animal stares out at us.

A new symbolic approach can shed light on what fascinates us in Rembrandt's art
and frees us
— and this is entirely new in art,
images not for their own sake
but for what we make of them.

We can thus put in a new perspective a great part of this singular artist's work.
One aspect of his genius lay in convincing influential members of society that he was rendering them faithfully, that they could recognize themselves in portraits that in fact already bore the marks of a truly revolutionary concept of painting.

Beginning around 1650, Rembrandt's style took on a greater freedom, became more openly expressed. His portraits are less restricted by the laws of the genre; his compositions are dictated by his subjects, following the deeper intuition of the artist. His strokes become denser; his use of impasto enables him to single out, ever more clearly, what interests him.

Ambiguity is less apparent with each successive painting.

This does not mean that Rembrandt's art becomes simpler.

The tremendous expressiveness in his treatment of the human element forces us to question how he creates in us such emotion.

The portraits of young girls, dating from 1651 (figs. 11, 384, 385), break away completely from the conventions of that time. Even as early as 1645, the fine portrait in the Dulwich College Gallery (fig. 386) announced this break.

And in what way is the 1645 Bathsheba in the Louvre (fig. 610) most expressive?
In her sad look?
in the radiance of her flesh?
— the weight of her belly, the curve of her hip?
— or in the way she abandons her foot to her servant's care?
or in that hand, so much like a Courbet, precisely outlined (like an individual who stands out from the group)?
— or in the old woman's attentive gaze, as a sliver of light catches on her bonnet, below her ear?

The fullness of the work is not conveyed by all of this at once, bathed in a golden hue — and some have spoken of the "bituminous" tones of Rembrandt! —
but is set in motion by two waves,
that of Bathsheba's robes in front,
and that of the costly fabric in the rear, which link the
two figures like an arch stretching to the horizon.

How much bigger is the painting of Hendrickje bathing in the river in the National Gallery, London (fig. 12). All parts of the composition, handled in large areas with heavy, sensitive brushwork, balance each other and resonate together. Here again, the human element takes precedence over the narrative.

But the movement
that fills the cloth and the column — with air? — in the background owes all its structural presence to lingering traces of the baroque.

To this, so coherent, how to connect the flat, precise stillness of the surface of the water
that cuts the calves of the young woman
— a sense of refreshing coolness
— in a reflection that reaches right up to us?

All of the figures from the years 1652 to 1654 produce in us a state of grace.
Using less and less decorative artifice, the painter's mastery is clearly shown.

The large *Nicolaes Bruyningh* in Cassel (fig. 395) creates a mood of tender emotion. The pleats of his collar find correspondence in the waves of his hair, emphasizing the delicacy of his features and his nostalgic regard. This is not only a portrait, but a moment of affecting humanity which moves us by its force and its intimacy.

11. Andromeda Chained to the Rock, 1632-39
Panel 34.5 × 25 cm G. 55
The Hague, Mauritshuis

And the way opens toward the last of Rembrandt's
portrayals where his self-portraits reach their
loftiest heights
and where another manner of painting is revealed
with all the richness of a flawless technique.

What an apotheosis is the end of his life
— from the bearded man in Leningrad to
the snub-nosed portrait in New York (fig. 426)
Or to this one: generous, immediate in its apparent
ease of execution, the *Old Man* in Cowdray Park
(fig. 428), in which face and hands have no
adornment, are deliberately unfinished in their
outline (only in the very white folds of the collar
and its strings has extreme care been taken).
Or yet this one.... but let us stop.
There is so much more to recognize and, above all,
to discover.

Maurice Guillaud

12. Hendrickje Bathing in a Stream, c. 1654-55
Panel 62 × 47 cm G. 289
London, National Gallery

Rembrandt and Symbolic Vision

Allegory and symbol: the two terms are often confused, and indeed, in both cases the meaning involves translating the conceptual into concrete images. That said, allegory and symbol point in totally different and almost opposed directions. In the case of allegory, the intent is to embody precisely conceived ideas in visible and intelligible equivalents: for example, Fortune is blindfolded to show that she is sightless and acts by chance. In the case of symbol, the message comes from the senses, is not thought out, not elucidated. Symbol attempts to communicate from soul to soul, by means of suggestion; the artist obscurely perceives an image that is the equivalent of what he feels, and hopes thereby to awaken in the spectator an analogous state of mind. Allegory is reasoned, indeed taught; symbol is spontaneous, intuitive; it is the bearer of an analogy whose impact and shock is expected to awaken an emotional response.

Allegory, which must release an idea, can be explained in dictionaries; it is part of an iconography. Symbol, which must prompt an intuition, acts like a vibrant chord, awakening the desired note in another, waiting chord; it renders concrete an interior impulse. That is to say that allegory refers to the world of ideas, that it is therefore the fruit of intentional thoughts, whereas symbol expresses what is felt: it is the projection of a yearning — sometimes still unconscious — to be made known. Allegory can repeat itself, codify itself; symbol is an invention and a quest. In art, allegory is within everyone's reach, since it is explained in advance; whereas symbol, to be valid, must be born of a creative impulse, since it can be explained only after the fact. In the strict sense, the use of symbol is a poetic act.

This can be clearly understood only by those who know how much our interior life is made up of two complementary parts. The one, turned toward the external world, is founded upon the senses and their experience, completed by the intellect and its capacity to formulate concepts and ideas. The other is turned toward our inner reality, that perceptible existence which we live and experience, whose roots draw on the unconscious.

That is to say that genius has far more to do with symbol than with allegory, since what symbol offers, what it has to say, is essentially the unexpressed. Such is the case with Rembrandt, and his symbolic quest was all the more intense in that what he had to say had not yet been said. He was one of the most radically new creative geniuses into the history of art. Destiny caused him to be born in that Northern school of painting dedicated, by the eminently middle-class society around it, to practical reality. The Flemish primitives of the fifteenth century, imbued as they were with the religious spirit of the late Middle Ages, made use of an iconography that had been rigorously formulated and sanctioned. In rendering it, they relied on a realism reinforced by the technical invention of painting in oils, with its capacity for detailed imitative effects. In the sixteenth century, the hold of religion weakened, and art devoted itself even more resolutely to the depiction of physical reality, becoming more and more anecdotal and everyday, culminating in seventeenth-century Dutch naturalism. The Northern European attempt to break free inspired in the sixteenth century by the prestige of the Italian Renaissance, was in Flanders marked only by new disciplines conceived and applied by the Romanists.

Such was the situation Rembrandt encountered when he was forced to make his own way. Born in Leiden, an eminently intellectual town, and graduated from the university by 1620, he made himself master of realist techniques; they enabled him, when he settled in Amsterdam in 1632, to begin a brilliant career as a portraitist (figs. 357, 359, 360, 368), giving full expression to his figurative powers. But already he felt the attraction of that inner life which the Dutch artists, involved as they were in capturing faithful images of the material world, or in following the Italians' stylistic recipes, had been led to neglect. The frozen figures of models, posing patiently in their finery, interested him less than the overt, fleeting signs of psychic life; a collective group, like the famous anatomy lesson of

13. Self-Portrait with a Dead Bittern, 1639
Panel 121 × 89 cm G. 191
Dresden, Gemäldegalerie

14, 15, 16. Dr. Nicolaas Tulp Demonstrating the Anatomy of the Arm, 1632
Canvas 169.5 × 216.5 cm G. 100
The Hague, Mauritshuis

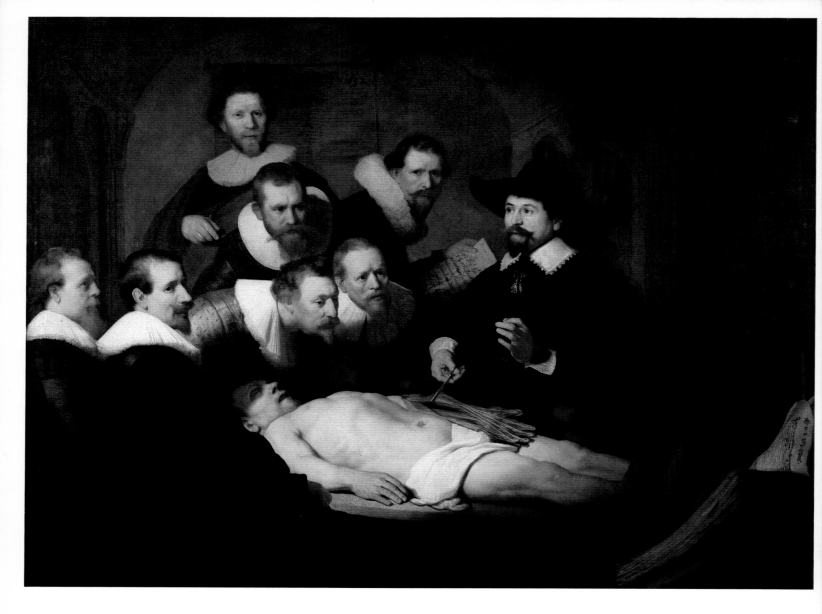

Dr. Tulp (fig. 14), is already a catalogue of the disciples' manifestations of attention, as visible in their physical attitudes as in their facial expressions. Alone with himself, Rembrandt looks into the mirror, grimacing even as he forces his face to act out his feelings — feelings that he then captures with his brush as well as with his graver (figs. 15, 16).

It was something that struck his first biographers, as early as the seventeenth century. Houbraken, who marvels at his etchings, emphasizes that they "perfectly express the movements of the soul." Again, he points out that in Rembrandt's drawings and prints "the emotions of the soul before different events are expressed so clearly in their essential traits that it is wonderful to watch them."

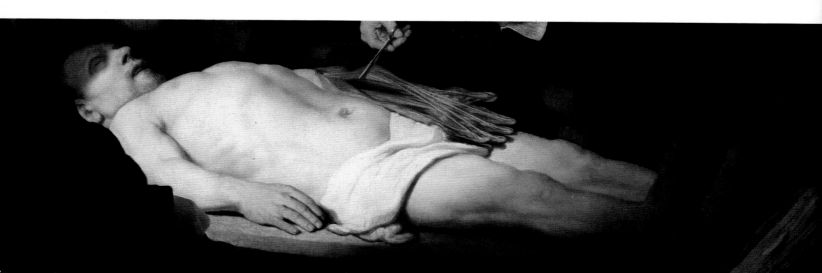

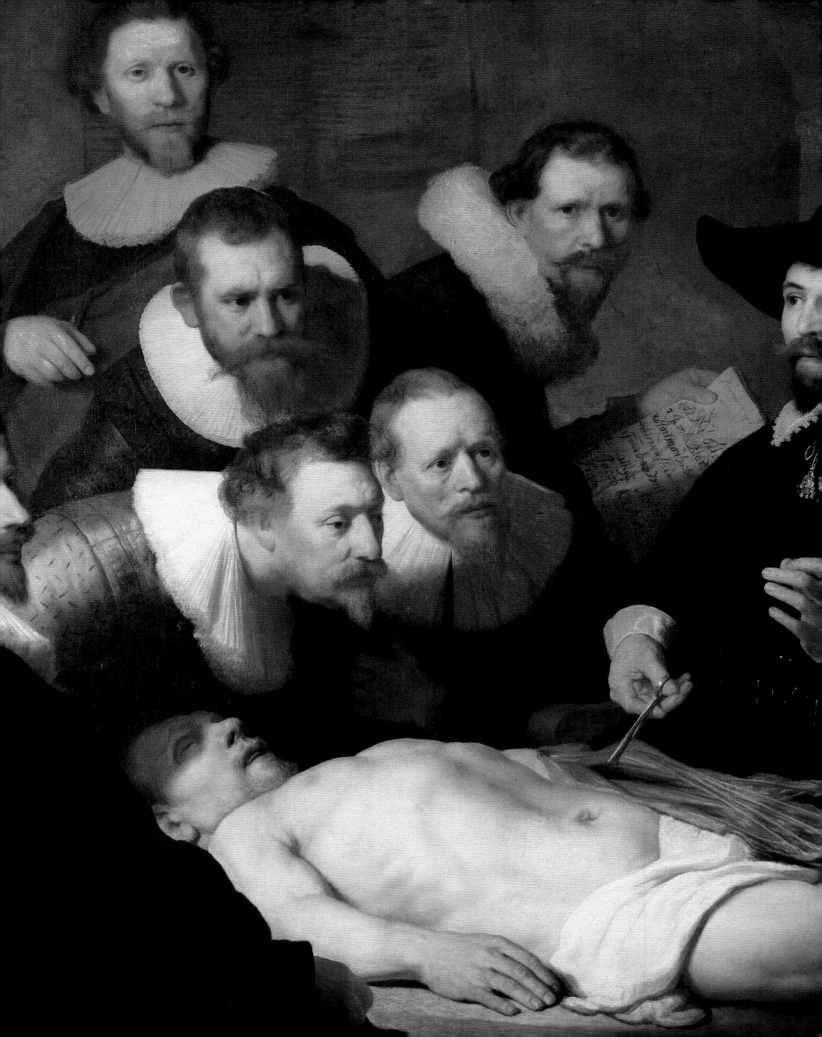

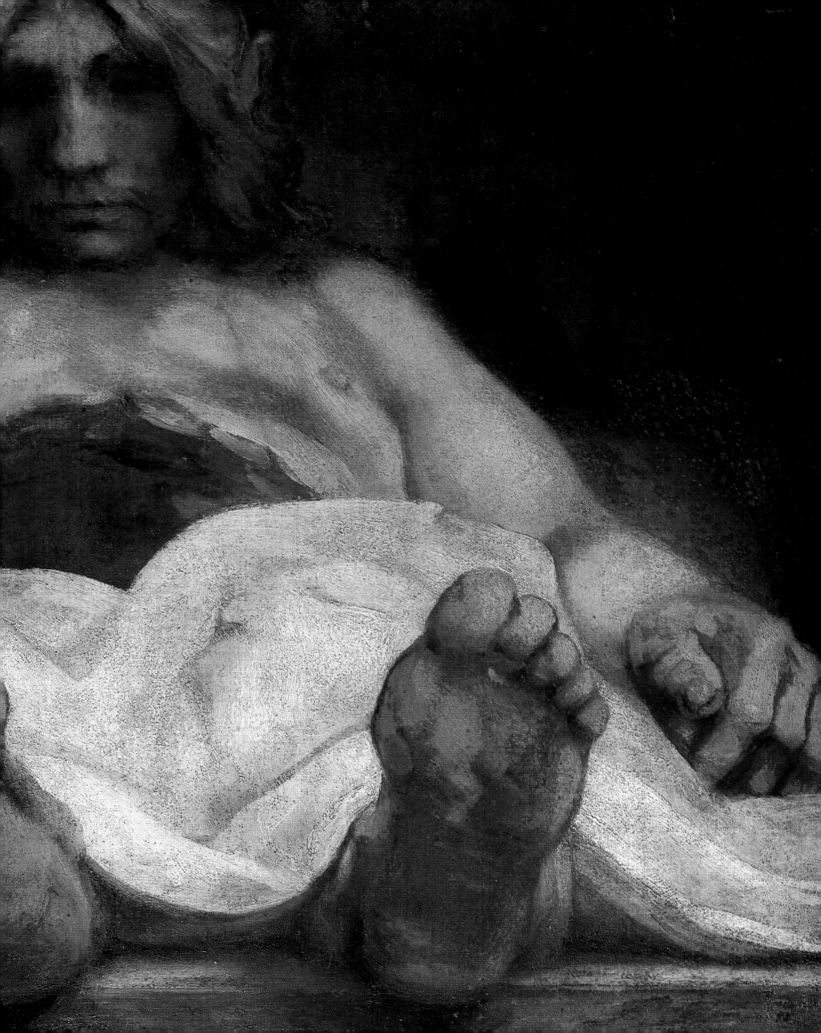

17. Detail of fig. 19

18. **The Anatomy Lesson of Doctor Joan Deyman, c. 1656**
(preparatory drawing with frame)
Pen and bistre 109 × 131 mm Ben. 1175
Amsterdam, Rijksprentenkabinet

19. The Anatomy Lesson of Doctor Joan Deyman, 1656
Canvas 100 × 134 cm G. 326
Amsterdam, Rijksmuseum

The irresistible fascination that drives Rembrandt more and more to make the visible world the expression of the secret world of the soul leads him to move from the study of precisely determined feelings to the depiction of the more mysterious emotion that accompanies indrawn meditation. He begins his series of old people's faces, finding a pretext as much in the portraits of his aged mother as in those of biblical figures. As early as 1630, he portrays Jeremiah and Tobias; he is fascinated by the luminous, wrinkled foreheads of philosopher, in meditation, whose image he renders repeatedly (fig. 593 A). In the words of Victor Hugo:

For one sees fire in young mens' eyes,
But in the eyes of the old, one sees light.

Indeed, from the effect of the inner life on the muscular system, he goes on to a more intimate quest: light, in its immaterial and impalpable energy, appears to him as a closer equivalent in the visible world for the intensities of the life of the psyche. A symbol was there already. He had acquired the technical skill to render light effects from his early masters, who, at the beginning of the seventeenth century, already echoed the Caravaggesque revolution. One early mentor, who taught him when he first came to Amsterdam for a few months in 1626, was Pieter Lastman, who had been a member of Elsheimer's following and who had been in contact with Caravaggism in Rome. Nor should one forget that even when still in Leiden, he had studied for three years under Jakob von Swasenborch, who, thirty-five years his senior and outside the currents that were then in vogue, already had an attraction for "the other world." In his *Hell*, now housed in the Leiden Museum, Swasenborch had rendered this other world by contrasting its different reds with the clarity of the ordinary world, whose reflection could still be seen, lighting the passage from one to the other. Thus Rembrandt acquired the feeling that to leave the concrete world of matter and evoke the impalpable and invisible world of the inner life, a different, essentially evocative light was called for. Surely this is the latent meaning of his *Belshazzar Sees the Writing on the Wall* (fig. 601) of about 1635, now in the National Gallery, London, where the intrusion of the supernatural in the delights of the physical world and "earthly nourishments" is marked by the brutal burst of another light, where is inscribed the famous handwriting on the wall, "MENE, MENE, TEKEL, UPHARSIN." The development of this secret idea led Rembrandt to dwell on the enigma of the blind, who seem to pay with physical sightlessness for the revelation of interior sight: such a one was Tobias in the Bible, and so too, in classical antiquity, was the poet Homer, whose dead-eyed image Rembrandt was to use.

"What then do they see in the sky, all these blind?" asks Baudelaire. In 1653, in the Metropolitan Museum painting (fig. 20), Rembrandt places Aristotle — the silent incarnation of rational, experimental, lucid thought — before the enigma posed by the bust of the bard: a confrontation laden with meaning between the world of logical, verified knowledge and that of inexplicable revelation. This is what the great mystics evoke, in their eagerness to exceed tangible reality and the evidence of the senses, to open themselves to the blaze of the irrational, to a going beyond. The texts attributed to Dionysius the Areopagite, in the first century, already assert that "the secrets of God appear in the Darkness, clearer than light, of silence, master of secrets.... They flood the souls who are eyeless with marvelous splendors." "It is in the mysterious darkness that good without limit hides," says Tauler, in the fourteenth century. Similarly, in the Orient, the Persian Sufi al-Hallaj, who was crucified in 922, confided: "the dawn I love rises at night, resplendent, and never sets."

Rembrandt, through his quest for shadow, for old people with closed eyes, for the blind, obeys the same revelation, the same fascination, and translates it by the same symbol. This constant obsession leads him to scrutinize the enigma of thought turned totally inward in meditation; in this lies the origin of a theme to which, from the beginning, he endlessly returns: that of the Philosopher. Rembrandt portrays him retired from the world, in his cell. Sometimes the exterior light seeps in through the window, dissipating the darkness of his retreat just enough to make possible his reading, the source of his reflections. But Rembrandt never fails to attenuate even that intrusion of the world of "the outside": the philosopher flees the daylight by placing his hand over his eyes or even by closing them, the better to isolate himself in his meditation. The *Spiritual Exercises* of Ignatius of Loyola commended: "This meditation will be practiced with the windows closed, for the darkness of the place helps greatly to impress the mind with the awful aspect of death," that final cutting off of physical experience. But a painter had already blazed the trail. It was El Greco who was surely the first to open painting to the rebirth of the spiritual

20. **Aristotle with a Bust of Homer, 1653**
Canvas 143.5 × 136.5 cm G. 286
New York, Metropolitan Museum of Art

that took place in the seventeenth century. The Dalmatian painter Giulio Clovio described him during his stay in Rome, between 1570 and his departure for Spain, seated "in fine weather with a spring sun... in the dark studio, with the curtains drawn so fast that objects could hardly be discerned. Far from the lights of the world, El Greco meditated," refusing to go out "because the light of day disturbed his inner light." Thus, in the chain of great solitary geniuses, El Greco precedes Rembrandt.

At issue then is penetration by the other light, that revealed at Emmaus to the disciples at table with Christ without knowing it (figs. 652, 653, 655) — that light which the servant cannot see. The theme is one that Rembrandt takes up as early as 1628-29 (Musée Jacquemart-André), then in 1648 (Louvre), and again in 1660 (Louvre), albeit with the collaboration this time of a pupil. Yet was it not the theme of *Belshazzar Sees the Writing on the Wall* in 1635, and again that of the etching *Faust* (fig. 28), about 1652? In the latter work, over and above the book open for meditation, the supreme revelation blazes forth in a circular and mysterious sign, one that curiously evokes the form — also symbolic — of the Buddhist mandalas of Tibet. Around 1657, the St. Paul of the painting housed by the National Gallery of Art, Washington, D.C. (fig. 615), still seeks revelation in the sacred volume. Some four years later, the St. Matthew of the painting now in the Louvre (fig. 616) neither sees nor looks at the angel murmuring the ultimate secret in his ear: the angel is behind him, outside the visible world, just as the angel who appeared before the prostrate Tobias had flown out of that same world. "After having spoken," says the Bible, "he vanished from their sight, and they could see him no longer."

Where does it come from, the truth that is not revealed to our senses and that goes beyond the powers of logical thought? Don't we commonly use

21. Old Man Shading His Eyes with His Hand, W.B. 259, p. 39

a symbol to designate its source, however immaterial, when we speak of the heart? In *The Jewish Bride,* now in the Rijksmuseum (fig. 622), Rembrandt guides the hands of the man and woman toward the heart's secret, toward its muffled beatings. Silent, their gaze lost, the two listen attentively to the source of those impulses that lead our souls to go beyond our persons, regardless of logical reasoning and concrete evidence, and toward that warm and generous pulsation.

Isn't it the same secret whose presence Rembrandt pursues in his *David and Saul* of around 1658 (Mauritshuis, The Hague, fig. 613)? The old king's anger and jealousy are left behind, for from David's harp arises the *song*, invisible, impalpable, inexplicable; and Saul lets drop the hand, inert, that had grasped the spear to do murder. The sobs that transform him come from the depths of his being, and he moves to hide his weeping eyes in the heavy drapery which, were it pulled, would efface everything from sight; only the music we do not hear would remain. Then would reign the "oscura noche de fuego amoroso," the dark night of the fire of love, which St. John of the Cross invoked and which he told us was "due to the sublimity of the divine wisdom that so far exceeds the capacity of the soul that it is darkness for it."

And surely that is why Rembrandt, painter of the visible, wished to sink into the night and silence, to seek there a light and a music that transport us beyond our limits.

René Huyghe
Académie Française

22. Student at a Table by Candlelight, W.B. 148, p. 39

23. St. Jerome in a Dark Chamber, W.B. 105, p. 39

24. The Artist Drawing from the Model, W.B. 192, p. 39

25. Homer Dictating to a Scribe, c. 1661-63
Pen and bistre, brush heightened with white, gray and brown washes
145 × 167 mm Ben. 1066
Stockholm, Nationalmuseum

26. The Artist Drawing from a Model, 1639
Pen and bistre, wash 185 × 160 mm Ben. 423 (recto)
London, British Museum

27. The Moneychanger, 1627
Panel 32 × 42 cm G. 19
Berlin-Dahlem, Gemäldegalerie

28. Faust, W.B. 270, p. 39

29. The Phœnix or the Statue Overthrown, W.B. 110, p. 40

4 Nude Man Seated and Another Standing, with a Woman and Baby Lightly Etched in the Background

c. 1646
Etching - 194 × 128 mm
Three states

Third state. The upper outline of the loincloth of the seated man has been filled in. Small white areas due to failure in biting in the first state have been shaded in drypoint in the second state. Fine parallel burin intaglios have been added on the white areas of the shoulder and neck of the seated man.

W.B. 194-III; BB 46-1 (four states)

Provenance: A. de Peters, 1784

There are two drawings of the nude man standing (Benesch 709 and 710) in London and Vienna, and a similar drawing by a pupil (Benesch A 55).

21 Old Man Shading His Eyes with His Hand

c. 1639
Etching and drypoint - 138 × 115 mm
One state only

Impression on Chinese paper with a light surface tone.

W.B. 259; BB 38-3

Provenance: A. de Peters, 1784

This striking etching, symbolizing "Thinking Man," was unfortunately entirely altered in the eighteenth century. Trible, the merchant who acquired the copperplate, had it completed in 1770 by G.-F. Schmidt after a drawing of Nicolas Blaise. Fifty impressions were made, as indicated by the inscription on one of them: *Engravé par Schmidt; 50 épreuves seulement* (Engraved by Schmidt; 50 prints only).

22 Student at a Table by Candlelight

c. 1642
Signed in lower right corner : *Rembrandt*

Etching - 146 × 133 mm

One state only

W.B. 148; BB 42-6

Provenance: A. de Peters, 1784

The signature, in general barely visible, is not visible at all on this much inked impression.

23 St. Jerome in a Dark Chamber

Signed and dated: *Rembrandt f. 1642*
Etching - 151 × 173 mm
Two states

First state. The hand curtain falls in a nearly straight line.

W.B. 105-I; BB 42-E

Provenance: J.-L. de Beringhen, 1731

The white of the paper models the shapes and gleams faintly through the meshwork of deep and tight intaglios brimming with ink. Rembrandt's mezzotint has as yet nothing in common with that of Ludwig von Siegen (1642) or that of Prince Rupert (1654). Fine impressions of this black etching, so mysteriously modeled by whites, are rare. The copperplate, having been so heavily worked, is fragile. The lion, the cardinal's hat, the skull, and the upper part of the crucifix, which enable the subject to be identified, are barely visible. The faint distinctness of both staircase and window endow the space with a metaphysical dimension.

In the same year, Rembrandt etched a similar subject, *Student at a Table by Candlelight* (W.B.148, fig. 22).

In 1633 he painted a philosopher meditating in a more colorful interior (Paris, Musée du Louvre, Bredius 431).

24 The Artist Drawing from the Model

c. 1639
Etching, drypoint and burin - 233 × 185 mm
Two states

Second state. Both the easel and the drapery hanging over the model's arm have been shaded. The background has been thoroughly reworked. A pot has been drawn under the model's stand. The press that was to be seen in front of the easel has been removed.

W.B. 192-II; BB 47-2

Provenance: J.-L. de Beringhen, 1731

There is a preparatory drawing in London (Benesch 423).

No other state of this plate is available. It is probably sheer luck that this unexpectedly "modern" print should have come down to us. It reveals the artist's way of proceeding, step by step. Each of his characteristic manners can be made out in it, from the lightly sketched to the perfectly finished. Rembrandt drew his whole subject rapidly with his point on the copperplate. He then came back to details, lengthening his model's legs, lowering the stand, and so on.

Regarding the technique, Courboin has judiciously remarked: "The technical preparation of this plate enables us to believe that Rembrandt used some transparent ground. The initial layout, which chance alone allows us to find intact in this plate, should normally be invisible through the layer of the engraver's ordinary black ground." (Exhibition Catalogue, n°. 164). Rembrandt has portrayed himself in his studio at his model's feet (as inspired by a print by Pieter Feddes van Harlingen, *The Pygmalion)*; the studio is as it has often been described.

28 Faust

c. 1652
Etching, drypoint and burin - 210 × 160 mm
Three states

First state. The pile of books on the right, near the margin, is shaded with diagonal lines; in the second state these were reinforced with additional, fine lines. In the third state, a triangular area of horizontal lines made with the burin appears on the pile of books.

W.B. 270-I; BB 52-4 (four states)

Provenance: J.-L. de Beringhen, 1731

In Clement de Jonghe's inventory, dating from 1679, this print is called "The Alchemist." In Röver's inventory (1730) it is called "Dr. Faustus"; the same title is used in the Huls sale catalogue of 1735, followed by Gersaint in 1751: "Portrait of a Philosopher, or Doctor, known in Holland as Dr. Fautrieus" (G. 250). The adaptation into Dutch of Marlowe's play had made Dr. Faustus a popular character in the seventeenth century. Although there have been numerous studies of this print, its meaning remains mysterious. A figure whose head is replaced by a luminous inscribed disk points to a mirror at which Dr. Faustus is looking. It has recently been discovered that the cabalistic anagram in the disk corresponds to the inscriptions on an amulet: ALGAR ALGASTNA AMRTET/GAG-LRAM ADAM THE/INRI.

H.v.d. Wall has suggested that this figure may be Lilio Sozzini, founder of a religious sect, the Socinians, who held that the Bible was an inspired rather than an historical work (*Oud Holland*, 1964).

29 The Phoenix or the Statue Overthrown

Signed and dated: *Rembrandt f. 1658*
Etching and drypoint- 182 × 184 mm
One state only

W.B. 110; BB 58-A

The dating and subject of this print are controversial. The date is hardly legible. In it Rovinski deciphered 1650, Claussin 1659, Middleton and H. von Seidlitz 1658, Charles Blanc 1648, and last Hind, Björklund, Barnard, White and Boon 1658. The allegory has also been diversely interpreted. For Middleton, the etching alludes to the Battle of the Dunes won in 1658 by Turenne against the Spaniards; Vosmaer sees in it the symbol of the raising-up again of the United Provinces. For Blanc, it represents the Peace of Münster of 1648; for others still, the destruction of the statue of the duke of Alba in Antwerp, or Death and Immortality, if not Rembrandt's own difficult situation.

The artist did indeed have enormous financial problems in 1658. His art collections were sold and his possessions, house and furniture were dispersed. Isn't this featherless phœnix, this overwhelmed genius above whom glory still hovers the image of the artist's destiny, an image loaded with bitter and provoking irony?

30, 31 The Boat House (Grotto with a Brook)

Signed and dated : *Rembrandt 1645*
Etching and drypoint - 127 × 134 mm
Three states

First state. The prow of the boat, with very pronounced contours done in drypoint, is high. It was lowered in the next state and the shadows of the cave and the boat were lightened with a burnisher.

Provenance : A. Firmin-Didot, 1877. Price 750 F.

Third state. The prow and the entrance to the cave are again shaded and the contours have been sharpened in drypoint. The front of the boat is smaller. The artist has used a surface-tone effect above.

Unique impression.

W.B. 231-I, III; BB 45-C

One drawing is preserved (Benesch 817).

32 The Ship of Fortune

Signed and dated: *Rembrandt. f. 1633*
Etching - 113 × 184 mm
Two states

First state. Before the plates was reduced to 166 mm in width. Etched crosshatching has not yet been added on Fortune's back; the partly worn away signature has not yet been covered with new intaglios.

W.B. 111-I; BB 33-E

This curious etching served as an illustration to a Dutch poem published in Amsterdam in 1634: *Der Zee-Vaert Lof* (*In Praise of Seafaring*) by E. Herckmans. It appears at the beginning of

chapter III, "Anno mundi 3935, Aetate Romae 723." In that year, the temple of Janus was closed shortly after the Battle of Actium; such is the event alluded to in chapter III of the poem. It may be assumed that the print represents the battle in an allegorical way. Fortune, in the person of a female nude, sails her boat away. The vanquished hero on his fallen horse is Mark Antony. The statue with a Janus face and the temple to the left evoke the closing of the temple by Augustus.

34 Death Appearing to a Wedded Couple from an Open Grave

Signed and dated: *Rembrandt. f. 1639.*
Etching - 110 × 80 mm
One state only

W.B. 109; BB 39-C

Provenance: A. de Peters, 1784

After the macabre dances of the Middle Ages came individual representations of Death. Here Rembrandt has taken up the theme of Man, Woman and Death, which Albrecht Dürer and Hans Sebald Beham had already tackled before him. In the present image Death is a skeleton, with the emblematical scythe and hourglass.

30, 31. The Boat House (Grotto with a Brook), W.B. 231-I, III, p. 40

32. The Ship of Fortune, W.B. 111, p. 40

33. The Abduction of Proserpina, 1632-39
Panel 83 × 78 cm G. 57
Berlin-Dahlem, Gemäldegalerie

34. Death Appearing to a Wedded Couple from an Open Grave, W.B. 109, p. 40

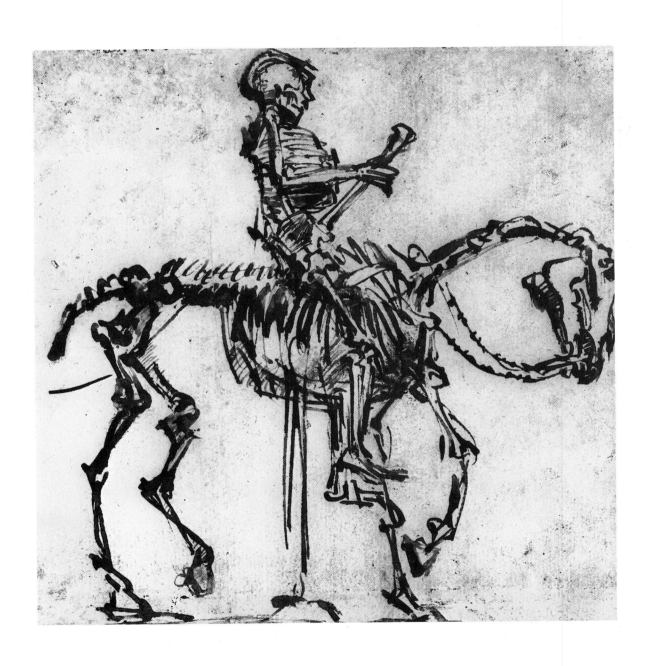

35. Human Skeleton Mounted on the Skeleton of a Horse, c. 1649
Pen and bistre 157 × 154 mm Ben. 728
Darmstadt, Hessisches Landesmuseum

36, 37, 38. The Conspiracy of Julius Civilis: the Oath, c. 1660
Canvas 196 × 309 cm (cut down) G. 354
Stockholm, Nationalmuseum

39. Six's Bridge (detail of fig. 46)

50

40. St. Jerome Reading in an Italian Landscape, W.B. 104, p. 69

Rembrandt: The Landscape and Man

Landscapes play a special role in Rembrandt's work. They are present, and pregnant with meaning, in every aspect of it — his drawings, etchings, paintings.

Included in this book are all of Rembrandt's etchings of landscapes, and a generous selection from among those that he painted or drew (in pen and ink, with or without wash, or in pencil), so as to achieve the most complete understanding possible of a genre in which Rembrandt invented a new way of grasping the outside world.

Rembrandt incorporated few landscapes in his paintings, most of them dating from the brief period between approximately 1635 and 1645.

Some of these landscapes form the background to the main subject, as in the astonishing *Polish Rider* (Frick Collection, New York, fig. 400). More often,

they constitute the framework for his biblical scenes, as in the *Holy Family* (Louvre, Paris), in *Saint John the Baptist Preaching* (Berlin-Dahlem, fig. 650), in the two versions of *Christ and the Woman of Samaria* (figs. 646, 647), and, especially, in *The Rest on the Flight into Egypt* (fig. 634).

Landscape Etchings

There are twenty-seven etchings of landscapes, and these can be dated more easily (see the annotations by Mme Gisèle Lambert, below). The first such etching, the *Small Gray Landscape: A House and Trees Beside a Pool* (fig. 42), dates from 1640; the last, *Landscape with Sportsman and Dog* (fig. 47), from 1653. In addition, there is the landscape setting, barely indicated, that he devised at the age of twenty for *The Rest on the Flight [into Egypt]* (fig. 490); and the much more developed one, executed many years later, in 1653, in *The Flight into Egypt* (fig. 486), for which he altered a plate prepared by Seghers for the latter's own etching of a landscape. In addition there are landscapes in the depictions of two saints at prayer, *Saint Jerome* (figs. 40, 43) and *Saint Francis* (figs. 466, 467), and in *Christ and the Woman of Samaria* (figs. 506, 507).

Some of the background landscapes are strikingly beautiful, regardless of whether they are very lightly drawn, as in *The Rat Catcher* (fig. 173) or *The Good Samaritan* (figs. 443, 444), or more sculptural, as in *The Descent from the Cross* (fig. 560). The subtlest one of all, barely a suggestion of a landscape, dominates the background of the decorative and moving *Baptism of the Eunuch* (fig. 450).

Landscape Paintings

From the very beginning, Rembrandt's landscapes differed sharply from those of the other Dutch masters, such as van Goyen and Ruysdael. Rembrandt was not at all concerned with realistically reproducing what he saw, or with using the usual harmonious colors. On the contrary, he executed his landscapes in strongly contrasted, dense tones. His use of light is dictated by the inherent drama of the scene, not by the established rules for depicting reality. The arrangement of each landscape is based on imaginary forms, and the subjects are wholly the inventions of the artist (figs. 123 to 131).

For Rembrandt, landscape was more than a mere physical setting. It became a sounding board for ideas that were totally new at the time — a way of transcribing his innermost feelings regarding the representation of light and the construction of space. In this respect, Rembrandt prefigured the grandiose, imaginary landscapes in Goya's "black paintings" now in the Prado, Madrid.

41. The Shepherd and His Family, W.B. 220, p. 69

42. Small Gray Landscape, W.B. 207, p. 69

Landscape Drawings

In order to understand to what extent the extraordinary effects of light that characterize most of Rembrandt's painted landscapes were actually motivated by aims other than that of merely "illuminating" the scene (fig. 130), and in order to grasp, at the same time, the artist's inherent need to render space through non-narrative elements, we must look closely at his drawings. In his landscapes, he is motivated by one overriding concern: never again can landscape be looked at for its own sake. For Rembrandt, it exists only in relation to the human dimension.

The same might be said of those whose portraits Rembrandt painted: what counts is not so much the characteristics of a given model as the attempt to convey his essence as a human being. This becomes even more obvious when we look at the way Rembrandt portrays Christ: he is more Jesus the man than God, son of God.

In his six-volume catalogue (1954-57), Otto Benesch lists over 1,400 drawings — studies, sketches, portraits or figures — by Rembrandt. A number of them are landscapes, but it is difficult to say exactly how many, for, since the publication of Benesch's catalogue raisonné, some of the drawings have been attributed to other artists — to Rembrandt's pupils, or to followers. Many drawings have disappeared since the seventeenth century, as the result of the numerous sales and exchanges of works of art that have taken place, but there is always hope that these drawings will come to light again.

The fifteen landscape drawings now at Chatsworth, England, were purchased early in the eighteenth century for the Duke of Devonshire by the son of Govert Flinck, Rembrandt's pupil. We are grateful to the Trustees of the Chatsworth Settlement for permission to publish twelve of them here (figs. 99-104, 106, 108, 110-112, 116).

Rembrandt's Compositions

Although Rembrandt apparently drew many of his landscapes *in situ*, we have good reason to wonder how faithfully he actually reproduced them. In his sketches as in his most finished drawings, there are certain constants, such as a type of composition in which the dominant note is the human element. In those works in which no figures are represented, the existence of man is symbolized by features that bear witness to his presence. Virtually none of Rembrandt's landscapes violates this rule.

Admittedly, it would have been difficult to avoid including in these landscapes either human figures or signs of their presence, because the sites that Rembrandt chose to draw were always situated quite close to cities — particularly to Amsterdam. Rembrandt was a city dweller *par excellence,* and led a sedentary life; he never displayed any pronounced interest in travel, and confined his rare trips to the environs of the city where he lived. Moreover, one Dutch landscape looks very much like another; the horizon is always an undefined fusion of sky, water, and earth. Yet never in the course of his limited travels did Rembrandt make sketches of a particular place for the sake of its "technical" interest alone — whether for a detail of the structure of a ship, or of the construction of a dike, or even of a canal.

Only man interested Rembrandt, man everywhere present, in person, through his habitat, or through his work. The flat open spaces in Rembrandt's drawings are rife with observations which, accurate though they may be, are nonetheless suspect, for they always occupy carefully chosen points in the composition, arranged according to a rigid system of construction.

Rembrandt had none of Turner's topographical curiosity. For each of his landscape drawings — done, of course, "on location" — Rembrandt chose an angle from which to view the scene before him so that it would correspond to his deep-seated compositional needs and to his intuitive rules. The significance of these rules is suggested by the fact that he added to each landscape as many figures, or objects denoting them, as he deemed necessary.

The Bastion at Amsterdam and *Landscape with a Cottage and Hay Barn*

Comparing the drawings and the etchings will help us to analyze their content. Let us take as our first examples *The Bastion at Amsterdam: Het Blanwhoofd* (fig. 113), a drawing with the centrally positioned, dominant form of a mill, a dwelling place; and *Landscape with a Cottage and Hay Barn* (figs. 44, 45), an etching whose composition is likewise dominated by a central, massive form. (We must bear in mind that the image an artist etches into a plate will appear in reverse when the prints are made; as a result, the etched landscapes should be read left to right, while the drawings must be read right to left. This is the direction in which Rembrandt generally worked, starting from the right foreground and moving leftward and back into the distance. His self-portraits, however, generally move in the opposite direction — from left to right — since they are derived from a mirror image that is itself reversed.)

The comparison begun above bears out the constant: Rembrandt's landscapes achieve their eloquence because of, and through, their human element. In both the drawing and the etching, the figurative mass in the center is challenged, offset by a detail that

43. St. Jerome Reading in an Italian Landscape (detail of fig. 40)

catches our eye and becomes the focus of our feeling for the scene. By de-centering his composition in this way, Rembrandt shows what is his real concern.

In the drawing, on the left a man is walking away from us with his dogs; in the etching, to the right of the cottage there is also a man walking his dog. In each case, even though the human figures are extremely small in relation to the rest of the composition, we cannot take our eyes off them. By placing the focus of his composition off-center, Rembrandt completely alters the way we perceive the massive form situated directly in the middle; although interesting in itself, this form does not really come to life except insofar as it relates to the human figures.

Rembrandt underscores man's supremacy still further by using movement to suggest the passage of time. The man in the drawing must be walking, for only the illusion of movement can counterbalance the impact of the buildings that stand out against a sweeping horizon, enlivened by the presence of boats. With time thus frozen, this landscape drawing takes on the look of a snapshot.

The man in the etching, on the other hand, is made to appear static by contrast with the group of children fishing in the central foreground. Time is suspended; the entire landscape is redolent of calm and serenity.

The music of each work complements the music of the other, as do the moments of inner life from which they spring. In spite of their differences (for technical reasons, it takes longer to produce an etching than a drawing), their melodic lines are similar; both vibrate within the great human symphony that wells up everywhere in Rembrandt's work.

In *The Bastion at Amsterdam*, the broad pencil strokes with which the man is drawn enhance his importance, indicating that our reasoning is sound.

We could almost make a game of this exercise, observing other works by Rembrandt and verifying whether it is the human presence, so strongly emphasized, that gives to each landscape its genuine impact.

Almost always, whether in etchings or in drawings, Rembrandt's landscapes stand out against an empty

44, 45. Landscape with a Cottage and Hay Barn: Oblong, W.B. 225, p. 70

sky. In his paintings, however, Rembrandt uses cloud banks and their movements to enrich the range of emotions conveyed.

View over the Amstel and Six's Bridge

Very unlike the previous example is the *View over the Amstel*, a handsome drawing now in the Rijksmuseum, Amsterdam (fig. 115). The superb composition is flat and horizontal; water and sky intermingle, seeming to bathe the whole. The drawing would be no more than remarkably descriptive were it not that in its very center Rembrandt included a boat and, in it, a man rowing — a minute black dot that creates tension and brings the entire scene to life. The drawing radiates outward from that infinitesimal point; instead of being static, the composition vibrates with contained movement that corresponds to the suggested movement of the rower in his skiff.

The composition of *Six's Bridge* (figs. 39, 46), a famous etching, obeys similar rules: the two people in the center give meaning to a landscape that is hardly visible in the distance, so low and flat is the horizon, but which fills the foreground, where the trees and the boat can be read as contrasting symbols of nature and of human activity. The foreground recedes

harmoniously along two oblique lines that converge on the two men in the middle who lean on the railing of the little bridge — which, as a result, appears amplified, out of scale.

Why is this one of Rembrandt's most popular etchings? Not just because it is so delicate and poetic, as if it were a rapid pencil sketch — and indeed, according to tradition, it was executed *in situ* — but because of the sensitivity with which Rembrandt expresses an essential rapport that was his own — between man, the industrious social being, and nature, the surrounding void. Like the *View over the Amstel, Six's Bridge* revolves around a central point, but this time the pivotal element is itself static; man is the center of gravity, the distillate of dispersed movement.

Again, in the drawing of the *Cottages Beneath High Trees* (fig. 95), though the human figure — that carefully centered black shape — is minute, its presence is so powerful that it overwhelms its whole environment.

Stormy Landscape

In this majestic little painting (fig. 126), now in Brunswick, the wild landscape — like the other

46. Six's Bridge, W.B. 208, p. 70

landscapes just discussed — converges toward the center, but this time in the foreground, where two people can be seen walking in the shade. In this funnel-shaped composition, the turbulence of the storm revolves around an invisible axis. Is it some cosmic whirlwind, culminating in man — or is it man himself who roils up the elements?

View of the Amstel with a Bather, Landscape with Sportsman and Dog, and Saint Jerome Reading in an Italian Landscape

There is no landscape at all, or hardly any, in the Berlin-Dahlem *View of the Amstel with a Bather* (fig. 107); disproportionately large, the bather in the foreground takes up the whole composition. What a revealing scene this is! The artist, out for a walk in the country, offers up his vision of the outer world. It is difficult to assign an accurate date to this drawing, but an etching made by Rembrandt at about the same time (fig. 64) contains a landscape with four figures of such exaggerated expressiveness that we may take the liberty of supposing that the subject is allegorical: man at every stage of his life, searching for his original innocence, before the Fall.

In another etching, *Landscape with Sportsman and Dog*

(fig. 47), the subject is handled in a way that makes us stop and think once again about the relationship between man and the outer world. A figure stands firmly in the middle of the scene as if posing for a photograph, against a rustic background punctuated by hills. Has he just left his village? What is he about to hunt, and where?

This etching dates from 1653. In that same year, Rembrandt, then aged forty-seven, produced *The Three Crosses* (figs. 556 to 558); the amazing etching *Flight into Egypt* (fig. 486), for which he reworked a plate made by Seghers; and the *Saint Jerome Reading in an Italian Landscape* (figs. 40, 43). *Aristotle with a Bust of Homer* (fig. 20; cf. p. 21, René Huyghe's essay, "Rembrandt's Symbolic Vision"), the large painting now in the Metropolitan Museum, New York, also dates from 1653. In all of these works, which are imbued with mystery, emotion, and contemplative inspiration, space plays a decisive role; Rembrandt uses it as no artist had before, to express his quest and his questioning.

Possibly the most beautiful of his outdoor scenes is his *Saint Jerome*. Here, Wisdom is in opposition to Society (and is doubtless threatened by it), for this

47. Landscape with Sportsman and Dog, W.B. 211, p. 70

Saint Jerome is a thinker, given more to reflection than to prayer. A few economical strokes suffice to create him; he is aglow with light. The composition is locked into place by one continuous line linking the old tree, the lion, the rock, and the ravine. The flood of light is strong enough to flow past that barrier. As if the light were projected by the saint's contemplative powers, it reaches the base of the knoll; at the summit are houses grouped together and topped off by an imposing tower.

In the shade of the tree (the source of thought?), the lion is on guard, atop his steep rock.

Landscape with Farm Buildings and Cottage Among Trees

There are a few landscapes in Rembrandt's work that are devoid of human figures. *Landscape with Farm Buildings* (fig. 104) was sketched from life. In this drawing Rembrandt delineated the piece of wood from which the articles of everyday activity were hung; it is almost disproportionately large, compared with the farm buildings.

Cattle occupy the entire left-hand portion of the drawing. One cow, lying down, is depicted with great care; near her is another, this one in calf. The same domestic animal, shown drinking in the foreground of *Landscape with a Cow* (figs. 80, 81), an etching dating from 1650, emphasizes the pastoral side of a scene that is pure fantasy. In *Cottage Among Trees* (fig. 98), a drawing now in the Metropolitan Museum, New York, we move ahead along a narrow path that will bring us up against the fence. There is total calm, save for the imagined rustling of leaves. The house stands on a Rousseauesque knoll; beyond it, the plains stretch out to meet the low-lying hills. At the rear, near the spot where a laden wagon waits, we can discern the curved shape of a peasant's hat: a farmer is walking back toward the house. Nothing else is astir in this world of suspended movement, captured by the precise, yet spontaneous strokes of Rembrandt's pen. Broad patches of brown wash add to the effect of the colored paper, unifying the whole.

Here again Rembrandt introduces a human being into the scene in the form of a tiny shape, barely visible, but, as always, placed at some crucial point in the composition. By focusing our attention on this contrapuntal presence, Rembrandt actually brings the figure of man center stage, underscoring his relationship with the world around him. Like an obsession, this theme infuses all of Rembrandt's work.

Clump of Trees with a Vista and Other Etchings

Clump of Trees with a Vista (figs. 52 to 54), one of the most beautiful of the artist's tree-filled landscapes,

perfectly illustrates this hypothesis. By placing side by side two small circles almost identical in diameter, Rembrandt suggests a woman, bent over her work (isn't that a washboard, just below her?). The diagonal on which the scene is constructed ends just above the woman. Both the composition and the particularly effective use of the drypoint technique make this a remarkable etching. Its evolution from the unfinished to the second state is astounding.

Among the finest of the drawings Rembrandt made in the course of his country outings is *Farmstead with Pigeon Loft* (fig. 103), where, in a lane, a woman (barely visible) sits sewing. Equally impressive are the etchings *Cottage with a White Paling* (figs. 58, 59) and *Landscape with a Road Beside a Canal* (figs. 55 to 57), and the drawing *Farmstead Beneath Trees* (fig. 97).

Similar tiny figures occupy the centers of two drawings in the collection at Chatsworth (figs. 103 and 104). The figures fade into the distance in *The Amsteldijk at Trompenburg* (fig. 112), and they stand out against the horizon in the etching (figs. 80, 81) mentioned above (this time, however, they are not people, but animals). They appear again in *Landscape with a Hay Barn and a Flock of Sheep* (figs. 71, 72), which underwent significant changes from one state to the next. Still more revealing are the two small figures in *The Windmill* (figs. 82 to 84), and the man with the scythe in *Landscape with an Obelisk* (figs. 73, 74).

In fig. 117, the superb, lofty tower that overlooks the bustling harbor is given human interest by the inclusion, alongside, of the little man who catches a breath of air in the shade of the tree. There are also figures like this one in the foreground of the painting now in Cracow (fig. 127), and still others — very tiny — in the lower right-hand corner of *Landscape with a Castle* (fig. 125), now in the Louvre. Rembrandt even drew himself sketching the landscape, observing himself surveying the scene, in *Cottages and Farm Buildings with a Man Sketching* (fig. 62); and again, in other works (figs. 99 and 102), at the edge of the road. In the drawing at Chatsworth, *Entrance to a Village with a Windmill* (fig. 111), one person sits on the grass and another on a bench as a woman retreats into the shade beneath the trees. The thin wash, delicately applied over the pen strokes, reflects Rembrandt's sensitivity to these "slices of life"; he transcribes them with such feeling that he involves himself and us in them, totally.

Water

Water is omnipresent in Dutch landscapes — not only in sweeping seascapes filled with movement, but also in the canals which form the basic structure of the land. Paths, as well as dikes, run alongside them. The

48. The Omval, W.B. 209, p. 70

farms are few and far between; trees are rare, and are grouped in small clumps. The rustic quality of the wet earth is conveyed by the rapid strokes of Rembrandt's pen — so free, and, at the same time, so accurate in their effect — reinforced by the areas of wash (or, in the etchings, by lines that shade). The seeming excesses of his pen-and-ink technique merely accentuate his expressive accuracy. When preparing an etching, Rembrandt drew with the utmost precision, but he used his pen to virtually sculpt his drawings. Achieved with a certain violence, his drawings seemed to many of his contemporaries to be unfinished.

In his etchings of landscapes, Rembrandt made very gentle use of his art, as if the open space around him — beyond that contained in the sheet of paper — gave him a more serene grasp of things. He indulged in renditions which, from one so original, might seem banal — were it not that he imbues them with all the non-narrative content of an obsessive existential sensibility.

The Omval: An Inward Look

The paradoxical composition of *The Omval* (fig. 48) is particularly striking. Its true subject is not the one that is readily apparent; Rembrandt couches it in an allegory whose various elements suggest added meanings, without shedding real light.

The landscape is divided into two parts. The scene on the right takes place by the water; it is charming and almost impressionistic. Standing quite near us, a very large man out for a stroll (is he, perhaps, meant to represent us?) watches a boat glide along. A canopy shields the talkative passengers from the sun. The scene has everything we could want: light, warmth, reflections in the water, and, in the background, a mill silhouetted against a luminous horizon. Lending depth to the center of the etching, a sailboat and other small craft idle along the bank, which is defined, at the rear, by houses, sheds, and trees. A lesser artist would have been content with this slight but pleasing scene for its own sake, but Rembrandt abruptly offsets it with an area of a very different nature, dominated by a large tree with a massive trunk and dead branches, at the base of a knoll covered with grass and trees. (In the etching of Saint Jerome [fig. 465] dating from 1648, there is a similar tree, in which the lion is hiding.)

By creating such a contrast, Rembrandt half-hides, half-reveals the main subject of the scene.

A similar approach marks some of his other etchings, drawings, and paintings — as, for instance, *The Boat House* (figs. 30, 31), an etching dating from the same year, 1645. Who is hiding in the boat that disappears into the dark passage from which the water flows?

Less allegorical than this enigmatic example is *Landscape with Trees, Farm Buildings and a Tower* (figs. 65 to 67), in which Rembrandt inserts figures into a perfectly straightforward landscape. It may be necessary to look twice in order to make out the figure who brings the human element into the scene.

But let us return to *The Omval* (fig. 48) with its hidden meaning. Because the dark hole next to the tree catches our attention and intrigues us, our eyes get used to the dark, and we begin to discern what is inside.

Although *The Omval* has been identified as a Virgilian scene, with a young man placing a crown on a young girl's head, for us it bears a very different significance. Since Rembrandt employs means that contrast so harshly with the delicacy of his ostensibly anecdotal subjects — a waterscape, a pair of lovers — his means must bear a deeper, more original relationship to the actual significance of this work; it has to be more than a charming narrative exercise.

Here, Rembrandt plainly juxtaposes heterogeneous scraps of information, but they do not give us the key to a work in which the obscure becomes the essential, and the obvious becomes irrelevant. Is that couple in the shadows hiding, looking for privacy? Or—Rembrandt being Rembrandt—are they there to tell us that discipline leads to strength, whereas gratification merely weakens?

Considered from that angle, this work — a landscape, after all — might also have been meant to represent the contrast between the outer world, teeming with impudence and promiscuity, and the secret plenitude of the inner life. Having inferred this much, we might stop there, satisfied with the course of our reasoning. We might even find pleasure in it — as we have always done when we have allowed Rembrandt to be our guide.

This book brings together the prevailing visions of a rare genius. Just try to leaf quickly through it; it will prove impossible. Every page is a trap. In no time, we feel the effect of the message emanating from each work: we want to renounce the too-enthralling outer world and to come to grips once again with our own inner being.

On each page the artist tells us, with profound awareness, about his blind need to exist as a human being. Face to face with Society, he must constantly focus his gaze inward in an effort to reassure himself that his life (the only important thing that he possesses, besides his art) is actually real.

When he turns this perpetual scrutiny of the inner self toward others, it provides the key that allows him access not only to their characters — for he does not paint individuals — but their essential reality as living persons. When the same attitude is applied to landscape, the very notion of landscape is radically transformed. Such analytical content, added to the constants of composition that have already been discussed, leads Rembrandt to alter the traditional nature of landscape. He — or, rather, the requirements of his subconscious — adds a new dimension to it, translating it into images that spring from his innermost being.

The Three Trees: The Inner Macrocosm; Light

At least once, in *The Three Trees* (figs. 49 and 51), an etching dating from 1643, Rembrandt violated this quality of intimacy with his landscapes. This is the only etching in which the sky itself becomes an actor on Rembrandt's stage; a storm rages across it with dizzying effect, such as no other etcher or painter ever achieved before or after.

Rembrandt thoroughly mastered this art of painting through etching; he did not hesitate to combine, on one and the same plate as the subject dictated, all possible techniques, or all the pictorial effects necessary to communicate the essence of his subject.

Much nearer to our own time, Picasso repeated such feats of virtuosity; even when working in such a restrictive medium, he succeeded in expressing with the utmost freedom a whole world of painting, sculpture, and drawing.

Likewise Rembrandt, three hundred years earlier, incorporated drawing and painting into his etchings; with a curiosity that never flagged, he always attempted something new. The number of states of many of his etchings doubtless indicates that he was constantly in search of the "why" behind each work — that he took a maieutic approach to his own art, rather than looking for the "how" by pursuing formal perfection. His *Three Trees* is cosmic in scope; its composition could easily be that of a painting. In the formidable series of etchings, *Christ Crucified Between Two Thieves* and *The Three Crosses* (figs. 555 to 558), made ten years later, in 1653, his work again attained the same amplitude.

In *The Three Trees,* as noted, the sky is the leading actor. The lateral effect of drenching rain is created by means of quick hatching strokes across the upper left-hand corner. The rain seems to flow down between us and the foreground, where we can discern figures and animals, just as a film director today might stage a torrential downpour right up against the lens of the camera.

The storm — the action — is indicated by two other zones of cloud that Rembrandt delineates using two contrasting techniques, to achieve an entirely new effect. One zone, across the top of the etching, is made up of intertwining strokes suggesting the gusty wind that is driving the clouds leftward where the rain is pouring down, almost onto us. In the distance, beyond the placid group of figures (similar to those in a scene that Rembrandt often depicted, *The Rest on the Flight into Egypt),* another cloud threatens to come nearer and release the second stage of the storm. It appears sculpted, modeled with strokes that look blurred, even rubbed out (Degas, later, applied the ink of his monotypes in the same way, as a solid mass — but here we are dealing with an etching). The wind is blowing so hard that it seems to be pushing the cloud out of the sky. On the right, the light pierces the horizon in a dazzling rush behind the trees, which stand upright like human figures on the edge of the plateau, where a farmer is bringing in the hay. On top of the plateau a man sits, as we ourselves might, facing that immensely liberating, luminous space, contemplating what we cannot see — what is, perhaps for that very reason, the most beautiful sight of all. (What is a work of art? Is it what we see, or perhaps what is left to our imagination?)

On the plain, bustling with the activity in the fields, a herdsman gazes at the rain drenching the countryside nearby, while a flock of large birds in the upper reaches of the restless air tries to stabilize its formation and get back on course. Falling diagonally, the light creates a violent chiaroscuro, a dynamic confrontation between black and white. The white has so much energy that it is hardly white; it contains all the colors of the spectrum. This is a pagan vision, in which no god is present; yet the light exalts it to the highest level of the Absolute.

Stormy Landscape

At about the same period, Rembrandt quite naturally turned to painted landscapes, in which the sky played a leading role. The atmosphere in *Stormy Landscape* (fig. 126), mentioned earlier, is as threatening as that in *The Three Trees,* but this time the wind blows at ground level. Amidst a patch of light, it attacks the trees, bending them over and creating a zone of hyperactivity that captures our attention, deepening our overall perception of the work.

Rembrandt continued to utilize this device: he employed light in a completely deliberate, empirical way — very unlike Caravaggio's didactic chiaroscuro — so that, in his landscape paintings, light takes on a special, symbolic dimension, becoming almost a sort of warning to mankind, a gesture of unmitigated defiance toward a menacing outside world.

In *Landscape with a Stone Bridge* (fig. 120 to 122), a cone of light, like a powerful beam from a projector,

49. The Three Trees, W.B. 212, p. 70

51. The Three Trees (detail of fig. 49)

spotlights a clump of trees in the middle distance. One tall tree stands out. The wind is trying to bend it; it becomes a noble and magnificent personage, like the old men depicted in Rembrandt's paintings, lucid and lonely, imbued with awareness of life.

In the painting now in Cracow, referred to earlier (fig. 127), a tree overlooks an illuminated, empty valley. Still another tree oversees the varied aspects of rural life in the *Landscape with a Stone Bridge,* where the velvety sky seems to breathe inspiration into the scene.

Each of these tree - personages occupies the center of the painted landscape, while the human figures are hidden in the shadows, experiencing the full impact of their assault. The potency of the trees stems from the light that radiates through them, attracting our gaze, in an effect that is not merely plastic, or even new (for, at about the same time, Claude Lorrain apotheosized light), but which seems to give them the power of speech — as if they were trying to break out of their isolation and communicate with the outside world. God does not respond to the cry of these giants; only man can hear it and understand it, for he is the true creator of it. Indeed, is man the originator of everything?

The world of Rembrandt's *Landscape with a Coach* (figs. 130, 131) is quite the opposite of that of the *Stormy Landscape.* It is swarming with activity that is foreign to us. Is the man standing in the very front of the scene, observing it, meant to be Rembrandt? Or ourselves? Here, Rembrandt lays before us an inhabited space which he describes complacently, without much emotion, as if he had landed on another planet.

The painting appeals to us because of the extreme clarity with which the light selects the details, and because the space in it seems deeper than deep, even infinite.

The gradual shift from darkness in the front to brightness in the very center of the composition is achieved by the radiant bursts of light in the neutral passages of the composition, between the narrative

50. Sheet with Two Studies: A Tree, and the Upper Part of a Head of the Artist Wearing a Velvet Cap, W.B. 372, p. 70

elements. The light barely grazes the trees and the buildings, as if the intervening void were meant to be more important than the areas whose significance is obvious. For those who take a purist view of landscape, the rift in the clouds can justify the division between light and dark, but its principal function is to elevate the luminous void of the earthly world to a different — absolute ? — reality.

God is not to be found here, either. The work is the product of a constant effort to define the Self — continually explored, yet perpetually unattainable.

Of all Rembrandt's landscapes, a drawing now in the Fogg Art Museum, Boston (fig. 91), is the most devoid of human presence. It is almost Japanese in its treatment. The lane opens its arms before us, amid the inviting solitude of a winter landscape.

Maurice Guillaud

52, 53, 54. Clump of Trees with a Vista, W.B. 222, p. 71

Rembrandt f. 1652.

55, 56, 57. Landscape with a Road beside a Canal, W.B. 221, p. 71

58, 59. Cottage with a White Paling, W.B. 232, p. 71

60, 61. Landscape with Three Gabled Cottages Beside a Road, W.B. 217, p. 71

Analytical notes on the landscapes etchings

Rembrandt etched twenty-seven landscapes from 1640 to 1645 and then from 1650 to 1653. Between 1651 and 1653, they were all executed with drypoint. In 1650, the artists' produced only landscapes, except for the Shell *etching. Their format is wider than it is high and the composition takes up only a small part of the height, giving an impression of immensity. The artist looked around him for his landscapes, and one of his students, van Hoogstraten, quoted this phrase of his master: "Around you in your own country, you will find so much beauty that your life will be too short for you to understand and express it."*

Although Rembrandt was inspired by reality, nevertheless he always interpreted it, and the identification of the various sites has often been a source of dispute. Rembrandt's landscapes are altogether different from topographically identifiable places.

40, 43 St. Jerome Reading in an Italian Landscape

c. 1653
Etching, burin and drypoint - 260 × 208 mm
Two states

First state. Before the alterations to the struts of the bridge on the right; these were later reworked in drypoint, the base of the left strut being made wider.

Impression on Japanese paper with a light surface tone.

W.B. 104-I; BB 53-3

Provenance: J.-L. de Beringhen, 1731

There is a preparatory drawing in Hamburg (Benesch 886, fig. 572).

In a landscape inspired by Titian or Campagnola, the saint, entirely sculpted in light, matches the sunny hillside relief. The interplay of shapes animating the space between the branch of the tree and the seated saint, as well as the elliptical form composed by the man and the lion, give the composition its structure. The technical variations in the rendering of the animal, from the simple etched lines to the velvety drypoint curves, create outlines, volume and coloring, to the benefit of the subtlety of the whole.

41 The Shepherd and His Family

Signed and dated: *Rembrandt f. 1644*
Etching - 95 × 67 mm
One state only

There are traces of earlier work on the plate, notably two circles still visible in the proof.

W.B. 220; BB 44-A

42 Small Gray Landscape: A House and Trees Beside a Pool

c. 1640
Etching - 38 × 82 mm
One state only

W.B. 207; BB 40-3

62. Cottages and Farm Buildings with a Man Sketching, W.B. 219, p. 71

The uniformity of bite and inking gives this small landscape, powerfully constructed by a network of serried lines, a particular gray tone, which creates an entire atmosphere.

44, 45 Landscape with a Cottage and Hay Barn: Oblong

Signed and dated : *Rembrandt f 1641*
Etching - 130 × 319 mm
One state only

W.B. 225; BB 41-A

Rembrandt etches his first large landscape and can thus develop his transparent backgrounds on either side of the realistic buildings in the foreground. Visible, on the left, is the town of Amsterdam and on the right a manor house, perhaps that of Kosteverloren or of Uytenbogaert. The barn, consisting of four wooden uprights and a movable roof that can be raised or lowered according to the amount of hay needing protection, is a construction typical of the Dutch countryside.

39, 46 Six's Bridge

Signed and dated: *Rembrandt f. 1645*
Etching - 130 × 225 mm
Three states

Third state. The hats of the two figures on the bridge are shaded. Neither had been in the first state, and only one of them was shaded in the second.

W.B. 208-III; BB 45-A

Provenance: A. de Peters, 1784

Gersaint tells the following story about this plate: "We have already said that Rembrandt was closely tied to Burgomaster Six, whose country house he often visited. One day when they were together, a servant came to announce dinner; they realized on the way to the table that there was no more mustard; the burgomaster sent a servant to get some from the village. Rembrandt, knowing well the slowness of servants in that region, who, when they said in reply to an order *anstons,* which means *in an instant,* took at least a half hour to turn up; Rembrandt, *I say,* who had a lively personality, bet the burgomaster that he could etch a plate before the servant returned with the mustard. The wager was accepted; and, as Rembrandt always had with him plates that were prepared with varnish, he took one, and etched on it the landscape that could be seen from the room they were in; in fact, the plate was etched before the servant's return, and Rembrandt won the bet; it is true that this piece was etched with no great pains but, be that as it may, it is amazing that it was indeed completed in so short a time." However, this place has not been identified as that in which the Six family owned property but as a site on the Amstel, near the Klein-Kosteverloren properties, owned by a burgomaster of Amsterdam. The tower of the Ouderkerk church can be seen on the left.

47 Landscape with Sportsman and Dog

c. 1653
Etching and drypoint - 129 × 152 mm
Two states

Second state. A cottage and a hay barn, visible in the first state behind the small figures on the left, have been burnished out.

Fine impression on Japanese paper.

W.B. 211-II; BB 53-1

Provenance: A. de Peters, 1784

This is the last landscape etched by Rembrandt and one of the few, together with the *Canal with an Angler and Two Swans* (W.B. 235, fig. 76) where the artist has replaced his usual horizons with a mountainous Italianate landscape drawn with a light and delicate needle.

48 The Omval

Signed and dated: *Rembrandt 1645*
Etching and drypoint - 186 × 226 mm
Two states

Second state. The right side of the brim of the hat worn by the character with his back turned, on the right, has been reduced with a burnisher.

W.B. 209-II; BB 45-B (one state)

"De Omval" is the name given by the natives to the bend in the Amstel rather than to the village which can be seen here on the opposite bank. A couple is visible under the trees on the left. The young man is crowning his companion with flowers. This is the first landscape in which the artist has used drypoint to establish a more marked contrast between the foreground, which is very dense, and the delicate vision of the opposite bank. This manner later inspired many etchers of the nineteenth century.

49, 51 The Three Trees

Signed and dated: *Rembrandt f. 1643*
Etching, drypoint and burin - 213 × 279 mm
One state only

A very fine grain appears in various places on the impression. It is probably the result of using a bite made of flowers of sulfur, or of work with a scraper and burnisher. J. Spingler supposes that Rembrandt used a plate that had previously been etched by Hercules Seghers. Among the clouds, one can, in fact, see arms and legs remaining from a badly erased composition.

Impression on yellowish paper.

W.B. 212; BB 43-B

Provenance: bought in 1816, 150 F.

This is the largest of Rembrandt's landscapes and one of the only ones, together with the *Landscape with Trees, Farm Buildings and a Tower* (W.B. 223, figs. 65, 66, 67), in which the sky is animated. Light spreads over the countryside as the sky clears at the end of a storm, emphasizing successive planes, some somber, some luminous. This state of change in nature, which is a theme unique in Dutch etching of the first half of the seventeenth century, is treated for the first time in this landscape. The print has always been much sought after by collectors.

50, 722 Sheet with Two Studies: A Tree, and the Upper Part of a Head of the Artist Wearing a Velvet Cap

c. 1642

Etching - 78 × 69 mm
Only one state
W.B. 372; BB 42-1

52, 53, 54 Clump of Trees with a Vista

Signed and dated from the second state: *Rembrandt f 1652*
Drypoint - 156 × 211 mm
Two states

First state. The landscape is simply roughed out; the right section of the print is white. Impression with slight, fairly even surface tone.

Second state. The landscape is finished. The foliage is modeled with strokes of drypoint of a varying smoothness. A distant prospect, drawn in line, appears in the right section of the print.

The cut-down plate measures no more than 124 × 211 mm.

W.B. 222-I, II; BB 52-D

The print is considered one of the oldest and most beautiful landscapes executed solely with drypoint. Three drawings (Benesch 1272, 1273, 1274) and one painting (Bredius 453) are related to this print.

55, 56, 57 Landscape with a Road Beside a Canal

c. 1652
Drypoint - 75-79 mm × 211 mm
One state only

One of the first proofs characterized by being printed on Japanese paper.

W.B. 221; BB 52-6

Provenance: A. de Peters, 1784

In the distance, on the right, the village of Ouderkerk can be seen.

58, 59 Cottage with a White Paling

Signed : *Rembrandt f.*; dated from the third state : *1648*

Etching and drypoint - 130 × 159 mm
Three states

First state. The dyke on the left is not yet shaded. The plate is not dated.

W.B. 232-I; BB 52-E

A drawing after a lost original is preserved (Benesch C 41).

60, 61 Landscape with Three Gabled Cottages Beside a Road

Signed and dated: *Rembrandt f 1650*
Etching and drypoint - 161 × 202 mm
Three states

First state. The white patches that appear on the ground in front of the first cottage were shaded in the next state by horizontal lines.

Fine impression on Japanese paper.

W.B. 217-I; BB 50-D

Provenance: A. de Peters, 1784

62 Cottages and Farm Buildings with a Man Sketching

c. 1645
Etching - 131 × 210 mm
One state only
W.B. 219; BB 45-2

Provenance: A. de Peters, 1784

63 The Goldweigher's Field

Signed and dated : *Rembrandt 1651*
Etching and drypoint - 121 × 321 mm
One state only

Proof and counterproof

63. The Goldweigher's Field, W.B. 234, p. 71

One of the early fine impressions loaded with drypoint strokes.

W.B. 234; BB 51-A

The usual title of this print, *The Goldweigher's Field*, originated from the description in Gersaint's catalogue (1751): "N° 226. A landscape, known in Holland, under the name of the field of the goldweigher who was called Wytenbogardus" (W.B. 281, figs. 271, 272). Gersaint was confusing it with the *Landscape with Trees, Farm Buildings and a Tower* (W.B. 223, figs. 65 to 67). We see here the country house, called Saxenburg, of the Amsterdam merchant Christoffel Thysz, the owner of Rembrandt's house on Saint Anthony Street in Amsterdam. Above all, though it is, a panoramic view of Haarlem that extends before our eyes. A half-dozen of the counterproofs are preserved. This high number is easily explained: the view of the town is reversed on the proof.

One drawing is preserved (Benesch 1259), and one painting closely resembles this landscape (Van Regteren Altena, 1954, p. 1).

64 The Bathers

Signed and dated: *Rembrandt. f 1651* (the *5*, originally a *3*, has been corrected in drypoint)
Etching - 108 × 137 mm
Impression little reduced in height
Two states

First state. The uneven plate edges were trimmed in the second state, easily discernible at a spot caused by acid corrosion in the upper center.

W.B. 195-I; BB 51-B

It may be argued that this work by Rembrandt foreshadows Expressionism rather than Impressionism, as is often stated.

65, 66, 67 Landscape with Trees, Farm Buildings and a Tower

c. 1651
Etching and drypoint - 124 × 320 mm
Four states

First state. The tower is topped by a small dome. Black spots, due probably to splashes of varnish from the bite, appear in the sky at left. Impression with slight surface tone, printed on yellowish paper formerly identified as Chinese paper (inventory of the Collection A. de Peters).

Second state. The tower is still topped by a small dome. The black spots in the sky on the left have been burnished out. Impression with more marked surface tone which intensifies the disquieting atmosphere of the landscape.

Fourth state. The dome was erased in the preceding state. The space between the entrance to the bridge and the buttresses is covered with new oblique lines. The plate has been thoroughly wiped and no surface tone remains, which contributes to a relaxation of the atmosphere.

W.B. 223-I, II, IV; BB 50-4

Provenance: A. de Peters, 1784

This is one of the only landscapes that offers vast white spaces in the foreground matching those in the sky. The site has been variously identified but it is now agreed to be the house of the tax collector Jan Uytenbogaert, known as the "goldweigher." This house was on the road to Amstelveen. As the result of a misunderstanding, for a long time another landscape print, always known by the name of *The Goldweigher's Field* (W.B. 234, fig. 63) was associated with Uytenbogaert.

68, 69, 70 Landscape with a Milkman

c. 1650
Etching and drypoint - 66 × 174 mm
Two states

First state. No landscape is seen behind the houses.

Second state. A landscape is added in the background on the left. The water of the canal, the road, the ground in front of the farm on the left, and the left side of the barn are more shaded. The water covers a part of the road leading to the farm and reaches the gate.

W.B. 213-I, II; BB 50-2

Recently the person on the right has been identified as a hunter with a dog rather than a milkman. There is a preparatory drawing at Oxford (Benesch 1227).

71, 72 Landscape with a Hay Barn and a Flock of Sheep

Signed and dated: *Rembrandt f 1652* (the *d* reversed)
Etching and drypoint - 83 × 175 mm
Two states

First state. With nothing behind the figures on the dyke on the left-hand side.

Impression on Japanese paper.

Second state. A distant prospect now appears on the left. Some lines are added to the landscape on the right, the field in the center, the hayrick, the road, the trees and the buildings on the left. A branch extends from the clump of trees near the road.

W.B. 224-I, II; BB 52-A

Provenance: A. de Peters, 1784

There is a drawing at Oxford (Benesch 1226).

This seems to be the same farm represented in the *Landscape with a Milkman* (W.B. 213, figs. 68 to 70), seen from the other side.

64. The Bathers, W.B. 195, p. 72

65, 66, 67. Landscape with Trees, Farm Buildings and a Tower, W.B. 223, p. 72

68, 69, 70. Landscape with a Milkman, W.B. 213, p. 72

71, 72. Landscape with a Hay Barn and a Flock of Sheep, W.B. 224, p. 72

73, 74 Landscape with an Obelisk

c. 1650
Etching and drypoint - 85 × 162 mm
Two states

First state. The cottage and the paling behind the wheelbarrow on the right are not shaded. Strokes of drypoint abound.

Second state. The cottage and the paling on the right are shaded. The base of the column, as well as the water and the plants in the foreground on the right, are more heavily shaded. Strokes of drypoint have been eliminated. A slipped stroke on the right of the obelisk appears in both states.

W.B. 227-I, II; BB 50-3

Provenance: A. de Peters, 1784

The obelisk was represented entire, then enlarged. One can still make out its apex at the top of the print, underneath the pyramidal structure. This is the only monument that Rembrandt portrayed with accuracy. Situated on the road leading to Haarlem, it is one of the landmarks placed around the town of Amsterdam to mark the limits of its jurisdiction.

75 Landscape with a Square Tower

Signed and dated: *Rembrandt f. 1650*
Etching and drypoint - 88 × 157 mm
Four states

Fourth state. A slipped stroke that did not exist in the preceding states crosses the signature obliquely.

W.B. 218-IV; BB 50-C

Provenance: A. de Peters, 1784

The tower of the old city hall of Amsterdam rises, quite

73, 74. Landscape with an Obelisk, W.B. 227, p. 78

unexpectedly, next to a group of cottages seen from a dyke. This is inspired by the constructions of Domenico Campagnola (Venice, 1500; Padua, 1564).

76 Canal with an Angler and Two Swans

Signed and dated : *Rembrandt f. 1650* (the *d* is reversed)
Etching and drypoint - 83 × 108 mm
Two states

Second state. The meadow is shaded with oblique lines. Crosshatching covers the oblique lines which shaded the trees in the background. The contour of the trees on the right has been reinforced.

W.B.235-II; BB 50-A

Gersaint affirms that the *Canal with an Angler and Two Swans* and the *Canal with a Large Boat and Bridge* (W.B. 236, fig. 77)

were etched on the same copperplate and were part of a single landscape. It seems, however, that only the atmosphere conveyed by these two landscapes connects them; the perspectives are different. In this print, we find again those mountains of Italianate inspiration that can be seen in the *Landscape with Sportsman and Dog* (W.B. 211, fig. 47).

77 Canal with a Large Boat and Bridge

Signed and dated : *Rembrandt f. 1650* (the *d* and the *6* inverted)
Etching and drypoint - 83 × 109 mm
Two states

Second state. The trees in front of the square tower have been shaded, and the contour of the hill has been modified to include three small vertical lines sticking up on the right.

W.B. 236-II; BB 50-B

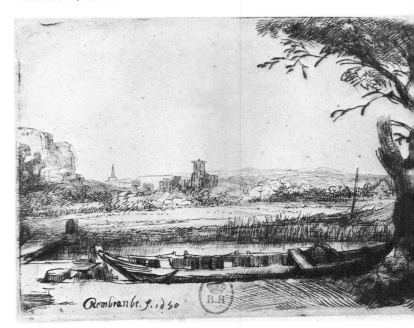

75. Landscape with a Square Tower, W.B. 218, p. 78

77. Canal with a Large Boat and Bridge, W.B. 236, p. 79

76. Canal with an Angler and Two Swans, W.B. 235, p. 79

78, 79. Landscape with a Cottage and a Large Tree, W.B. 226, p. 82

80, 81. Landscape with a Cow, W.B. 237, p. 82

78, 79 Landscape with a Cottage and a Large Tree

Signed and dated : *Rembrandt f 1641*
Etching - 129 × 321 mm
One state only

W.B. 226; BB 41-B

As in the preceding landscape, Rembrandt establishes a contrast between the almost oppressive realism of the building in the foreground and the marvelously evanescent background. Here the outlook is totally transformed, and this effect is achieved by the use of a single technique.

80, 81 Landscape with a Cow

c. 1650
Etching and drypoint - 105 × 130 mm
Two states

Second state. The ground to the right of the cow, white in the preceding state, is shaded.

W.B. 237-II; BB 50-I (three states)

82, 83, 84 The Windmill

Signed and dated : *Rembrandt f. 1641*

82, 83, 84. The Windmill, W.B. 233, p. 82

Etching - 146 × 210 mm
One state only

The network of lines in the center is due to the cracking of etching ground. A slight graining to the left is probably due to the use of a sulfur tint.

W.B. 233; BB 41-C

The windmill is situated near one of the bastions of the ramparts of Amsterdam called *"de Paseeder"*; it is not, as was long believed, Rembrandt's windmill. The latter, which no longer exists, was to be found in the town of Leiden, near the ramparts.

A more accurate drawing is preserved (Benesch 810).

85, 86 View of Amsterdam from the Northwest

c. 1640
Etching - 111 × 154 mm
One state only

W.B. 210; BB 40-4

This view of Amsterdam, which is very precise, appears in reverse, suggesting that Rembrandt etched it directly on the copper while looking at the landscape near his house. The lightness of the lines, which barely mark the copper, makes the city look disembodied under the luminous white sky and beyond the limpid countryside.

87, 88 Cottage Beside a Canal : A View of Diemen

c. 1645
Etching - 141 × 209 mm
One state only

A delicate grain around the trees to the left characterizes the first impressions. It is due perhaps to a bite using flowers of sulfur. It suggests a slight mist.

W.B. 228; BB 45-1

Rembrandt created in etching a crystalline town, luminous and marked out with trees drawn with glass-thin lines. None of his other landscapes achieves this degree of poetic beauty. It is a miragelike vision.

85, 86. View of Amsterdam from the Northwest, W.B. 210, p. 83

87, 88. Cottage Beside a Canal: A View of Diemen, W.B. 228, p. 84

LANDSCAPES
DRAWINGS

89. View of Diemen, c. 1649-50
Pen, bistre, wash on brownish paper 90 × 170 mm Ben. 1229
Haarlem, Teylers Museum

90. Diemerdijk with View of Houtewael from the West, 1651
Pen, bistre, wash 132 × 182 mm Ben. 1262
Rotterdam, Boymans-van Beuningen Museum

91. Winter Landscape, c. 1649-50
Pen and bistre on clean antique laid paper 68 × 160 mm Ben. 845
Cambridge, Massachusetts, Fogg Art Museum

92. Two Cottages, 1637
Silverpoint on prepared vellum 134 × 80 mm Ben. 341
Rotterdam, Boymans-van Beuningen Museum

93. Courtyard of a Farmhouse, c. 1636
Pen, bistre, wash 164 × 226 mm Ben. 464
Budapest, Museum of Fine Arts

94. Cottage near the Entrance to a Wood, 1644
Pen, bistre, wash with some black and red chalk 298 × 452 mm Ben. 815
New York, Metropolitan Museum of Art, Lehman Collection

95. Cottages Beneath High Trees, c. 1657-58
Pen, brush in bistre 195 × 310 mm Ben. 1367
Berlin-Dahlem, Staatliche Museum

96. Landscape with a Mill (detail of fig. 114)

97. Farmstead Beneath Trees, c. 1654
Red pen and bistre, wash 108 × 178 mm Ben. 1289 (recto)
Stockholm, Nationalmuseum

98. Cottage Among Trees, c. 1650-51
Pen and bistre, wash on brownish paper 171 × 275 mm Ben. 1249
New York, Metropolitan Museum of Art

99. Village Inn on the Highroad, c. 1652
Pen and bistre 100 × 226 mm Ben. 1314
Chatsworth, Derbyshire, Devonshire Collection (1036)

100. Farm Buildings Surrounded by Trees, c. 1650
Pen and wash in bistre 110 × 217 mm Ben. 1248
Chatsworth, Derbyshire, Devonshire Collection (1035)

101. Cottage by a Large Tree, c. 1652
Pen and bistre 175 × 267 mm Ben. 1282
Chatsworth, Derbyshire, Devonshire Collection (1046)

102. View of Sloten, c. 1650
Pen and bistre 96 × 180 mm Ben. 1237
Chatsworth, Derbyshire, Devonshire Collection (1039)

103. Farmstead with Pigeon Loft, c. 1650 Pen and bistre, wash 130 × 199 mm Ben. 1233 Chatsworth, Derbyshire, Devonshire Collection (1037)

104. Landscape with Farm Buildings, c. 1652
Pen and bistre, wash 116 × 202 mm Ben. 1294 (recto)
Chatsworth, Derbyshire, Devonshire Collection (1041)

105, 106. Bend in the Amstel near Kostverloren, c. 1651
Pen and brush in bistre, washes in bistre 136 × 246 mm Ben. 1265
Chatsworth, Derbyshire, Devonshire Collection (1021)

107. View of the Amstel with a Bather, c. 1654-55
Pen and bistre, wash with some white 146 × 273 mm Ben. 1352
Berlin-Dahlem, Staatliche Museum

108. View of the River Ij near Amsterdam, c. 1649-50 Pen and wash in bistre with some white on grayish paper 76 × 244 mm Ben. 1239 Chatsworth, Derbyshire, Devonshire Collection (1030)

109. View of the Amstel and *Het Molentje,* c. 1654 Pen and bistre, wash with some white 82 × 226 mm Ben. 1353 Cambridge , Fitzwilliam Museum

110. River Amstel at the Omval, c. 1653 Pen and wash in bistre 108 × 197 mm Ben. 1321 Chatsworth, Derbyshire, Devonshire Collection (1026)

111. The Entrance to a Village with a Windmill, c. 1649-50 - Pen and bistre, wash 143 × 180 mm Ben. 1217 - Chatsworth, Derbyshire, Devonshire Collection (1040)

112. The Amsteldijk at Trompenburg, c. 1649-50 - Pen and wash in bistre with some white on prepared paper - 130 × 217 mm Ben. 1218 - Chatsworth, Derbyshire, Devonshire Collection (1022)

113. The Bastion at Amsterdam, 1641
Black chalk on brownish paper 166 × 275 mm Ben. 813
Rotterdam, Boymans-van Beuningen Museum

114. Pastures with a Windmill, c. 1641
Pen and wash 142 × 288 mm Ben. 802
Chantilly, Musée Condé

115. View over the Amstel, 1648-50
Pen and wash on vellum 132 × 232 mm Ben. 844
Amsterdam, Rijksprentenkabinet

116. Cottage by the River, c. 1650
Pen and bistre, wash 133 × 200 mm Ben. 1232
Chatsworth, Derbyshire, Devonshire Collection (1033)

117. Montelbaan Tower at Amsterdam, c. 1652-53
Pen and bistre 145 × 144 mm Ben. 1309
Amsterdam, Rembrandt's House

118. The Western Gate at Rhenen, c. 1647-48
Pen and bistre, wash 165 × 226 mm Ben. 826
Haarlem, Teylers Museum

119. The Ruins of the Old City Hall in Amsterdam after the Fire, 1652
Pen and wash with red chalk 150 × 201 mm Ben. 1278
Amsterdam, Rembrandt's House

120, 121, 122. Landscape with a Stone Bridge, c. 1637
Panel 29.5 × 42.5 cm G. 196
Amsterdam, Rijksmuseum

123.   Winter Landscape, 1646
Panel 17 × 23 cm G. 267
Cassel, Gemäldegalerie

124. River Landscape with Ruins, 1650-58
Panel 67 × 87.5 cm G. 344
Cassel, Gemäldegalerie

125. Landscape with a Castle, c. 1643
Panel 44.5 × 70 cm G. 268
Paris, Musée du Louvre

126. Stormy Landscape, c. 1639
Panel 52 × 72 cm G. 200
Brunswick, Herzog Anton Ulrich Museum

127. Landscape with the Good Samaritan, 1638
Panel 46.5 × 66 cm G. 199
Cracow, Czartoryski Museum

128. Landscape with the Baptism of the Eunuch, 1636
Canvas 85.5 × 108 cm G. 195
Hanover, Niedersaechsisches Landesmuseum

129. Stormy Landscape with an Arched Bridge, 1632-39
Panel 28 × 40 cm G. 197
Berlin-Dahlem, Gemäldegalerie

130. Landscape with a Coach, 1640-49
Panel 46 × 64 cm G. 266
London, Wallace Collection
131. Landscape with a Coach (detail)

132. Two Tramps, a Man and a Woman, W.B. 144, p. 122

133. Beggar Man and Beggar Woman Conversing, W.B. 164, p. 122

134. Ragged Peasant with His Hands Behind Him, Holding a Stick, W.B. 172, p. 122

135. Beggar Leaning on a Stick, W.B. 163, p. 122

136, 137. The Blindness of Tobit, W.B. 153-II, V, p. 122

138, 139. The Leper ("Lazarus Klap"), W.B. 171-I, III, p. 122

141. Polander Standing with Arms Folded, W.B. 140, p. 122

A Peasant in a High Cap, Standing Leaning on a Stick
B. 133, p. 122

142. Beggar Woman Leaning on a Stick, W.B. 170, p. 122

143. Beggar with a Crippled Hand Leaning on a Stick, W.B. 166 p. 122

144. Old Beggar Woman with a Gourd, W.B. 168, p. 123

132 Two Tramps, a Man and a Woman

c. 1634
Etching - 64 × 48 mm
One state only

Impression with a light surface tone.

W.B. 144; BB 34-2

Provenance : A. de Peters, 1784

133 Beggar Man and Beggar Woman Conversing

Signed and dated: *RHL (in monogram) 1630* (the *3* was originally a *2*)
Etching - 78 × 66 mm
One state only

This is one of the early impressions with rough and uneven plate edges.

W.B. 164; BB 30-A

134 Ragged Peasant with His Hands Behind Him, Holding a Stick

c. 1630
Etching with touches of drypoint - 93 × 68 mm
Six states

Third state. The plate, originally 93 × 78 mm, was cut down. Several drypoint touches are visible on the cap. Various areas were to be shaded in the later states. A pillar and an arch were added to the right in the sixth state.

W.B. 172-III; BB 30-7

135 Beggar Leaning on a Stick, Facing Left

c. 1630
Etching - 86 × 46 mm
One state only

W.B. 163; BB 30-2

136, 137 The Blindness of Tobit

A Sketch
c. 1629
Etching - 79 × 56 mm
Five states

Second state. The plate had been 63 mm wide but has been cut down on the left. Tobit's cloak has been more heavily shaded, as has the space to the left of his stick.

Fifth state. In the third state, the doorway was shaded with diagonal strokes; in the fourth, the shoes were shaded with vertical strokes. The doorway is now covered with vertical strokes from top to bottom.

W.B. 153-II, V; BB 29-5

Provenance: A. de Peters, 1784

138, 139 The Leper ("Lazarus Klap")

Signed and dated from the second state onwards: *RHL (in monogram) 1631*
Etching
Seven states

First state. The plate's dimensions were originally 102 × 76 mm. This single known version was printed on the verso of an impression of *Beggar Man and Woman* (W.B. 183, fig. 148). It was then cut down to 100 × 78 mm.

This Paris impression is unique.

Provenance: J.-L. de Beringhen, 1731

Third state. The plate was cut down to 93 × 64 mm in the second state. A triangular white area, due to failure in biting on the fold on the right-hand side of the cloak, has been shaded.

Fifth state. The face was shaded in the fourth state. Cut down further, the plate now measures 88 × 63 mm. A white spot at the back of the neck has been shaded.

This impression was cut down again to 86 × 61 mm.

W.B. 171-I, III, V; BB 31-Q

Provenance: A. de Peters, 1784

In Dutch, *Lazarus klap* means the leper's clapper; made of wood, it rattled when shaken by the leper, who had to announce his presence so that no one should come near him. A clapper was later used by deaf-mutes, but in this case to draw people closer.

140 A Peasant in a High Cap, Standing Leaning on a Stick

Signed and dated : *Rembrandt f. 1639*
Etching - 84 × 44 mm
One state only

W.B. 133; BB 39-B

Provenance: A. de Peters, 1784

There are eight known copies of this piece.

141 Polander Standing with Arms Folded

c. 1635
Etching - 52 × 48 mm
One state only

This is one of the earliest impressions with rough, uneven edges. Their later trimming was to cause a slight reduction in the dimensions of the plate.

Impression with a light surface tone.

W.B. 140; BB 35-7

142 Beggar Woman Leaning on a Stick

Signed and dated: *Rembrandt f. 1646*
Etching and drypoint - 82 × 63 mm
One state only

W.B. 170; BB 46-A

Here the artist's manner is close to that of his delicately drawn little figures representing well-defined characters such as *The Quacksalver* (W.B. 129, fig. 166), *The Blind Fiddler* (W.B. 138, fig. 167), the *Polander Standing with Arms Folded* (W.B. 140, fig. 141), etc.

143 Beggar with a Crippled Hand Leaning on a Stick

c. 1629
Etching - 97 × 44 mm
Five states

Second state. Crosshatching was added to the shoulder and the cloak at bottom left. The plate was reduced to 93 × 42 mm in the third state and to 90 × 42 mm in the fourth. Vertical crosshatching was added to the shadow of the cloak in the fifth state.

W.B. 166-II: BB 30-15

Provenance: A. de Peters, 1784

In his numerous sketches of beggars dated approximately 1628 to 1631, Rembrandt has given greater importance to the clothes and attitudes of his subjects than to their actual character. A loose, shabby cloak, a battered cap, a stick, a bundle are the main attributes of these figures, often seen in profile or from the back. The artist has filled one-half of his sketch with large, open lines, leaving the other half of the plate white and untouched. These contrasts give life to his subjects.

144 Old Beggar Woman with a Gourd

c. 1630
Etching - 103 × 47 mm
Two states

Second state. The trimming of the originally uneven plate edges accounts for the plate's reduction (first state: 106 × 49 mm). A horizontal line has been added at the bottom of the plate.

W.B. 168-II; BB 30-16

145 Man in a Coat and Fur Cap Leaning Against a Bank

c. 1630
Signed: *RHL* (in monogram, in reverse)
Etching - 112 × 79 mm
Three states

First state. The upper outline of the bank against which the man leans is indicated by a single line which does not quite reach the plate mark. In the second state it was to be continued to the edge of the plate by two lines meeting at an angle. A white vertical strip on the bank at the lower left, due to failure in biting, was corrected in the third state. A single impression of this last state is in the Cabinet des Estampes, Paris.

W.B. 151-I; BB 30-6

146 Beggar with His Left Hand Extended

Signed and dated from the second state onwards:
RHL (in monogram) *1631*
Etching - 77 × 50 mm
Four states

First state. A large dog is asleep on the right. The shading on the cloak is only outlined. In the second state the plate was reduced to 63 × 41 mm.

From the second to the fifth state considerable hatching was added to the cloak.

This is one of the two known impressions from the Cabinet des Estampes, Bibliothèque Nationale, Paris.

W.B. 150-I; BB 31-0

147 Beggar Seated Warming His Hands at a Chafing Dish

c. 1630
Etching - 78 × 47 mm
Two states

Second state. The left underside of the beggar's bundle has now been shaded. It was left unfinished in the first state, where the area bordering the edge of the plate had also been left white. The plate edges are more even in this state than in the first.

W.B. 173-II; BB 30-I

This subject, borrowed from Jacques Callot, has become, in Rembrandt's vision, totally emancipated from its source.

148 Beggar Man and Woman

c. 1628
Etching - 100 × 78 mm
One state only

Again a unique impression from the Bibliothèque Nationale, Paris. This was printed on the reverse of a unique impression of *The Leper* ("Lazarus Klap" W.B.171, figs. 138, 139).

W.B. 183; BB 31-16

Provenance: J.-L. de Beringhen, 1731

149 A Stout Man in a Large Cloak

c. 1628
Etching - 113 × 74 mm
One state only

This unique impression was printed on the reverse of the first state of *Seated Beggar and His Dog* (W.B. 175, figs. 150, 151) also a unique impression.

W.B. 184; BB 31-15

150, 151 Seated Beggar and His Dog

Second state inscribed: *RL* (in monogram) *1631*
Etching and burin - 110 × 81 mm
Two states

First state, without burin, c. 1629. This plate was printed on the reverse of an impression of *A Stout Man in a Large Cloak* (W.B. 184, fig. 149). This single impression was further cut down to 113 × 74 mm.

Second state. The plate was probably reworked in burin by a pupil of Rembrandt.

W.B. 175-I, II; BB 31-P

The discovery of the first state—a lightly sketched beggar—has made it possible to assign the second state to Rembrandt. One should compare the two pieces to distinguish the master's manner from that of his pupil.

152 Sheet of Studies of Men's Heads

c. 1630-31
Signed: *RHL* (monogram in reverse)
Etching - 119 × 91 mm (trimmed impression).
Only one state

One of three known impressions of the complete plate; it was later cut into five pieces, from which impressions were made (W.B. 143, 300, 303, 333 and 334). The fragments were reworked.

W.B. 366; BB 31-3

Provenance: J.-L. de Beringhen, 1731

153 Beggar Man and Beggar Woman Behind a Bank

c. 1630
Signed from first to fourth state: *RHL* (in monogram)
Etching, drypoint and burin - 113 × 82 mm
Nine states

146. Beggar with His Left Hand Extended, W.B. 150, p. 123

145. Man in a Coat and Fur Cap Leaning Against a Bank
W.B. 151, p. 123

147. Beggar Seated Warming His Hands at a Chafing Dish
W.B. 173, p. 123

148. Beggar Man and Woman, W.B. 183, p. 123

149. A Stout Man in a Large Cloak, W.B. 184, p. 123

150, 151. Seated Beggar and His Dog, W.B. 175, p. 123

152. Sheet of Studies of Men's Heads, W.B. 366, p. 123

154. Head of a Man in a Fur Cap, Crying Out, W.B. 327, p. 132

153. Beggar Man and Beggar Woman Behind a Bank, W.B. 165, p. 132

155. Peasant with His Hands Behind His Back, W.B. 135, p. 132

156. Two Studies of Beggars, W.B. 182, p. 132

157. Beggar Sitting in an Armchair, W.B. 160
Amsterdam, Rijksmuseum

158. Peasant Family on the Tramp, W.B. 131, p. 132

159. Beggar with a Wooden Leg, W.B. 179, p. 132

160. Beggar in a High Cap, Standing and Leaning on a Stick, W.B. 162, p. 132

161. A Peasant Replying *Dats Niet* ("That's nothing"), W.B. 178, p. 132   **162. A Peasant Calling Out *Tis Vinnich Kout* ("It's very cold"), W.B. 177, p. 132**

163. Polander Standing with His Stick, W.B. 142, p. 132   **164. Polander Leaning on a Stick, W.B. 141, p. 133**

165. The Skater, W.B. 156, p. 133

166. The Quacksalver, W.B. 129, p. 133

167. The Blind Fiddler, W.B. 138, p. 133

Second state. The plate, originally 116 × 85 mm, has been reduced to 113 × 80 mm. From the fifth state onwards much shading was added to the bank, consequently changing its shape. From the sixth to the ninth state crosshatching was introduced in various areas of the plate. The beggars gradually filled the whole space.

W.B. 165-II; BB 30-5

Provenance: A. de Peters, 1784

This is a strange composition in which the beggars seem to come out of the bank itself: a shapeless bank or rather a shadow replica of the beggars, a symbol of their condition. The broad, deep intaglios in burin gradually give way to lighter and finer drypoint lines, as one gazes from the heavily shaded bank to the merely sketched beggar woman.

154 Head of a Man in a Fur Cap, Crying Out

c. 1629-30
Etching - 35 × 29 mm
Three states

The plate originally measured 37 × 33 mm but was cut down in the second state.

Third state. Crosshatchings have been added on the right shoulder; the slipped stroke on the cap, was burnished out in the second state.

W.B. 327-III; BB 30-14

155 Peasant with His Hands Behind His Back

Signed and dated : RHL (in monogram) 1631
Etching and burin - 60 × 50 mm
Four states

Fourth state. Simply etched in the first state, the plate was shaded in burin in the second and third states; in the present state further shading has been added to the neck, both on the highlight and the shadow.

W.B. 135-IV; BB 31-M

156 Two Studies of Beggars

c. 1629
Etching - 91 × 75 mm
One state only

This impression from the Bibliothèque Nationale, Paris, is unique.

W.B. 182; BB 31-18

Provenance: J.-L. de Beringhen, 1731

158 Peasant Family on the Tramp

c. 1652
Etching - 114 × 93 mm
Two states

First state. Acid biting has failed on the peasant's pack. It was corrected in the next state.

W.B. 131-I; BB 52-3

159 Beggar with a Wooden Leg

c. 1630
Etching - 114 × 66 mm
Two states

First state. The rough, uneven plate edges were trimmed in the second state, causing the beggar's stick to touch the plate mark.

W.B. 179-I; BB 30-4

Provenance: A. de Peters, 1784

160 Beggar in a High Cap, Standing and Leaning on a Stick

c. 1630
Etching - 156 × 122 mm
One state only

W.B. 162; BB 31-1

Provenance: A. de Peters, 1784

Callot's etchings of beggars were among the first prints to be bought by Rembrandt. Rembrandt's liking for tramps, street characters and picturesques scenes was noted quite early in his career. As early as 1641 Joachim von Sandrart wrote: "He preferred to deal with simple, not overrefined subjects and picturesque scenes." In 1699, Roger de Piles, commenting on Rembrandt's art, stated: "Although he was spiritually a good man and earned a great fortune, he was naturally inclined to talk to people of low extraction. Some people concerned for his reputation wanted to draw his attention to it. 'When I want peace of mind, it is not honor but freedom that I seek' was his answer to them."

161 A Peasant Replying: 'Dats Niet' ("That's nothing")

Signed and dated: Rembran f 163 (the letters d and t and the figure 4 are missing)
Etching - 111 × 39 mm
One state only

W.B. 178; BB 34-F

Two prints by Hans Sebald Beham have the same captions (Bartsch 188 and 189).

162 A Peasant Calling Out: 'Tis Vinnich Kout' ("It's very cold")

Signed and dated: Rembrandt f. 1634
Etching - 112 × 39 mm
One state only

W.B. 177; BB 34-E

163 Polander Standing with His Stick

Signed and dated: RHL (in monogram) 1631
Etching - 56 × 21 mm
One state only

Impression with a light surface tone.

W.B. 142; BB 31-B

164 Polander Leaning on a Stick

c. 1632
Etching - 82 × 43 mm
Six states

First state. The outline of the seat of the trousers is a single line, becoming a double line in the next state. The outline of the bank and the foliage between the left leg and the stick were burnished out in the third state, to be replaced by a single line in the sixth state. From the third state onwards, additional shading was gradually added to the figure.

Impression with a light surface tone.

W.B. 141-I; BB 32-5 (five states)

165 The Skater

c. 1639
Etching and drypoint - 62 × 59 mm
One state only

This is one of the early impressions characterized by much drypoint burr.

W.B. 156; BB 39-1

166 The Quacksalver

Signed and dated : *Rembrandt f. 1635*
Etching - 78 × 36 mm
One state only

W.B. 129; BB 35-G

There are eight known copies of this piece. Several of Rembrandt's small figures, which are very finely etched and as animated as this one, look as though they were marionettes or puppets.

167 The Blind Fiddler

Signed and dated: *RHL* (in monogram) *1631*
Etching - 78 × 54 mm
Three states

First state. Before the heavy reworking of the fiddler's clothing in burin.

W.B. 138-I; BB 31-A

It has been suggested, because of some lines along the top margin, that the copperplate was originally larger and had possibly contained other figures.

168 Woman at a Door Hatch Talking to a Man and Children (The Schoolmaster)

Signed and dated : *Rembrandt f. 1641*
Etching - 93 × 63 mm
One state only

W.B. 128; BB 41-N

Provenance: A. de Peters, 1784

169 Man Drawing from a Cast

c. 1641
Etching - 94 × 64 mm
Three states

Second state. The area of shadow behind the cast's head to the left has been worked over.

W.B. 130-II; BB 41-4

170 The Goldsmith

Signed and dated: *Rembrandt f. 1655*
Etching and drypoint - 77 × 57 mm
Two states

First state. Without the vertical lines shading the lower part of the beam.

Impression on Japanese paper.

W.B. 123-I; BB 55-D

Provenance : J.-L. de Beringhen, 1731

The goldsmith protectively holds a piece of sculpture (a mother and children representing Charity) that he is completing. He seems to be at one with his anvil and his work. The golden hue of the Japanese paper helps to suggest the color and brightness of the metal.

No such metal sculpture of similar dimensions is known to exist from that time, although there is a similar but larger wooden sculpture of a mother and children.

171 The Golf Player (Le Jeu du Kolef)

Signed and dated : *Rembrandt f. 1654*
Etching - 95 × 144 mm
Two states

First state. The white areas along the top margin of the plate were shaded in burin in the second state.

W.B. 125-I; BB 54-A

Provenance: J.-L. de Beringhen, 1731

This game was very common in seventeenth-century Holland, although little known in France at the time. It was played in private gardens, as well as in inn and tavern gardens and courtyards. Gersaint has explained at length the rules of the game (G. 121): 'The game of *Kolef* is very common in Holland although very little known in France: people who own a country house often play it in their gardens. But it is usually played in taverns and inns situated out of town, where townfolk go to have a good time. The *Kolef* court varies in size; it may be from eight to twelve yards long, and about nine or ten feet wide. The place of the game proper is usually sanded and walled in, like our mall alleys. Several players can take part at one time, each playing for himself and against the others. At both ends of this alley, in the middle of it, is a round post about two feet in diameter and two feet six inches high; one plays with balls as big as our tennis balls, but these are knocked with a stick the end of which is sheathed in lead and crook-shaped. To begin with the balls are placed at one end of the alley; the skill consists of being the first to touch the wooden post at the other end of it. Because of the distance involved, it is rare to be able to strike it at the first blow; one attempts however to place one's ball as close to the target as possible and in as an advantageous position as possible in order to be able to hit it at the second blow; if one is skillful or vigorous enough to make the ball rebound from one post to the other one, at the opposite end, one is then in a position to be able to hit this post at the third blow rather than at the fourth; in so doing, one is almost sure of winning the game, because the winner is he who hits both posts with the least number of blows. There are some players who are skillful enough to be able to hit both posts with two blows. Sometimes the game is played two against two, or four against four: it is then quite a busy game."

172 The Pancake Woman (La Faiseuse de Koucks*)

Signed and dated: *Rembrandt f. 1635*
Etching - 109 × 78 mm
Three states

Second state. The first state, merely sketched, has now been completed. Shadows have been added to the hat and clothes of the pancake maker, which were almost white in the earlier state, as well as to the boy leaning over immediately behind her, and to the cat and the basket at her feet. Crosshatching has also been added to the skirt of the woman holding a child on the extreme left.

W.B. 124-II; BB 35-I (five states)

There is a preparatory study of the whole print (Benesch 409) in Amsterdam. A study for the small boy and dog occurs in a drawing in the Louvre (Benesch 112).

The old woman, the central character of the composition, at the heart of the movement around her, has been drawn from life. She is much more highly finished than the other figures, who are merely sketched.

* The French title, *La Faiseuse de Koucks,* has been explained by Gersaint, who gives a definition of the *Kouck* : "The *Kouck* is a sort of pancake that is very thin and little cooked. It is made of flour, eggs and milk mixed together to form a liquid dough that is thrown into the pan with melted butter that is not yet brown; generally, the pan used is wide and the dough fills it completely. In Holland these *Koucks* are often served after meals; they are piled up, one on top of the other, and come away as loosely as the leaves of a book. As they are soft and thin, they are folded five or six times before being eaten." (G. 110)

173 The Rat Catcher

Signed and dated : *RHL* (in monogram) *1632* (the last two numbers reversed)
Etching - 139 × 126 mm
Three states

Third state. The foliage and the right side of the box held by the child are shaded with parallel diagonal lines with the burin.

W.B. 121-III; BB 32-C

Provenance: A. de Peters, 1784

There are eleven known copies of this print. This was the first genre subject executed by the artist; the very picturesqueness of the scene must have made it attractive.

174 The Strolling Musicians

c. 1635
Etching - 140 × 115 mm
Two states

First state. Before shading was added to the headgear of the beggar, the boy and the woman, and to the baby's chest.

W.B. 119-I; BB 35-8

Provenance: A. de Peters, 1784

175 Beggars Receiving Alms at the Door of a House

Signed and dated: *Rembrandt. f. 1648*
Etching, burin and drypoint - 166 × 130 mm
Three states

First state. The areas behind the cap of the old man giving alms and on the half-door and wall in front of him have been shaded in open crosshatching; these parts were worked over using very fine horizontal crosshatching in the second state. Very fine drypoint intaglios were subsequently added to various areas of the plate.

W.B. 176-I; BB 48-C

176 The Flute Player ("L'Espiègle")

Signed and dated from the second state onwards:
Rembrandt. f. 1642 (the *2* reversed)
Etching and drypoint - 117 × 145 mm
Four states

First state. A dark shadow extends immediately above the girl's hat. It was burnished white and replaced by lightly drawn foliage in the second state, and then restored in drypoint in the third state. The face in the upper part of the foliage to the right was ultimately burnished out and the plate reworked in various areas in the fourth state.

W.B 188-I; BB 42-D (five states)

Provenance: A. de Peters, 1784

177 The Hog

Signed and dated: *Rembrandt f 1643*
Etching and drypoint - 145 × 184 mm
Two states

First state. Without the crosshatching added to the boy's face and the baby's ear flap.

W.B. 157-I; BB 43-A

The hog inspired quite a number of seventeenth-century Dutch painters, although none of them has represented the animal about to be slaughtered. The child on the right-hand side of the plate is holding an inflated bladder, an emblem of death in seventeenth-century Holland.

This very uncommon image has always caught the viewers' attention. Describing Rembrandt's art with great precision, as regards the rendering of the modeling in the artist's *Hog,* Charles Blanc commented further: "One day, while I was in the Cabinet des Estampes of the Bibliothèque [Nationale] closely examining this fine piece on the curator's desk, one of our most famous engravers, Henriquel Dumont, walked in. Noticing this amazing print, he came near the desk and after contemplating it for some time he exclaimed: "This Rembrandt is truly the magician of our art!" (Bl. 350)

178 A Man Making Water

Signed and dated: *RHL* (in monogram) *1631*
Etching - 83 × 49 mm
One state only

W.B. 190; BB 31-C

179 A Woman Making Water

Signed and dated: *RHL* (in monogram) *1631*
Etching - 81 × 64 mm
One state only

W.B. 191; BB 31-D

Provenance: A. de Peters, 1784

180 The Monk in the Cornfield

c. 1646
Etching and drypoint - 48 × 66 mm
One state only

W.B. 187; BB 46-2

Provenance: A. de Peters, 1784

181 "Ledikant" or "Le lit à la française"

Signed and dated: *Rembrandt. f. 1646* (the two *6*s in reverse)
Etching, burin and drypoint - 126 × 225 mm
Five states

Fourth state. The lines on the sleeve of the man's right arm were burnished out and redrawn in the third state. The cloth on the small table near the bedstead has been shaded with diagonals. The plate, originally 150 × 224 mm, was cut down for the first time in the second state and further reduced to 125 × 177 mm in the fifth state, where the wall and doorway were cut away.

W.B. 186-IV; BB 46-D (four states)

Gersaint was the first to give a title to this etching. The Dutch had referred to it as *Ledikant*, which means a "state bed." The woman has either three or four arms, depending on the commentators. Rembrandt, in changing her position, deliberately forebore to rub out the first arm, on the bed.

182 Girl with a Basket

c. 1642
Etching - 87 × 63 mm
Two states

Second state. Vertical lines shade the forehead on the left, beneath the hat. The cheek is outlined from the right eye to the mouth. A horizontal line appears at the end of the strokes on the bridge of the nose. It is possible but not certain that the difference in dimensions visible in this proof is due to the evening up of the edges.

W.B. 356-II; BB 42-3

184 Sick Woman with a Large White Headdress

c. 1641-42
Etching with touches of drypoint - 63 × 52 mm
Only one state

W.B. 359; BB 42-4

This head has been identified as a portrait of Saskia when sick; the same woman can be seen in *The Hundred Guilder Print.*

185 The White Negress

c. 1630
Signed in the first state only: *RHL* (in monogram reversed)
Etching -
Two states

First state. The plate is 113 × 83 mm. Impression with considerable surface tone.

Second state. The plate has been cut down to 98 × 78 mm, thus removing the monogram. Not reproduced.

W.B. 357-I, II; BB 30-17

186 The Spanish Gypsy "Preciosa"

c. 1642
Etching - 133 × 113 mm
One state only

W.B. 120; BB 42-2

There is a preparatory drawing in Brussels (Benesch 737).

Regarding this print, Gersaint has written: "The subject is derived from a Spanish story which has been dealt with in a Dutch tragedy I saw in Amsterdam. I believe this print was etched to serve as an illustration to the printed drama."

Thereafter Gersaint summed up the story (G. 116): "A Gypsy kidnapped a young Spanish Princess. She brought her up with great care but afterwards made her her companion in all her adventurous outings. She kept closely guarded the secret of the princess's high birth. However, one day the gypsy was walking through a wood with her protégée when a Prince, hunting there, was surprised at the beauty of the young lady; he approached her, spoke to her and fell immediately head over heels in love with her. Some time later, he discovered by chance the secret of her birth and set himself to the task of abducting her from the hands of this gypsy in order to marry her."

Blanc thinks that the subject was inspired by *Preciosa*, a short story by Cervantes; Jan Six saw in it an illustration of *Het Leven van Konstance; waaruit volgt het toneelspel, De Spaensche Heidin de Tengnagel.*

All these characters are already Goya-like.

187 Old Woman Seated in a Cottage, with a String of Onions on the Wall

Signed and dated from second state onwards: *Rt. 1631*
Etching - 123 × 81 mm with border line (reduced impression).
Three states

Second state. The plate, originally 128 × 85 mm, has been cut down; the border line has been added.

W.B. 134-II; BB Rej. 11 (as inauthentic)

168. Woman at a Door Hatch Talking to a Man and Children (The Schoolmaster), W.B. 128, p. 133

169. Man Drawing from a Cast, W.B. 130, p. 133

170. The Goldsmith, W.B. 123, p. 133

171. The Golf Player (Le Jeu du Kolef), W.B. 125, p. 133

137

172. The Pancake Woman (La Faiseuse de Koucks), W.B. 124, p. 134

173. The Rat Catcher, W.B. 121, p. 134

174. The Strolling Musicians, W.B. 119, p. 134

175. Beggars Receiving Alms at the Door of a House, W.B. 176, p. 134

176. The Flute Player ("L'Espiègle"), W.B. 188, p. 134

177. The Hog, W.B. 157, p. 134

178. A Man Making Water, W.B. 190, p. 134

179. A Woman Making Water, W.B. 191, p. 134

180. The Monk in the Cornfield, W.B. 187, p. 135

181. "Ledikant" or "Le lit à la française," W.B. 186, p. 135

182. Girl with a Basket, W.B. 356, p. 135

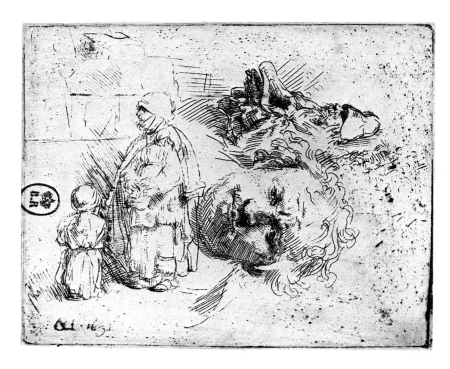

183. Sheet of Studies with the Head of the Artist, W.B. 370, p. 616

184. Sick Woman with a Large White Headdress (Saskia)
W.B. 359, p. 135

185. The White Negress, W.B. 357, p. 135

186. The Spanish Gypsy "Preciosa", W.B. 120, p. 135

187. Old Woman Seated in a Cottage, with a String of Onions on the Wall, W.B. 134, p. 135

188 The Artist's Mother in a Cloth Headdress, Looking Down

Signed and dated beginning with second state:
Rembrandt f. 1633
Etching - 43 × 41 mm
Two states

Second state. The hood shows additional shading, and there has been further work on the shoulders. The plate has been cut down from its original size, 63 × 59 mm; the one impression of the first state, now in the British Museum, does not show the plate marks.

W.B. 351-II; BB 33-F

Provenance: Mariette sale, 1775

189 The Artist's Mother, Head and Bust

Signed and dated in the second state: *RHL (in monogram) 1628 (the 2 reversed)*
Etching - 65 × 63 mm
Two states

Second state. In the first state, only the head had been completed and the bust was lightly sketched in. Here both headdress and bust are completed. Strokes have been added below the right eye.

W.B. 354-II; BB 28-A

Provenance: A. de Peters, 1784

190 The Artist's Mother: Head Only, Full Face

Signed and dated beginning with the second state: *RHL (in monogram) 1628 (the 2 reversed)*
Etching - 63 × 64 mm
Two states

Second state. In the first state, only the face was etched. The hood is now completed. The plate has been cut down from 85 × 72 mm. This is one of Rembrandt's earliest dated etchings. The impression is bordered with a line of brown ink.

W.B. 352-II; BB 28-B

The surprising way in which the face is positioned in the second state corresponds to a profound change in expression and accentuates the fact that the sitter is looking downward.

191 The Artist's Mother with Her Hand on Her Chest

Signed and dated: *RHL (in monogram) 1631*
Etching - 94 × 66 mm
Two states

First state. In the next state, the eyes and the right cheek were retouched, the shadow was strengthened by vertical lines, and the area below the hands was reworked.

W.B. 349-I; BB 31-G (four states)

Provenance: A. de Peters, 1784

192 The Artist's Mother (with Black Shawl)

c. 1631
Etching - 148 × 131 mm
Three states

Second state. Diagonal shading added to the shadow below the chair and to the left, where the shading extends to the margin. The plate was cut down to an oval in the third state.

W.B. 343-II; BB 31-8

Provenance: A. de Peters, 1784

193 The Artist's Mother Seated, in an Oriental Headdress

Etching - 145 × 129 mm
Three states

Second state. The shadow at the left of the plate stops at shoulder height, whereas in the first state it went as far as the top of the cap. The right sleeve has been reworked.

The third state is not by Rembrandt.

W.B. 348-II; BB 31-H

Provenance: Mariette sale, 1775

194 Woman Reading

Signed and dated: *Rembrandt f 1634*
Etching - 124 × 100 mm
Three states

Second state. The left sleeve is wider. The width of the plate has been reduced by 2 mm on the left, and the straight line of the border now cuts the corner of the page in the book. In the third state, there is a double outline around the tip of the nose, and a slipped stroke crosses the cheek. The third state is not by Rembrandt.

W.B. 345-II; BB 34-D

195 Saskia with Pearls in Her Hair

Signed and dated: *Rembrandt f 1634*
Etching - 87 × 67 mm
Only one state

W.B. 347; BB 34-C (two states)

196 The Little Jewish Bride (Saskia as St. Catherine)

Signed and dated: *Rembrandt f 1638* (reversed)
Etching and touches of drypoint - 110 × 78 mm
Only one state

W.B. 342; BB 38-A

197 Studies of the Head of Saskia, and Others

Signed and dated: *Rembrandt f 1636*
Etching - 152 × 127 mm
Only one state

W.B. 365; BB 36-B

The head in the middle has been identified as that of Saskia.

198 Sheet of Studies, with a Woman Lying in Bed

c. 1641-42
Etching - 151 × 132 mm
Only one state

W.B. 369; BB 38-2

199, 200 Three Heads of Women

c. 1637
Signed in the second state only: *Rembrandt*
Etching -
Three states

First state. Only the head at the top can be seen. One of the five known impressions, 124 × 100 mm (trimmed impression).

Provenance: J.-L. de Beringhen, 1731

Third state. The scratches and the signature which, along with two additional heads, had appeared in the second state, have been burnished out, 124 × 103 mm (trimmed impression).

W.B. 367-I, III; BB 37-3

It has been assumed that the head appearing in the first state is that of Saskia.

201 Three Heads of Women: One Asleep

Signed and dated: *Rembrandt f 1637*
Etching - 142 × 95 mm
Only one state

W.B. 368; BB 37-D

Provenance: A. de Peters, 1784

202, 203 The Great Jewish Bride

Signed and dated beginning with the third state: *R 1635* (reversed)
Etching with a little drypoint and burin - 221 × 170 mm
Five states

Second state. Only the upper half of the plate, with the head and background, has been etched; the other half is white. Very similar to the first state; slight shading has been added to the right side of the forehead, which had been white; above the left eye; on the cheek below the right corner of the left eye; and on the right wing of the nose. A white line, caused by a defect in the paper, appears to cross the hair in this impression.

Provenance: J.-L. de Beringhen, 1731

Fifth state. The lower portion of the plate was completed in the third state, and the hands and sleeves were shaded in the fourth. Here the stones of the pillar on the right are clearly shown by horizontal lines.

W.B. 340-II, V; BB 35-C

This strange and captivating portrait has been variously identified as the daughter of Ephraïm Bonus (W.B. 278, fig. 260), as Esther, as a Sibyl, as an actress, and as Saskia. The same woman was portrayed in 1638 under two alternative titles: *Saskia as St. Catherine* or *The Little Jewish Bride* (see below). Gersaint explains the title of *Jewish Bride* as follows: "She wears a string of pearls about her head (it was customary at this time, in Holland, for Jewish women who were about to be married to wear their hair in this manner." More recently, Landsberger, in his *Rembrandt, the Jews and the Bible* (Philadelphia, 1946, p. 74), has pointed out that a Jewish bride received her husband with her hair down and the *ketuba*, or Jewish marriage contract, in her hand.

204 Naked Woman Seated on a Mound

c. 1631
Signed : *RHL* (in monogram)

Etching - 177 × 160 mm
Two states

Second state. The hatching and crosshatching that shaded the top of the left thigh have been burnished out. The upper part of the right shoulder has been shaded by crosshatching. The white areas behind the woman's left calf and in the crook of her left arm have been shaded over.

W.B. 198-II; BB 31-5

Provenance: J.-L. de Beringhen, 1731

The light, falling upon the model, causes her whole figure to sag.

Together with *Diana at the Bath* (W.B. 201, fig. 205), this is one of the first etched nudes by Rembrandt characterized by a provoking naturalism, a naturalism that was yet to be mellowed several years later, in *Adam and Eve* (W.B. 28, fig. 434).

In 1681, André Pels was shocked by this nude. In outrage, he wrote: "Rather than taking the Greek Venus for his model, he has picked a washerwoman or a peat digger. One cannot deny that! Her breasts are baggy, her hands are deformed. His close observation has brought out everything, from the marks left by the blouse around her loins, to those left by the garters around her legs!" (*Gebruick en misbruick des toonels*, Amsterdam, 1681).

205 Diana at the Bath

c. 1631
Signed: *RHL. f.*
Etching - 178 × 159 mm
One state only

W.B. 201; BB 31-4

There is a preparatory drawing (Benesch 21).

206, 207 Woman at the Bath with a Hat Beside Her

Signed and dated: *Rembrandt. f. 1658*
Etching and drypoint - 158 × 129 mm
Two states

First state. The cap is as high as it is wide.

Two impressions: Impression on Japanese paper printed with surface tone in the shaded areas of the arms and the right leg. Impression on a golden-hued vellum with a light surface tone in the shaded areas.

Second state. The height of the cap has been reduced and its shape rounded like a turban.

Impression on Japanese paper.

W.B. 199-I, II; BB 58-C

From 1658 to 1661 Rembrandt etched a series of female nudes (W.B. 199, 200, 202, 203, 205, figs. 210 to 214, 216), totally different from his earlier ones (W.B. 198, 201, figs. 204, 205). If, according to Sandrart's relevant comments, "he fought against the academies and drew from nature alone," he was able to borrow from nature and decipher its aesthetic audacity. His supports, whether Japanese paper, vellum or Dutch paper, were to him a palette of lights with different nuances; inking was responsible for modeling. From one impression to the next, technical alterations were minimal and yet all the proofs are different, both in the general impression and in the specific expressions of the model's face.

188. The Artist's Mother in a Cloth Headdress, Looking Down
W.B. 351, p. 150

190. The Artist's Mother, W.B. 352, p. 150

189. The Artist's Mother, Head and Bust, W.B. 354, p. 150

191. The Artist's Mother with Her Hand on Her Chest
W.B. 349, p. 150

192. **The Artist's Mother (with Black Shawl)**, W.B. 343, p. 150

193. The Artist's Mother Seated, in an Oriental Headdress
W.B. 348, p. 150

208, 209 Woman Sitting Half Dressed Beside a Stove

Signed and dated: *Rembrandt f. 1658*
Etching, burin and drypoint - 227 × 186 mm
Seven states

Second state. The model's breasts and right side, lightly modeled in the first state, have been shaded with crosshatching. An indefinite lighting shapes the background elements.

This is one of the four known impressions.

Provenance: A. de Peters, 1784

Third state. Crosshatching has darkened the entire background. Additional horizontal and vertical intaglios and crosshatching have completed the light diagonal hatching shading the stove pipe. The structure of the niche has been altered by the introduction of a vertical wall to the left. Areas of light and shade have been clearly defined.

Seventh state. Several details have been gradually modified. In the fourth state, a damper key was inserted into the stove pipe. In the fifth state the hem of the skirt was ornamented with a drypoint pattern and the upper outline of the petticoat was shaded by additional crosshatching. In the sixth state the model's cap was removed, showing the woman's hair tied up in a bun. Lastly, a single unintentional scratch above the model's left breast distinguishes the seventh state from the sixth. The fold-mark in the paper to the right-hand side must have occurred in printing.

Impression on Japanese paper.

W.B. 197-II, III, VII; BB 58-B

In the second state this realistic subject was pervaded by a dreamlike atmosphere, due essentially to the lyricism expressed by the radiantly bright areas and lack of definition in the structural elements. From the second state onwards, a gradually deepening darkness, increasingly better defined shapes, and stronger contrasts between light and shade concentrate the viewer's attention on the woman's chest; like mother-of-pearl in the second state this has become ivory on the Japanese paper used for the seventh, thereby restoring realism to the subject.

210 Woman with the Arrow (Cleopatra)

Signed and dated: *Rembrandt f. 1661* (the *d* reversed)
Etching, drypoint and burin - 205 × 123 mm
Three states

Third state. In the second state, additional crosshatching was introduced in the area between the woman's foot and the hanging sleeve, as well as on her left cheek, although the latter is indistinct. The triangular area of white to the upper right of the date has been shaded. The signature has been redrawn. In various places this plate looks like a drawing or a soft-ground etching. It was laid flat for acid corrosion and, as a consequence, biting did not go far enough. The modeling was mainly achieved through reworking in drypoint and burin.

W.B. 202-III; BB 61-A (four states)

There is a preparatory drawing in London (Benesch 1147).

This is Rembrandt's last dated print; together with the *Negress Lying Down* (W.B. 205, figs. 213, 214), it is one of his most handsomely achieved etchings of a female body. The arrow is simply the shining braid of the bed curtain which the woman clasps in order to draw it aside. A man's face (Antony's?), modeled by faint gleams, emerges from the shading to the left.

211, 212 Woman Bathing Her Feet at a Brook

Signed and dated: *Rembrandt f. 1658*
Etching - 160 × 80 mm
One state only

W.B. 200; BB 58-D

Two impressions: Impression on Japanese paper. Impression on vellum with regular surface tone.

Provenance: A. de Peters, 1784

213, 214 Negress Lying Down

Signed and dated: *Rembrandt f. 1658*
Etching, drypoint and burin
Three states

First state. Several areas of white at the top of the plate were shaded in the third state; the pillow was shaded with crosshatching in the second state.

Unique impression on Japanese paper - 160 × 82 mm

Second state. Crosshatching has been added on the sheet.

Impression on Japanese paper - 158 × 81 mm

W.B. 205-I, II; BB 58-E

Provenance: Verstolk van Soelen's sale, 1847

Bartsch was apparently the first to give the etching its present title. In the catalogue of Amadée de Burgy's collection, established in 1755, the print was referred to as "Une femme dormant nue, les fesses au vent" ("Sleeping Female Nude, with Buttocks Uncovered"; n° 550). Here the modeling has been achieved by shading, not by the use of light. A tight meshwork of hatching defines the shapes, even describing their outlines. The modulations of the surface tone through inking and a selective wiping out filter the light that enlivens the nude.

This woman lying in the dark is strongly reminiscent of Titian's late female nudes.

215 Jupiter and Antiope

The Smaller Plate
c. 1631
Signed: *RHL* (in monogram)
Etching - 83 × 112 mm
Two states

Second state. A drapery covers the knees. The shading on the thighs has been burnished out. The edges of the plate have been trimmed and the corners rounded.

W.B. 204-II; BB 31-6

Hind was the first to give the present title to this etching. It is listed in de Jonghe's inventory under the title of "Venus and Satyr", and in that of Röver under the title of "Danae." Rovinski has entitled it "Sleeping Nude." Wilson and Blanc, discerning a shower of gold on the left-hand side, restored the title of "Danae and Jupiter" to the print.

216 Jupiter and Antiope

The Larger Plate
Signed and dated: *Rembrandt f 1659*
Etching, burin and drypoint - 140 × 206 mm
Two states

First state. Before reworking and inscription (top right) due to the interpolation of a different hand. This early impression has rough edges.

Impression on Japanese paper.

W.B. 203-I; BB 59-B

194. Woman Reading, W.B. 345, p. 150

195. Saskia with Pearls in Her Hair, W.B. 347, p. 150

196. The Little Jewish Bride, W.B. 342, p. 150

197. Studies of the Head of Saskia, and Others, W.B. 365, p. 150

198. Sheet of Studies, with a Woman Lying in Bed, W.B. 369, p. 150

199, 200. Three Heads of Woman, W.B. 367-I, III, p. 150

201. Three Heads of Women, One Asleep, W.B. 368, p. 151

202. The Great Jewish Bride, W.B. 340-II, p. 151

203. The Great Jewish Bride, W.B. 340-IV, p. 151

204. Naked Woman Seated on a Mound, W.B. 198, p. 151

205. Diana at the Bath, W.B. 201, p. 151

206. Woman at the Bath with a Hat Beside Her, W.B.199-I, p. 151

207. Woman at the Bath with a Hat Beside Her, W.B. 199-II, p. 151

208. Woman Sitting Half Dressed Beside a Stove, W.B. 197-II, p. 156

209. Woman Sitting Half Dressed Beside a Stove, W.B. 197-VII, p. 156

210. Woman with the Arrow (Cleopatra), W.B. 202, p. 156

211, 212. Woman Bathing Her Feet at a Brook, W.B. 200, p. 156

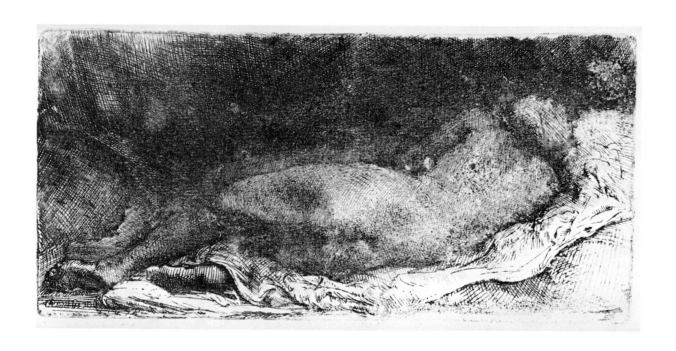

213. Negress Lying Down, W.B. 205-I, p. 156

214. Negress Lying Down, W.B. 205-II, p. 156

215. Jupiter and Antiope (The Smaller Plate), W.B. 204, p. 156

216. Jupiter and Antiope (The Larger Plate), W.B 203, p. 156

**217, 218. Nude Man Seated on the Ground with One Leg Extended
(Proof and Counterproof),** W.B. 196, p. 180

219. Nude Man Seated Before a Curtain, W.B. 193, p. 180

220. The Artist's Son, Titus, W.B. 11, p. 180

221. Portrait of a Boy, in Profile, W.B. 310, p. 180

222. The Card Player, W.B. 136, p. 180

223. Man at a Desk with Cross and Chain, W.B. 261, p. 180

217, 218 Nude Man Seated on the Ground with One Leg Extended

Signed and dated: *Rembrandt. f. 1646*
Etching - 97 × 168 mm
Two states

Second state. The rough plate edges have been trimmed and the corners rounded. The narrow white strip along the internal outline of the forearm has been shaded. Vertical intaglios have covered the upper part of the left thigh near the loincloth.

Impression and counterproof.

W.B. 196-II; BB 46-C

219 Nude Man Seated Before a Curtain

Signed and dated: *Rembrandt. f. 1646*
Etching - 165 × 98 mm
Two states

First state. The hair beside the right cheek is visible. This is one of the earliest impressions with uneven plate edges.

W.B. 193-I; BB 46-B

A drawing by a pupil of Rembrandt showing in reverse the same model in the same pose (Benesch A 48) is in the Cabinet des Estampes, Paris. There are several known prints of academic male nudes etched or drawn, c. 1646. They are not all by Rembrandt, although they are very close to the prints listed under W.B. 193, 194, 196 (figs. 219, 4, 217, 218). It has been suggested that master and pupils studied academic nudes from life.

220 The Artist's Son, Titus

c. 1656
Etching - 97 × 70 mm
One state only

The vertical line on the right is the result of an accident. Impression with surface tone on Japanese paper.

W.B. 11; BB 56-1

Gersaint (15) and Bartsch (11) see a self-portrait in this print. Claussin (11), Charles Blanc (236) and Middleton (165) think that it is a portrait of Titus, Rembrandt's son.

221 Portrait of a Boy, in Profile

William II, Prince of Orange
Signed and dated: *Rembrandt f 1641*
Etching - 95 × 67 mm
Only one state

The abundant light grain on the earliest impressions has not yet altogether disappeared.

W.B. 310; BB 41-K

222 The Card Player

Signed and dated : *Rembrandt f. 1641*
Etching - 88 × 81 mm
Two states

Second state. The background has been reworked and darkened. The white areas along the top margin have been filled in.

W.B. 136-II; BB 41-M (three states)
Provenance: A. de Peters, 1784

223 Man at a Desk with Cross and Chain

Signed and dated: *Rembrandt f. 1641*
Four states

Second state. A small white collar has been drawn with the burnisher.

W.B. 261-II; BB 41-L

Provenance: A. de Peters, 1784

224 The Persian

Signed and dated: *RHL* (in monogram) *1632* (the last two numbers reversed)
Etching - 109 × 79 mm
One state only

W.B. 152; BB 32-A

225 Old Man with a Flowing Beard

Signed and dated: *RHL* (in monogram) *1631*
Etching - 68 × 66 mm
Two states

Second state. Diagonal crosshatching has been added to the shadow to the left of the right shoulder. A tuft of hair has been added near the left ear, so that the hair forms a continuous line from temple to shoulder. The edges of the plate have been evened up.

W.B. 315-II; BB 31-F

Provenance: A. de Peters, 1784

226 Bust of an Old Man with a Flowing Beard

Signed and dated: *RHL* (in monogram) *1630*
Etching - 92 × 76 mm
One state

W.B. 325; BB 30-J

One drawing exists (Benesch 38).

227 Bust of an Old Man with Flowing Beard and White Sleeve

c. 1630
Etching - 71 × 64mm
Only one state

W.B. 291; BB 30-10

Two drawings exist (Benesch 37 and 41).

228 Bust of an Old Bearded Man, Looking Down

Signed and dated: *RHL* (in monogram) *1631*
Etching - 118 × 112 mm
(impression reduced from 119 × 117 mm)
Three states

Second state. Several intaglios outlining the cloak on the left shoulder have been burnished out, but they can still be made out. In the next state the plate was reduced to 119 × 106 mm, eliminating the last two figures of the date.

W.B. 260-11; BB 31-E

224. The Persian, W.B. 152, p. 180

225. Old Man with a Flowing Beard, W.B. 315, p. 180

228. Bust of an Old Bearded Man, Looking Down, W.B. 260, p. 180

226. Bust of an Old Man with a Flowing Beard, W.B. 325, p. 180

227. Bust of an Old Man with Flowing Beard and White Sleeve
W.B. 291, p. 180

229. Old Man with a Flowing Beard, W.B. 309, p. 190

230. Old Man with Beard, Fur Cap and Velvet Cloak, W.B. 262, p. 190

231. Bald-Headed Man, in Profile Right (The Artist's Father?)
W.B. 292, p. 190

232. Bald-Headed Man in Profile Right (The Artist's Father?)
W.B. 294, p. 190

233. Three Studies of Old Men's Heads, W.B. 374, p. 190

234. Man Wearing a Close Cap (The Artist's Father?), W.B. 304, p. 190

**235. Bust of a Man Wearing a High Cap, Three-Quarters Right
(The Artist's Father?)**, W.B. 321, p. 190

**236. Bearded Man in Furred Oriental Cap and Robe
(The Artist's Father?)**, W.B. 263, p. 190

237. The First Oriental Head, W.B. 286, p. 190

238. Old Bearded Man in a High Fur Cap, with Eyes Closed
W.B. 290, p. 190

239. The Second Oriental Head, W.B. 287, p. 191

240. The Third Oriental Head, W.B. 288, p. 191

229 Old Man with a Flowing Beard

Signed and dated: *RHL (in monogram) 1630*
Etching - 98 × 81 mm
Only one state

W.B. 309; BB 30-K

Provenance: A. de Peters, 1784

230 Old Man with Beard, Fur Cap and Velvet Cloak

c. 1632
Signed: *RHL (in monogram) fe*
Etching - 149 × 131 mm
Three states

First state. A patch of white showing below the right hand was shaded in the next state.

W.B. 262-I; BB 32-2 (four states)

231 Bald-Headed Man, in Profile Right

The Artist's Father?
Signed and dated in the first and second states: *RL (in monogram) 1630;* in the third state: *RHL (in monogram) 1630.*
Etching - 118 × 97 mm
Three states

First state. Only the head has been etched; the bust, lightly sketched in, was etched in the second state. The plate was then cut down at the shoulders in the third state so that it measured only 69 × 58 mm; the background was shaded.

W.B. 292-I; BB 30-G

Provenance: A. de Peters, 1784

Rembrandt's father was buried on April 27, 1630.

232 Bald-Headed Man in Profile Right

The Artist's Father?
Signed and dated : *RHL (in monogram) 1630*
Etching - 56 × 42 mm
Only one state

W.B. 294; BB 30-H (two states)

233 Three Studies of Old Men's Heads

c. 1630
Etching - 91 × 82 mm (trimmed impression).
Only one state

W.B. 374; BB 30-9

Provenance: J.-L. de Beringhen, 1731

234 Man Wearing a Close Cap

The Artist's Father?
Signed and dated beginning with the second state: *RHL (in monogram) 1630*
Etching - 97 × 75 mm
Five states

First state. Only the head has been completed; the body, lightly shaded, was completely shaded in the second state. In the third state the plate was cut down to 75 × 60 mm; a new monogram and the date were added at the upper left. In the fourth state, the background was shaded; in the fifth, the plate was reworked but not by Rembrandt.

W.B. 304-I; BB 30-E

Provenance: Prints Department, Rijksmuseum, Amsterdam (on the back of the etching, a stamp: von Lugt 240).

A painting exists (Bredius 77).

235 Bust of a Man Wearing a High Cap, Three-Quarters Right

The Artist's Father (?)
Signed and dated: *RHL (in monogram) 1630*
Etching - 103 × 84 mm
Two states

Second state. The plate has been cut down from 107 × 89 mm and its edges have been trimmed.

W.B. 321-II; BB 30-F

A painting of Rembrandt's father, dated 1630, is similar to this etching. It was engraved in reverse by van Vliet (Bartsch 24).

236 Bearded Man, in a Furred Oriental Cap and Robe (The Artist's Father?)

Signed and dated in second state: *RHL (in monogram) 1631*
Etching and burin - 147 × 130 mm
Four states

First state. Before monogram and date.

Third state. Hand at lower right burnished away.

W.B. 263-I; BB 31-J

Provenance: A. de Peters, 1784

237 The First Oriental Head

Signed and dated: *Rembrandt geretuc 1635*
Etching with a little drypoint - 151 × 125 mm
Three states

Second state. The white space that appeared on the left of the neck is now shaded over, and the bottom left-hand and top right-hand corners have been rounded off.

In the third state, the publisher's name, F. van Wyngaerde, and the figure 5 were added. The bottom left-hand corner of this impression has been restored.

W.B. 286-II; BB 35-E

Provenance: A. de Peters, 1784

This print is a copy in reverse of a print by Lievens (Bartsch 21), probably done by a pupil and retouched by Rembrandt. It has aroused considerable controversy.

238 Old Bearded Man in a High Fur Cap, with Eyes Closed

c. 1635
Signed: *Rembrandt*
Etching - 114 × 103 mm
Only one state

W.B. 290; BB 35-3

Reminiscent of the three Oriental heads, this print is in the style of Castiglione. Rembrandt already has firm control of his needle, and the freedom of line found in this etching is in perfect harmony with the strangeness of the expression.

239 The Second Oriental Head

c. 1635
Signed: *Rembrandt geretuckert*
Etching - 151 × 125 mm
Only one state

W.B. 287; BB 35-4

Copy in reverse of an etching by Lievens (Bartsch 20), done by a pupil and retouched by Rembrandt. This face strongly resembles that of Rembrandt's father.

240 The Third Oriental Head

Signed and dated: *Rembrandt geretuck 1635*
Etching - 157 × 134 mm
Only one state

W.B. 288; BB 35-F

Provenance: A. de Peters, 1784

Copy in reverse of an etching by Lievens (Bartsch 18), probably done by a pupil and retouched by Rembrandt. Vosmaer interprets the word "geretuck" which follows Rembrandt's signature as "geretuckerdt," a Dutch word meaning "retouched"; this would confirm the theories commonly held.

241 Jews in the Synagogue

Signed and dated : *Rembrandt f. 1648*
Etching and drypoint - 72 × 129 mm
Three states

First state. The right foot and the bottom of the coat of the figure to the left have been left white. They were shaded with burin intaglios in the next state.

W.B. 126-I; BB 48-D

Rembrandt was well acquainted with the Jews and "lived the Bible." The atmosphere of a sacred place is captured above all in the attitudes. This small piece has the impact of a snapshot.

242 Medea or The Marriage of Jason and Creusa

Signed and dated in the fourth state: *Rembrandt f. 1648*
Etching with touches of drypoint - 241 × 178 mm
Five states

Fourth state. The plate was completed in drypoint in the second state with the lengthening of Medea's robe in the right foreground; in the third state the cap worn by the sculpted seated figure of Juno was replaced by a crown in drypoint. Four verses in Dutch, the date and the signature were later added in the bottom margin of the plate, but these were all cut out in the fifth state.

W.B. 112-IV; BB 48-E

Provenance: A. de Peters, 1784

While still a secretary of the town of Amsterdam, the burgomaster Jan Six wrote *Medea*, a verse tragedy. He asked Rembrandt to etch an illustration for the printed version of his play. The artist accepted but, as Blanc has remarked, the scene represented does not illustrate any specific scene in Jan Six's drama, since in it the marriage of Jason and Creusa actually takes place offstage.

The plate was used to make several single prints before being used to make book illustrations.

Gersaint's comment (G. 124) on this print deserves to be quoted in part: "In the impression of the second state, which is most rare, the same Juno has on her head the simple little cap Dutch women usually wear as a night cap. This feature may in the eyes of people have appeared insufficiently decent for a Goddess; they consequently obliged Rembrandt to substitute a crown for it; but such mistakes regarding *costume*,* were quite habitual with this Master who, in his compositions, troubled himself little with complying exactly with contemporary usage regarding what suited and did not suit his subjects. He has almost always dressed his figures in the Dutch fashion, and at times, looking closely at his compositions, one cannot refrain from laughing. He has even often dealt with the most respectable subjects in so personal a manner, dressing his figures so originally, that one could only be shocked by them; it would be erroneous, however, to reproach him with any bad intention. He was simply carried away by habit. In spite of all these flaws of carelessness and indecency, one cannot but admire his compositions, however ridiculous they may appear, because of his fine use of light and shade (chiaroscuro) which pervades them all and because of the spirituality brightening up the faces of his characters; one feels compelled to forgive him all his flaws. I actually believe that he is the only artist for whom one feels such indulgence; indeed the parts in which he excells please so violently that they throw a thick veil of shadow upon the mistakes one could reproach him with."

He must have thought, in a like manner, that the antique temple much resembled the Dutch Reformed Church.

* Costume is a word appertaining to Painting by which is meant the manner in which a subject is dealt with, in accordance with time and place and to give consequently to each figure clothing and character in keeping with the story painted.

243 Samuel Manasseh ben Israel

Signed and dated: *Rembrandt f 1636*
Etching - 149 × 107 mm
Three states

Second state. The outline of the cheek, which had been slightly indented, has been rounded out. Diagonal strokes cross the earlobe. Crosshatching imparts additional shading to the fold of the cloak on the left. A few more touches were added to the third state.

W.B. 269-II; BB 36-C (four states)

Provenance: A. de Peters, 1784

Manasseh ben Israel (1604-1657), a Portuguese Jew, was a writer and a rabbi, and one of Rembrandt's friends. He had commissioned from Rembrandt the illustrations for his book, *La piedra gloriosa*, in 1655 (W.B. 36, figs. 459 to 462).

244 Man in a Broad-Brimmed Hat

Signed and dated: *RHL* (in monogram) *1638*
Etching - 77 × 64 mm (trimmed impression).
Only one state

W.B. 311; BB 38-C

241. Jews in the Synagogue, W.B. 126, p. 191   **242.** Medea or The Marriage of Jason and Creusa, W.B. 112, p. 191

Creus en Iason hier elckanderen, Trouw beloven:
Medea Iasons vrouw, onwaerdighlijck verschoven,

Werde opgehitst van spijt, de wraecksucht vpert haer aen.
Helaes! Ontrouwigheydt, wat komt ghij dier te staen!

Rembrandt f.1648.

245 Old Woman Sleeping

c. 1635-37
Etching - 69 × 53 mm
Only one state

W.B. 350; BB 37-1

246 Man in an Arbor

Signed and dated: *Rembrandt f. 1642*
Etching - 73 × 57 mm
One state only

W.B. 257; BB 42-A

247 Young Man in a Velvet Cap, or Seated Young Man, Thinking (Ferdinand Bol?)

Signed and dated: *Rembrandt f 1637*
Etching - 97 × 84 mm
Two states

First state. Dotted shading shapes the left cheek. On the right a second outline of the cap is visible. In the next state, the left cheek was lightened, and the double outline rubbed out.

W.B. 268-I; BB 37-C

Provenance: Purchased from Clement, print dealer, on November 18, 1885, for 300 F.

Degas made a sketch (Reff, notebook 10, p. 13) and a copy of this etching (Loys Delteil, 13).

248 The Fourth Oriental Head, or Young Man with Velvet Cap

c. 1635
Signed: *Rt*
Etching - 158 × 135 mm
Three states

First state. Prior to the addition in the next state of a lock of hair and the nose. In the third state, the publisher's name, *J. de Reyger ex.,* was added.

W.B. 289-I; BB 35-5

Copy in reverse of an etching by Lievens, to which a beard and a mustache have been added.

249 Bearded Man in a Velvet Cap with a Jewel Clasp

Signed and dated: *Rembrandt f 1637*
Etching - 96 × 83 mm
Only one state

W.B. 313; BB 37-B

Provenance: A. de Peters, 1784

250 Old Man with a Divided Fur Cap

Signed and dated: *Rembrandt f 1640*
Etching with drypoint - 150 × 137 mm
Two states

First state. Without the slipped stroke running from the left cheek to the cap.

W.B. 265-I; BB 40-A (three states)

Provenance: A. de Peters, 1784

251, 252 Clement de Jonghe

Signed and dated: *Rembrandt f. 1651*
Etching, drypoint and burin - 207 × 161 mm
Six states

First state. Without the arch at the top of the plate. The folds of the cloak farthest to the right are lightly shaded. Below the bar of the chair back is a white strip, which was shaded over in the second state.

Third state. An arch has been added with drypoint. Numerous lines darken the hat; its left edge, which had been irregular, is now a simple curve. A ribbon has been burnished in. The right eye is smaller and its expression different.

The shading of the face has been so changed since the second state that its expression is completely changed. In the fourth state, the arch was emphasized by etched diagonal lines on the right. In the fifth state, white spaces were burnished in: one, triangular, below the bar of the chair on the right; the other, near the hair on the left. In the sixth state, more shading was added throughout.

W.B. 272-I, III; BB 51-C

Provenance: A. de Peters, 1784

Clement de Jonghe (died 1679) was a well-known Amsterdam print publisher and dealer. The inventory compiled after his death in 1679 provided the first list of titled etchings by Rembrandt.

253 Jan Cornelis Sylvius

Signed and dated: *Rembrandt f 1633*
Etching and burin in the second state - 166 × 141 mm
Two states

First state. Before additional work on the upper lip, the cap, the collar, the cloak and the background.

W.B. 266-I; BB 33-H

Jan Cornelis Sylvius (1563/4-1638) was a preacher in Amsterdam, where he moved in 1610. On June 22, 1634, as Saskia's cousin and guardian, he gave his consent to her marriage. He died on November 19, 1638, at the age of seventy-four, as we are informed by the inscription around another, oval-shaped portrait of Sylvius, this one posthumous (W.B. 280, fig. 266).

254 Jan Lutma, Goldsmith

Signed and dated beginning with the second state: *Rembrandt f. 1656*
Etching, drypoint and burin - 199 × 150 mm
Three states

First state. Prior to the window in the background, the carafe, the signature, the date and the inscription to the right of the goldsmith's elbow *(Joannes Lutma Aurifex/Natus Groningae),* all of which were added in the second state.

Other parts were reworked in the third state.

W.B. 276-I; BB 56-C

Jan Lutma (1584-1669), born in Groningen, had moved to Amsterdam and become the most renowned goldsmith of his day. His embossed silver pieces, like the bowl we see near him, and his ornamental works were in great demand. An art lover and collector, he had been to Rome and brought back a great many prints. His son, Jan Lutma the younger, was an etcher, and it was he who inserted the inscription that appears in the second state.

255 Jacob Haaringh ("Young Haaringh")

Signed and dated: *Rembrandt f. 1655* (the *6* reversed)
Etching, drypoint and burin - 199 × 147 mm
Five states

First state. Prior to the horizontal curtain rod at the window, added in the second state, and to the landscape hung on the wall in the third state.

The signature and date are barely legible.

The landscape painting was burnished out of the fourth state. In the fifth state the plate was cut in two: one part showing the bust, the other showing the left hand and the hat.

Impression on Japanese paper.

W.B. 275-I; BB 55-E

Jacob Haaringh was a lawyer in Utrecht. His deep gaze in this portrait conveys an impression of inner life and a profound melancholy. In this etching Rembrandt plays off against each other dark and light areas, handled in similar ways.

256 Thomas Haaringh ("Old Haaringh")

c. 1655
Drypoint and burin - 195 × 150 mm
Two states

Second state. The curtain at the window is longer and wider and covers part of the window frame. Two "pillars of shadow" are visible in the center and to the right of the window.

Impression full of burrs.

W.B. 274-II; BB 55-I

Three areas of light provide rhythm: the window; the face and collar; and the hands and the arm of the chair. This is one of Rembrandt's finest etched portraits. Haaringh (died 1660) was bailiff of the Court of Inheritances and Insolvencies. It was he who was charged with seizing Rembrandt's collection of drawings and prints and selling the artist's belongings in 1657 and 1658.

257 Abraham Frans or Francen

c. 1657
Etching, drypoint and burin - 158 × 208 mm
Ten states

Of the first three states, only a very small number of prints were made.

Fourth state. This is one of the portraits that underwent the greatest amount of change; it has even been supposed sometimes that starting with the sixth state, the subject is no longer the same person. The stool on which Frans is seated in the first state becomes a chair in the second; in the third state, its back is partly burnished out. In the fourth state, this seat becomes an armchair, and a grotesque head terminates its back.

The curtain to the left of the window is partly removed in the third state, and completely in the fourth. Trees are now visible through the window. We can now see the right hand, holding the sheet of paper, and a drawing on the back of that sheet. The eyes are darker and the expression of the face has changed.

Fifth state. The frame of the triptych has been retouched, and the drawing on the back of the sheet of paper has become the bust of a man.

Sixth state. The plate has been reworked; the hair, eyes and mustache have been redrawn to such an extent that the sitter's appearance has changed altogether.

The plate continued to be reworked up to the tenth state. The seventh state became much lighter; the eighth was bathed in light; then the ninth and tenth states were darkened again.

This portrait is the only one in an oblong format.

Impression on Japanese paper, with surface tone.

W.B. 273-IV; BB 57-2

Abraham Francen (born 1613) was an apothecary and art lover, and one of Rembrandt's friends. He put up bond for Rembrandt when the artist had to render accounts to his son, Titus (receipt dated November 5, 1665). Francen became the guardian of Cornelia, daughter of Rembrandt and of Hendrikje Stoffels.

Gersaint describes him thus: "This amateur of the arts had such a passion for prints, and such inadequate means by which to satisfy his passion, that he often went without food and drink so as to be able to acquire the pieces he liked when the occasion arose."

258 Jan Six

Signed and dated beginning with second state: *Rembrandt f. 1647* (the *6* and *4* reversed)
Etching, drypoint and burin - 241 × 181 mm
Four states

First state. Before the signature and date were added. A stone window ledge comes halfway up to Jan Six's arm. The upper window is completely shaded. In the second state, the window ledge disappeared; in the second and third states, there were some changes in the shading of the window and the table. In the third state, the hair and face were retouched with the burin. In the fourth state, an inscription was added: JAN SIX AE. 29, and the reversed digits *6* and *4* in the date were rectified.

One of the two known proofs on Chinese paper with a wide lower margin, whose delicate whiteness enriches the overall appearance.

W.B. 285-I; BB 47-B (three states)

Provenance: Comte de Chabannes, 1755

Joly, keeper of the Cabinet du Roi in the eighteenth century, noted in his diary the acquisition of two impressions of this print: "On May 15, 1755, upon orders from M. Bignon, I acquired two impressions, one with letter and one without, of this rare portrait of Jan Six, the burgomaster, of which the king had only a fairly faithful India-ink copy. These two impressions were purchased publicly at the sale of the Comte de Chabannes, for the sum of 1,110 *livres*."

The impression of the first state had been sold for 864 *livres*.

The two preparatory drawings and the copperplate are in the Six collection; a third drawing is in the Fodor Museum, Amsterdam (Benesch 749 verso).

Rembrandt first etched, then used drypoint and burin for the darkest parts. He then reworked a number of places on the plate with drypoint so as to darken the shading and enhance the details. In this way he achieved the most subtle gradations of tone, the most delicate shading that an etching can yield. So transparent is the shading that it barely grazes each object, yet gives it shape and form. Similarly, the light endows Six's face with an immaterial quality, molding it without lines, like the face of Christ in the *Hundred Guilder Print*.

So sensitive is the Chinese paper that it brings out every degree of subtlety. The art of etching here reaches the utmost limit of its potential.

Jan Six (1618-1700) belonged to a family which had owned mills since the sixteenth century, when Charles VI founded a dyeworks for silk and other types of cloth. An industrialist and an art lover, Jan Six had done the tour of Italy. Like Rembrandt, he was curious about everything, and it is in his curio room that Rembrandt has chosen to show him. Six collected objets d'art, engraved stones, objects from antiquity, drawings, prints, and paintings. He met Rembrandt when the artist painted the portrait of Anna Wijmer, Six's mother. Six also wrote poetry, and in 1640, while Secretary of the city of Amsterdam, he wrote a tragedy entitled *Medea*, for which Rembrandt did an illustration in 1648 (W.B. 112, fig. 242). In 1654 Rembrandt painted his portrait. Six was appointed Commissioner of Marriages in 1656; in 1667 he entered the College of Magistrates; and it was not until 1691 that he became Burgomaster. He married Margaretha Tulp, daughter of the physician we see in the *Night Watch.*

Six collected all of the Rembrandt prints, which later appeared in the sale of the effects of Willem Six, his nephew, in 1734. It was that collection, bought by Houbraken, that Gersaint used in making his catalogue. With regard to this portrait of Six, Gersaint wrote in 1751: "The famous portrait of Burgomaster Six, which is of the utmost rarity today and which, when one does come across it, commands a surprising price in Holland; it is this master's most costly piece, and we can even go so far as to say that it is the only print ever to have been sold for such a high price; and we cannot but agree that quite aside from its rarity, it is one of the handsomest things Rembrandt ever did." Gersaint went on to describe the Six sale: "During one of my first travels to Holland, I chanced to be in Amsterdam at the time of the sale of his cabinet, which was filled with a great quantity of volumes of prints and numerous paintings by the best masters; I purchased at this sale several fine prints; and among others three or four portraits of the Burgomaster which, as there were some twenty-five of them, went for only 15, 16 or 18 florins each; but since that time this portrait has become so sought after, and collectors have pursued it so avidly, particularly as concerns the English, by whom everything this excellent master has done is extremely prized, that one of them was sold in Holland, in this very year 1750, to a London collector, for the sum of one hundred and fifty florins, which is equal to approximately three hundred fifteen pounds of our money. I do not believe that there has ever been an example of any print by any master whosoever which has gone for so high a price. M. l'Abbé Jolly de Fleury, Counselor in Parliament and Canon of Notre-Dame, possesses the first proof of this portrait in his collection of Rembrandt, as well as many other very rare pieces; as this portrait is not widely known in France, some people will at least be pleased to know that it is to be found in that country.... We must assume that this portrait of Burgomaster Six was already very rare at the time that M. de Beringhen assembled his collection; for although the said collector spared no effort to satisfy his ambitions, he was not able to acquire the portrait; and by way of consoling himself he had a pen-and-ink copy made, with an India-ink wash,

and so well did it imitate the original that it has often deceived persons who were not given any warning. This copy is to be seen in the Œuvre de Beringhen, in the Bibliothèque du Roi." (G. 265)

259 Jan Antonides van der Linden

c. 1665
Etching, drypoint and burin - 174 × 105 mm
Five states

First state. On the left, the farthest reaches of the foliage are outlined; they are shaded in the second state. Then the suit was reworked and the banister shown in greater detail.

W.B. 264-I; BB 65-I (six states)

In 1637, Jan Antonides van der Linden (1609-1664), doctor of medicine, was an inspector at the medical college in Amsterdam; in 1639, a professor in Franeker; and in 1651, professor at the University of Leiden. He was a friend of Nicolaas Tulp. He had the botanical garden of the Franeker Academy enlarged, and published a number of books on medicine. A year after van der Linden died, Rembrandt was commissioned to do this etched portrait of him; it was intended as the frontispiece to a book by van der Linden on Hippocrates but in fact was not used. Rembrandt based the portrait on a painting by Abraham van den Tempel, dated 1660.

260 Ephraïm Bonus

Signed and dated: *Rembrandt f. 1647*
Etching, drypoint and burin - 241 × 177 mm
Two states

Second state. In the first state, the ring was still burred and looked black; now it is white. The banisters are finished. The right side of the coat and the sleeve are more heavily shaded.

W.B. 278-II; BB 47-A

An oil sketch has been preserved (Bredius 252).

Ephraïm Bueno (1599-1665), known by his latinized name Bonus, was a Portuguese Jew who had settled in Amsterdam, where he was a noted physician and writer. In 1651, he was granted the status of burgher.

Rembrandt painted a portrait of Bonus, which is now in the Rijksmuseum, Amsterdam.

261, 262 Jan Asselyn

c. 1647
Signed and dated: *Rembr[andt] f 16*
(the last two figures are illegible)
Etching, drypoint and burin - 218 × 171 mm
Three states

First state. With a landscape painting on an easel in the background. Handwritten inscription in the lower margin: *Asseleyn alias Crabbetie.*

Impression on Indian paper.

Second state. The easel and painting have been burnished out, but traces of them remain. The background was completely removed in the following state.

Impression with slight amount of surface tone.

W.B. 227-I, II; BB 47-I (four states)

Jan Asselyn (1610-1652) was a painter in the Italian style (he had traveled to Italy), devoted to landscapes and ruins. He was the husband of Ferdinand Bol's sister. Because one of his hands was deformed, he was nicknamed "Crabbetje" (little crab). An anecdote about this etching is yet another addition, if one were needed, to the legends surrounding Rembrandt's work. The word *Ezel* in Dutch means both donkey and easel. In Amadée de Burgy's catalogue (The Hague, 1755), printed in Dutch with the French translation on facing pages, the portrait of Asselyn "Crabbetje" was described in French as "The same, with the donkey behind him. Exceptionally rare." This mistake on the translator's part was funny enough in itself; in addition it is said to have led to a still more comical incident in the nineteenth century. A German speculator, who had either seen de Burgy's catalogue or made the same mistake as the eighteenth-century translator, decided to fabricate a first state of the Asselyn portrait by means of a second plate on which he had a donkey etched, to be used with an ordinary impression of the portrait. The earnest German then sent his print to England and offered it to a wealthy art lover; fortunately, his prospective client was well informed, the fraud was revealed, and the laugh was on the German speculator. The English collector returned the impression to him, pointing out that he had given himself away by drawing his own picture in place of the easel. A look at the Burgy sale catalogue confirms that the first part of this story, at least, is true (p. 31, n° 227). The impression which gave rise to the linguistic confusion sold for 94.5 florins.

263 Arnold Tholinx, Inspector

c. 1656
Etching, drypoint and burin - 189 × 148 mm
Trimmed impression.

Two states

Second state. Horizontal lines shade what had been a light area on the breast, and light diagonal lines have been added to the right eyebrow. The drypoint burr on the beard and cloak is very worn.

W.B. 284-II; BB 56-2

A painting exists, at the Musée Jacquemart-André in Paris (Bredius 281).

There has been some confusion regarding this portrait. At the Amadée de Burgy sale, it was identified as that of Peter van Tol, a famous physician. Gersaint and Bartsch called the subject "Tolling, Avocat." Yet it is definitely a portrait of Arnoldus Tholinx, physician and inspector of the medical college in Amsterdam from 1643 to 1653.

Impressions of this etching are rare, possibly because it was done in the year that Tholinx died and not many impressions were made. Tholinx was the son-in-law of Dr. Nicolaas Tulp and brother-in-law to Jan Six. From Blanc's account of the sale of one of the impressions of this portrait, we can see how much interest it aroused: "This portrait, most handsomely engraved indeed, is of such a rareness that connoisseurs fight ardently over it when it chances to appear in some public sale. I can recall hearing a well-known French collector, living in London, tell how, at the Pole Carew sale, which took place in that city in 1835, an interesting scene occurred over an impression of Tolling, Avocat. Attending that sale were England's most illustrious art lovers: Lord Aylesford, Lord Spencer, Sir... Astley, William Esdaile, Chambers Hall, Wilson, Maberly; M. Donnadieu, our countryman and a great collector of autographs, drawings and prints; Chevalier de Claussin, who had written one of the catalogues of Rembrandt's work; and at the same, the wealthiest dealers in London: the Colnaghis, the Tiffins, the Smiths, the Graveses, the Evanses.

Finer prints were perhaps never seen. Almost the entire Pole Carew collection was derived from the collections of Barnard, Haring, Hibbert, and Lord Bute. The Asselyn portrait with the easel, that is to say, the first state, was sold for £39 18 shillings (close to 1,000 francs); the portrait of Anslo, the Anabaptist minister, reached £74 11 shillings (1,800 francs): the hundred guilder print had just risen to £163 (4,075 francs).

Finally, the Tolling, Avocat was put on display. The impression was an admirable one, almost unique, full of burr, with uneven edges, less closely worked than the one in the Amsterdam Museum. Mr. Pole Carew had bought it for only £56, at Mr. Hibbert's sale in 1809. The bidding was extremely fierce; every face was infused with the utmost emotion; M. de Claussin could hardly breathe. When the print came around to him, it had already gone up to £150! His hand trembled as he held it and examined it for some minutes through a magnifying glass; he then bid up the price by £5, but by the time the print had gone once around the table the price had risen to £200, that is, 5,000 francs! Poor de Claussin was quite pale; cold sweat trickled down his temples. He could bear it no longer. Realizing that his unknown competitor must be some powerful figure, he sought to soften this merciless opponent. He first stammered a few words in English, then continued in the same language, which he spoke almost as well as his native tongue: 'Gentlemen, you know me: I am Chevalier de Claussin; I have devoted part of my life to compiling a new catalogue of Rembrandt's work and to etching copies of the great master's rarest prints. For twenty-five years I have been looking for "Tolling, Avocat" and have seen it nowhere except in the national collections of Paris and Amsterdam and in the late Barnard's collection, which included the impression we see before us. If this impression eludes me today, then I can no longer hope at my age ever to see it again. I beg my competitors, therefore, to take into consideration the extent to which my book has rendered service to art lovers; the fact that I am a foreigner; the sacrifices which I have borne all my life for the sake of compiling a collection such as enables me to offer new and useful comments on Rembrandt's splendid work.... Gentlemen, a little generosity, if you please,' added de Claussin, whose eyes had filled with tears. The effect of this unexpected speech was quite sensational. Many of those present were touched by it; some, however, smiled and whispered that the same M. de Claussin who did not hesitate to bid a print up to four and even five thousand francs could often be seen in the streets of London, of a morning, on his way to fetch two sous's worth of milk in a little jug.... There was a moment of silence. But then a signal was made to the auctioneer, the last offer was announced — and the fatal hammer fell on the figure of £220! Only then was it learned that the happy purchaser was Mr. Verstolk van Soelen, a Dutch cabinet minister." (Bl. 188)

264 Cornelis Claesz Anslo

Signed and dated: *Rembrandt f. 1641*
Etching and drypoint - 185 × 157 mm
Slightly trimmed impression, edged with a line of brown ink.
Two states

First state. A white strip at the bottom of the plate was worked over in the second state.

Single impression, signed and dated by the artist, in black chalk.

The sitter's name, Anslo, is written in the margin in brown ink.

W.B. 271-I; BB 41-J (four states)

Provenance: M.-J. Bouillon, 3-1-1894, 4, 500 F.

The additional states mentioned by Björklund are those of the plate as retouched by Baillie.

There is a drawing (Benesch 758).

Cornelis Claesz Anslo (1592-1646) was a theologian and a Mennonite minister. It has been said that Rembrandt was a Mennonite, as were his pupils van Hoogstraten and Bernard Keilh. At the bottom of the print appear four lines of poetry by Vondel, handwritten, we are told, by Coppenol:

Ay Rembrandt! maal Kornelis Stem,
Het zichtbre deel is't minst van hem;
T'on zichtbre kent men slechts door d'Ooren.
Wie Anslo zien wil moet hem hooren.

O Rembrandt! Paint Cornelis's voice for us, for the visible part of this man is the least of him; only through our ears can we know the invisible part. Whoever wishes to behold Anslo must hear him.

265 Jan Uytenbogaert

Signed and dated beginning with the third state:
Rembrandt ft. 1635
Etching and burin - 225 × 187 mm
Six states

Fourth state. The plate was originally rectangular (250 × 187 mm), with the portrait within an oval; in the third state, the plate was cut down to an octagon. The plate has been reworked and four lines by Grotius have been added. This was the only time that Rembrandt ever etched a text below a portrait.

Impressions of the first three states are rare. Here the outline of the oval is continuous on the right and the curtain is shaded with horizontal lines on the upper right. In the next state, the guards were removed; in the sixth state, the plate was reworked but not by Rembrandt.
Watermark.

W.B. 279-IV; BB 35-D

Jan Uytenbogaert (1577-1644) was a theologian, leader of the Remonstrant sect, and an enemy of the orthodox Calvinists. Exiled from 1618 to 1626, he then settled in The Hague and visited Amsterdam occasionally. Rembrandt painted his portrait in 1633, when the Remonstrants held their general assembly.

243. Samuel Manasseh ben Israel, W.B. 269, p. 191

244. Man in a Broad-Brimmed Hat, W.B. 311, p. 191

245. Old Woman Sleeping, W.B. 350, p. 194

246. Man in an Arbor, W.B. 257, p. 194

247. Young Man in a Velvet Cap (Ferdinand Bol?), W.B. 268, p. 194

249. Bearded Man in a Velvet Cap with a Jewel Clasp
W.B. 313, p. 194

248. The Fourth Oriental Head, or Young Man with Velvet Cap, W.B. 289, p. 194

250. Old Man with a Divided Fur Cap, W.B. 265, p. 194

251. Clement de Jonghe, W.B. 272-I, p. 194

252. Clement de Jonghe, W.B. 272-III, p. 194

253. Jan Cornelis Sylvius, W.B. 266, p. 194

254. Jan Lutma, Goldsmith, W.B. 276, p. 194

255. Jacob Haaringh ("Young Haaringh"), W.B. 275, p. 195

256. Thomas Haaringh ("Old Haaringh"), W.B. 274, p. 195

257. Abraham Frans or Francen, W.B. 273, p. 195

258. Jan Six, W.B. 285, p. 185

259. Jan Antonides van der Linden, W.B. 264, p. 196

260. Ephraim Bonus, W.B. 278, p. 196

261. Jan Asselyn, W.B. 277-I, p. 196

262. Jan Asselyn, W.B. 277-II, p. 196

263. Arnold Tholinx, Inspector, W.B. 284, p. 197

264. Cornelis Claesz Anslo, W.B. 271, p. 198

anslo

Rembrand

f 1641

Cornelis Claesz Ansloo

265. Jan Uytenbogaert, W.B. 279, p. 198

266. Jan Cornelis Sylvius, Preacher, W.B. 280, p. 224

Spes mea Christus. Iohannes Cornelij Sylvius. Amstelodamobat functus S.S. Ministriaos 45. et 6. menses. In Frisia. in Tzummarum et Phirdum aos 4. In Balk et Harich uniuww.

Cuius adorandum docuit Facundia Christum,
    Et populis veram pandit ad astra viam,
Talis erat Sylvi facies. audivimus illum
    Amstelijs isto civibus oro loqui.
Hoc Frisijs praecepta dedit: pietasq̃. severo
    Relligiog. diu vindice tuta stetit.
Praeluxit. veneranda suis virtutibus. atas.
    Eruditq̃. ipsos fessa senecta viros.

Simplicitatis amans fucum contemsit honesti,
    Nec sola voluit fronte placere bonis.
Sic statuit: Iesum vita meliore doceri
    Rectius, et vocum fulmina posse minus.
Amstela, sis memor extincti. qui condidit urbem
    Moribus, hanc ipso fulsijt illo Deo.
                                        C. Barlæus.
Haud amplius depraedico illius dotes.
    Quas æmulor, frustraq̃ persequor versu.
                                        P. S.

267. Lieven Willemsz. van Coppenol (The Larger Plate), W.B. 283, p. 224

268. Lieven Willemsz. van Coppenol (The Smaller Plate), W.B. 282-III, p. 224

269. Lieven Willemsz. van Coppenol, W.B. 282-VI, p. 224

270. Lieven Willemsz. van Coppenol, W.B. 282-V, p. 224

271. Jan Uytenbogaert, "The Goldweigher", W.B. 281-I, p. 224

272. Jan Uytenbogaert, "The Goldweigher", W.B. 281-II, p. 224

266 Jan Cornelis Sylvius, Preacher

Signed and dated: *Rembrandt 1646*
Etching, drypoint and burin - 278 × 188 mm
Two states

Second state. A small area between the corner of the right eye and the eyebrow is covered with diagonal lines and shaded with crosshatching. Slight grain on the hands and face, in particular, may be the result of biting by a sulfur tint or of previous scraping of the plate.

W.B. 280-II; BB 46-E

Two preliminary drawings have been preserved (Benesch 762a and 763).

This is a posthumous portrait: Rembrandt made it eight years after Sylvius died. He gives the preacher great vitality by means of the hand projecting from the frame and the shadow that enhances the outline of the oval. Rembrandt had already made a portrait of Sylvius, dated 1633 (W.B. 266, fig. 253). Inscribed around this portrait is Sylvius's motto, *Spes mea Christus*, followed by: *Iohannes Cornelÿs Sylvius Amstelodamo-bat: functus SS. Minist: aõs 45. et 6. menses. In Frysiâ, in Tyemarum et Phirdgum aõs 4. In Balc et Harich unicum. In Minnerstgae aõs 4. Slotis aõs 2. In Hollandia, Slotis aõs 6. Amstelodami aõs 28. et 6. menses, ibidemque obÿt aõ 1638. 19. novembr. natus aõs 74.* At the bottom, in a wide margin, are eight Latin distichs by Barlæus in two columns:

Cuius adorandum docuit Facundia Christum,
  Et populis veram pandit ad astra viam,
Talis erat Sylvî facies. Audivimus illum
  Amstelÿs isto civibus ore loqui.
Hoc Frisÿs præcepta dedit: pietasq. severo
  Relligioq. diu vindico tuta stotit.
Prae luxit, veneranda suis virtutibus, ætas.
  Erudytq. ipsos sossa senecta viros.
Simplicitatis amans fucum contemsit honesti,
  Nec sola voluit fronto placero bonis.
Sic statuit: Jesum vita melioro doceri
  Rectius, et vocum fulmina posso minus.
Amstola, sis memor extincti qui condidit urbem
  Moribus, hanc ipso fulsÿt illo Deo. C. Barlæus

Haud amplius deprædico illîus dotos,
Quas æmulor, frustraque persequor versu. P.S.

267 Lieven Willemsz. Van Coppenol, Writing Master

The Larger Plate
1658
Etching, drypoint and burin - 329 × 289 mm
Six states

First state. The background is blank; it was covered by a broad curtain in the second state. The right arm is lightly shaded. The right sleeve and the curtain were worked over in the later states. By the sixth state, the plate was cut down to only 159 × 133 mm and the head alone remained.

Impression on Japanese paper with slight surface tone on the right sleeve and the top of the column.

One of the seven impressions of the first state that still exist.

W.B. 283-I; BB 58-F

Provenance: J.-L. de Beringhen, 1731

A drawing exists (Benesch 766).

Coppenol (1599 - after 1667) was a schoolmaster and calligrapher. This is Rembrandt's largest etched portrait.

268-270 Lieven Willemsz. Van Coppenol, Writing Master

The Smaller Plate
c. 1658
Etching, drypoint and burin - 259 × 190 mm
Six states

Third state. The compass and set squares which were added in the second state have been hung on the wall, just above the writing master's right hand. Vertical and diagonal lines shade Coppenol's forehead and right cheek; close lines also shade the child's head and the lower part of his collar.

Fourth state. The circular disk which had been above the child's head has been replaced by a triptych showing a Crucifixion, hung on the wall (not reproduced).

Provenance: A. de Peters, 1784

Fifth state. The triptych has been imperfectly burnished out. 230 × 190 mm (trimmed impression)

Sixth state. The circular disk has been reinstated; in the background, traces of the triptych remain.

Provenance: A. de Peters, 1784

W.B. 282-III, IV, V, VI; BB 58-1

A drawing exists (Benesch 766).

271, 272 Jan Uytenbogaert, "The Goldweigher"

Signed and dated: *Rembrandt f. 1639*
Etching and drypoint - 252 × 204 mm
Two states

First state. Face lightly sketched in.

Provenance: J.-L. de Beringhen, 1731

Second state. The face is completed.
Trimmed impression - 248 × 204 mm

Provenance: A. de Peters, 1784

W.B. 281-I, II; BB 39-D

The plate was known as "The Goldweigher" in the eighteenth century. Jan Uytenbogaert (1606-1689), a distant cousin of the theologian of the same name (see above; W.B. 279, fig. 265), had been Receiver-General in Amsterdam for a year when Rembrandt made this etching. Rembrandt had come in contact with Uytenbogaert when he delivered paintings of the Passion to Frederick Henry, prince of Orange. Although this portrait looks like a genre scene, Rembrandt has infused it with symbols.

Gersaint wrote of the first state: "I have seen another and singular impression of this portrait, which is almost never to be found, and which one could not wish to behold except on a whim; its singularity lies in the fact that every part of the plate has been completed, as has the previous one, with but one exception: the Receiver-General's head, which is suggested by a mere line." (G. 261)

273. **Portrait of Saskia in a Straw Hat, 1633**
Silverpoint on prepared vellum 185 × 105 mm Ben. 427
Berlin-Dahlem, Kupferstichkabinett

274. Sheet of Studies with Five Heads, 1637
Silverpoint on prepared vellum 134 × 80 mm Ben. 341 (recto)
Rotterdam, Boymans-van Beuningen Museum

275. Studies of Men on Horseback, 1637
Pen and bistre 200 × 150 mm Ben. 360(verso)
Rotterdam, Boymans-van Beuningen Museum

276. Woman with a Child Seen from Behind, 1633-34
Pen and bistre 99 × 62 mm Ben. 228
Rotterdam, Boymans-van Beuningen Museum

277. Beggar Couple with Children and a Dog, c. 1648
Black chalk 105 × 100 mm Ben. 751
Vienna, Albertina

278. Study of a Woman Teaching a Child to Walk, c. 1646
Pen and bistre 160 × 165 mm Ben. 706
Stockholm, Nationalmuseum

279. Studies of Beggars and of an Old Woman with a Crying Child, c. 1633-34
Pen and bistre with wash heightened with white 218 × 186 mm Ben. 218
Berlin-Dahlem,Kupferstichkabinett

280. The Naughty Boy, 1635
Pen and brown ink with wash heightened with white 206 × 143 mm Ben. 401
Berlin-Dahlem, Kupferstichkabinett

281. Study of a Boy with a Child 1635
Pen and bistre with wash 100 × 82 mm Ben. 274
Rotterdam, Boymans-van Beuningen Museum

282. Woman Going Downstairs with a Child in Her Arms, c. 1636
Pen and bistre 187 × 133 mm Ben. 313
New York, Pierpont Morgan Library

283. Woman with a Child Frightened by a Dog, c. 1636
Pen and bistre 184 × 146 mm Ben. 411
Budapest, Museum of Fine Arts

284. Study of a Peasant Woman Wearing a Zeeland Costume, c. 1638-40
Pen and bistre, wash 220 × 150 mm Ben. 315
Haarlem, Teylers Museum

285. Portrait of Titia van Uylenburgh, 1639
Pen and brown ink with wash 177 × 147 mm Ben. 441
Stockholm, Nationalmuseum

286. Young Woman at Her Toilet, c. 1632-34
Pen and bistre, washes in bistre and India ink, 238 × 184 mm Ben. 395
Vienna, Albertina

236

287. Polish Officer, c. 1631
Red chalk 245 × 175 mm Ben. 45
Leningrad, Hermitage

288. Life Study of a Young Man Pulling a Rope, c. 1645
Brush, red pen and wash heightened with white
290 × 178 mm Ben. 311
Amsterdam, Rijksprentenkabinet

291. Standing Man in a Fur Cap, 1630
Pen and bistre with wash 115 × 66 mm Ben. 36
Rotterdam, Boymans-van Beuningen Museum

289. Two Men in Conversation, 1642-43
Black chalk 84 × 65 mm Ben. 676
Rotterdam, Boymans-van Beuningen Museum

290. Bearded Old Man in a Cloak with Fringes, 1633-34
Pen and bistre 167 × 127 mm Ben. 238
Rotterdam, Boymans-van Beuningen Museum

292. Standing Beggar with a Leather Bag, c. 1629
Black chalk 290 × 167 mm Ben. 31
Amsterdam, Rijksprentenkabinet

293. Old Man with His Arms Extended, c. 1629
Black chalk 254 × 190 mm Ben. 12
Dresden, Kupferstichkabinett

294. Various Sketches: center, An Oriental Talking to an Old Man in European Dress; right, Half-figure of a Woman
Pen and bistre, wash 127 × 126 mm Ben. 142 (recto)
Chatsworth, Derbyshire (H. de G. 833)

294 A. Studies of Beggars Walking on Crutches, c. 1636
Pen and bistre 152 × 185 mm Ben. 327
London, British Museum

295. Portrait of an Old Man (Rembrandt's Father), c. 1630
Red and black chalk with wash 189 × 240 mm Ben. 56
Oxford, Ashmolean Museum

296. The Standing Syndic, c. 1662
Pen and bistre with wash corrected in white on a sheet of paper from
a cashbook 225 × 175 mm Ben. 1180
Rotterdam, Boymans-van Beuningen Museum

297. Portrait of Margaretha de Geer, 1635-40
Pen and bistre with wash 127 × 110 mm Ben. 757
Rotterdam, Boymans-van Beuningen Museum

298. Old Man Seated in an Armchair, 1631
Red and black chalk 225 × 145 mm Ben. 40
Haarlem, Teylers Museum

299. Portrait of Saskia Seated, c. 1634-35
Pen and brown ink 140 × 107 mm
Leningrad, Hermitage

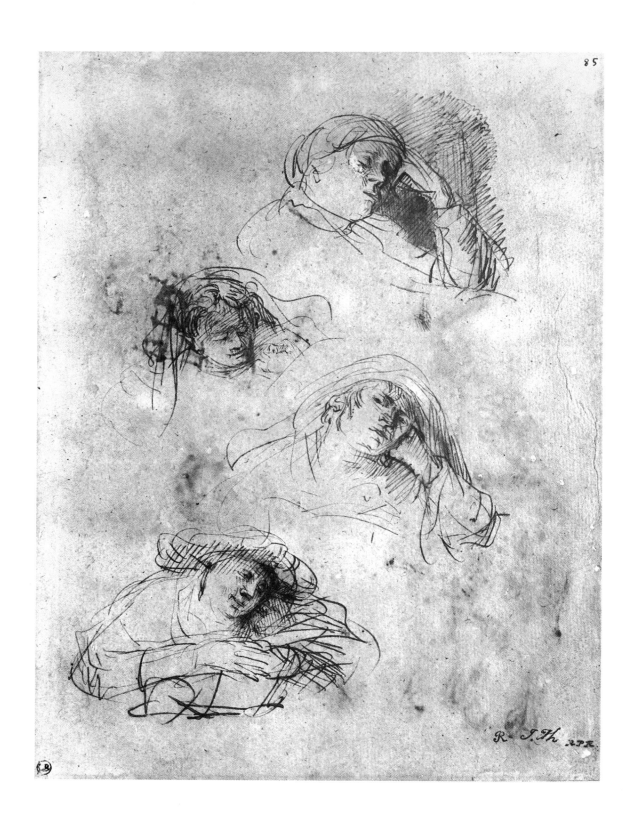

300. Four Studies of Saskia , 1636-37
Pen and bistre 200 × 150 mm Ben. 360 (recto)
Rotterdam, Boymans-van Beuningen Museum

301. Saskia at a Window, 1633-34
Pen and bistre with wash 236 × 178 mm Ben. 250
Rotterdam, Boymans-van Beuningen Museum

302. Saskia Sitting Up in Bed, c. 1639-40
Pen and brush in bistre 150 × 138 mm Ben. 255
Dresden, Kupferstichkabinett

303. Seated Girl, in Profile to Left, Half Nude, 1637
Black chalk 200 × 154 mm. Ben. 376 (recto)
Rotterdam, Boymans-van Beuningen Museum

304. Female Nude with her Head Bent Forward, c. 1657-58
Pen and brush in bistre with wash 135 × 283 mm Ben. 1137
Amsterdam, Rijksprentenkabinet

305. A Girl Sleeping, c. 1655-56
Brush and bistre with wash 245 × 203 mm Ben. 1103
London, British Museum

306. The Music-makers, 1626
Panel 63 × 48 cm G. 18
Amsterdam, Rijksmuseum

307. The Prophetess Hannah (Rembrandt's Mother), 1631
Panel 60 × 48 cm G. 27
Amsterdam, Rijksmuseum

308. Rembrandt's Mother, 1639
Panel 79.5 × 61.7 cm G. 190
Vienna, Kunsthistorisches Museum

▲▲ 309. Rembrandt's Mother, c. 1630
Panel 58.5 × 45 cm G. 37
Windsor Castle, Royal Collection

▲ 310. Rembrandt's Mother, c. 1630
Panel 35 × 29 cm G. 35
Essen, Collection of Mr. Harald von Bohlen und Halbach

▲ 311. An Old Man in a Cap, c. 1628
Panel 47 × 39 cm G. 36
The Hague, Mauritshuis

263

312. An Old Man in a Fur Hat, 1630
Panel 22 × 17.5 cm G. 42
Innsbruck, Museum Ferdinandeum

▲ **313. Head of a Man, 1625-31**
Panel 48 × 37 cm G. 31
Cassel, Gemäldegalerie

314. Officer with a Gold Chain, 1631
Canvas 81.1 × 75.7 cm G. 46
Chicago, Art Institute

315. The Amsterdam Merchant Nicolaes Ruts, 1631
Panel 115 × 85.5 cm G. 53
New York, The Frick Collection

▲ **316. Young Man with a Cock's Feather in His Cap, 1631**
Panel 55 × 45 cm G. 51
San Diego, San Diego Museum of Art

317. Young Man with Plumed Hat, 1631
Panel 81 × 67 cm G. 52
Toledo, Ohio, Toledo Museum of Art, Gift of Edward Drumond Libbey

268

▲ 318. Old Man with a Jewelled Cross, 1630
Panel 67.5 × 56 cm G. 50
Cassel, Gemäldegalerie

319. Portrait of a Youth, 1632
Panel 56.5 × 42 cm G. 101
Cleveland Museum of Art, Bequest of John L. Severonee

320. Young Man Sharpening a Quill, c. 1632
Canvas 101.5 × 81.5 cm G. 111
Cassel, Gemäldegalerie

▲ **321. Young Man in a Turban, 1631**
Panel 63.5 × 50 cm G. 106
London, Buckingham Palace, Royal Collection

**322. Man in Oriental Costume
("The Noble Slav"), 1632**
Canvas 152.7 × 111.1 cm G. 103
New York, Metropolitan Museum of Art
Bequest of William K. Vanderbilt 1920

323. Man in Oriental Costume, 1633
Panel 85.8 × 63.8 cm G. 152
Munich, Alte Pinakothek

▲ **324. Bearded Old Man with a Gold Chain, 1632**
Panel 59.3 × 49.3 cm G. 109
Cassel, Gemäldegalerie

▲ **325. Bald-headed Old Man, 1632**
Panel 50 × 40.5 cm G. 107
Cassel, Gemäldegalerie

▲ 326. Young Man with a Pointed Beard, 1632
Panel 63.5 × 48 cm G. 119
Brunswick, Herzog Anton Ulrich Museum

327. Portrait of an Amsterdam Citizen as a Militiaman
"Joris de Caullery", 1632
Canvas 101 × 82.5 cm G. 124
San Francisco, M.H. de Young Memorial Museum

328. Young Woman with a Fan, 1632
Canvas 72 × 54 cm G. 118
Stockholm, Nationalmuseum

329. Amalia van Solms, 1632
Canvas 68.5 × 55.5 cm. G. 112
Paris, Musée Jacquemart-André

▲ 330. Young Woman in a Pearl-trimmed Beret, 1632
Canvas 68.5 × 53.5 cm G. 114. Zurich, Private Collection

331. Saskia van Uylenburgh, c. 1633
Panel 60.5 × 49 cm G. 174. Washington, D.C., National Gallery of Art

332. Saskia, 1633
Panel 52.5 × 44.5 cm G. 134. Dresden, Gemäldegalerie

333. Saskia, c. 1634
Panel 99.5 × 78.8 cm G. 175. Cassel, Gemäldegalerie

334. Man in Oriental Costume
(detail of fig. 323)

335. Saskia with a Veil
(detail of fig. 338)

336. Portrait of a Young Woman
(detail of fig. 423)

337. Saskia
(detail of fig. 333)

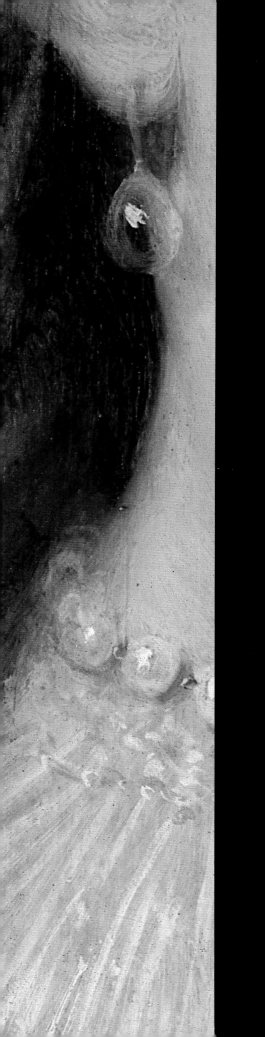
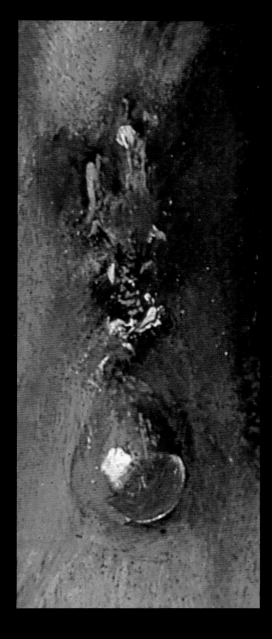
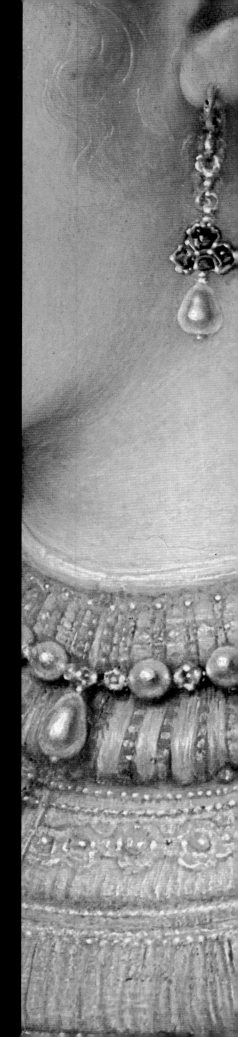

338. Saskia with a Veil, 1633
Panel 66.5 × 49.7 cm G. 132
Amsterdam, Rijksmuseum

339. Sophonisba Receiving the Poisoned Cup, 1634
Canvas 142 × 153 cm G. 69
Madrid, Prado

340. Saskia as Flora, 1635
Canvas 123.5 × 97.5 cm G. 96. London, National Gallery

341. Saskia as Flora, 1634
Canvas 125 × 101 cm G. 92. Leningrad, Hermitage

342. Saskia with a Flower, 1641
Panel 98.5 × 82.5 cm G. 226
Dresden, Gemäldegalerie

343. Saskia (Posthumous Portrait), 1643
Panel 72 × 59 cm G. 241
Berlin-Dahlem, Gemäldegalerie

**344. Philips Lucasz, Councillor of the
Dutch East India Company, 1635**
Panel 79.5 × 59 cm G. 178
London, National Gallery
345. Portrait of a Lady, 1635
Panel 77 × 64 cm G. 181
Cleveland Museum of Art, Bequest of Mrs Francis F. Prentiss

▲**346. Young Woman with Flowers in Her Hair**
1634 Panel 71 × 53.5 cm G. 167
Edinburgh, National Gallery of Scotland
On loan from the Duke of Sutherland's Collection

347. Young Woman with Flowers in Her Hair
(detail of fig. 346)

348. Maria Trip
(detail of fig. 368)

349. Young Girl at Half-open Door
(detail of fig. 380)

350. Susanne van Collen, Wife of Jan Pellicorne,
and Her Daughter, Eva Susanna
(detail of fig. 364)

351. Lucretia
(detail of fig. 424).

▲ 352-353. Lady and Gentleman in Black, 1633
Canvas 131 × 107 cm G. 130
Boston, Isabella Stewart Gardner Museum

354. Portrait of an 83-year-old Woman, 1634
Panel 68.5 × 54 cm G. 156
London, National Gallery

355. The Shipbuilder and His Wife, 1633
Canvas 115 × 165 cm G. 139
London, Buckingham Palace, Royal Collection

356. Portrait of a Seated Man, c. 1633
Panel 90 × 68.7 cm G. 153
Vienna, Kunsthistorisches Museum

▲ **357. Portrait of a Seated Woman, c. 1633**
Panel 90 × 67.5 cm G. 154
Vienna, Kunsthistorisches Museum

358. The Poet Jan Hermansz. Krul, 1633
Canvas 128.5 × 100.5 cm G. 138
Cassel, Gemäldegalerie

359. Portrait of a Young Man, 1633
Canvas 125 × 100 cm G. 140
Cincinnati, Taft Museum, Bequest of Mr and Mrs Charles Phelpo Taf

360. Portrait of a Lady with a Fan, 1633
Canvas 127 × 101 cm G. 141
New York, Metropolitan Museum of Art,
gift of Helen Swift Neilson 1943

361. A Scholar in His Study, 1634
Canvas 141 × 135 cm G. 93
Prague, Národuí Gallery

▲▲ **362. A Turk, c. 1630-35**
Canvas 98 × 74 cm G. 182
Washington, D.C., National Gallery of Art

▲ 363. Jan Pellicorne and His Son, Caspar, c. 1635
Canvas 155 × 123 cm G. 176
London, Wallace Collection

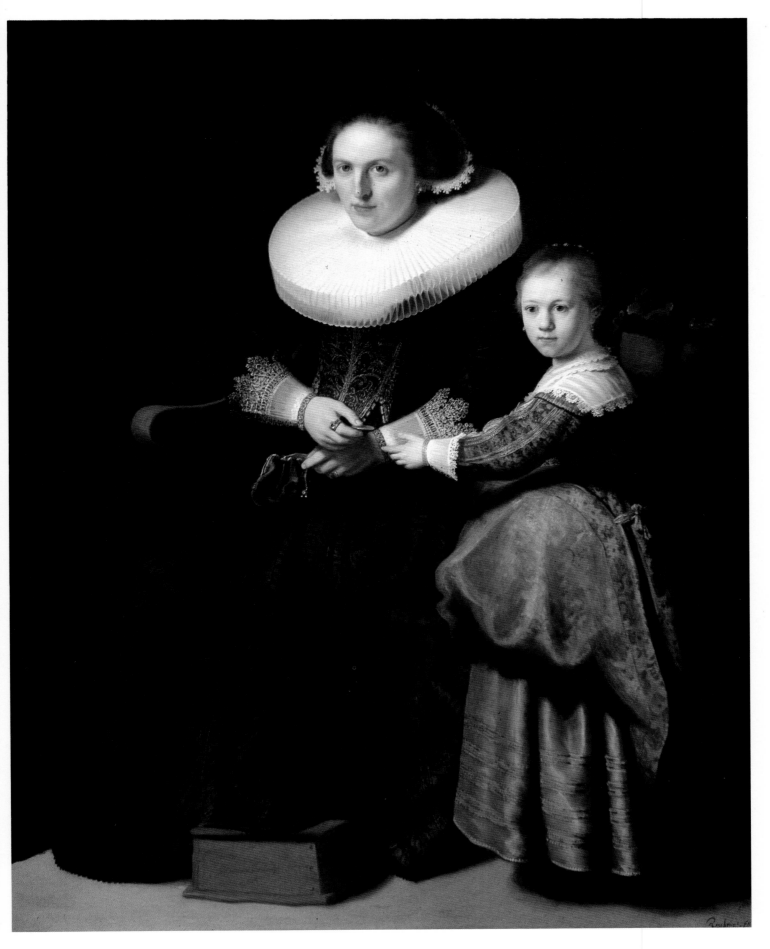

▲ 364. Susanna van Collen, Wife of Jan Pellicorne,
and Her Daughter, Eva Susanna, c. 1635
Canvas 155 × 123 cm G. 177. London, Wallace Collection

365. Man Standing in Front of a Doorway, 1639
Canvas 200 × 124.2 cm G. 192. Cassel, Gemäldegalerie

366. A Polish Nobleman, 1637
Panel 97 × 66 cm G. 186. Washington, D.C., National Gallery of Art

367. Alotte Adriaensdr, 1639
Panel 64.7 × 55.3 cm G. 193
Rotterdam, Boymans-van Beuningen Museum

368. Maria Trip, Daughter of Alotte Adriaensdr, 1639
Panel 107 × 82 cm G. 194
Amsterdam, Rijksmuseum (on loan from the van Weede Family Foundation)

369. Nicolaas van Bambeeck, 1641
Canvas 105 × 84 cm G. 232
Brussels, Musée Royal des Beaux-Arts

370. The Mennonite Minister Cornelis Claesz. Anslo in Conversation with a Woman, 1641
Canvas 176 × 210 cm G. 234
Berlin-Dahlem, Gemäldegalerie

371-372. Agatha Bas, Wife of Nicolaas van Bambeeck, 1641
Canvas 104.5 × 85 cm G. 233 London, Buckingham Palace

**373-374. The Militia Company of Captain Frans Banning Cocq
("The Night Watch"), 1642**
Canvas 363 × 437 cm G. 239
Amsterdam, Rijksmuseum

375. An Old Man in Rich Costume, 1643
Panel 72.5 × 58.5 cm G. 243
Woburn Abbey, Collection of the Duke of Bedford

376. The Art Dealer Clement de Jonghe, 1644
Canvas 92.5 × 73.5 cm G. 250
Buscot Park, Berkshire, Faringdon Collection

377. Man Holding a Glove, c. 1644
Panel 81 × 67 cm G. 245
New York, Metropolitan Museum of Art, Bequest of Benjamin Altman 1913

378. The Framemaker Herman Doomer, 1640
Panel 74 × 53 cm G. 230
New York, Metropolitan Museum of Art,
Bequest of Mrs H. O. Havemeyer 1929

379. The Painter Hendrick Martensz-Sorgh, 1647
Panel 74 × 67 cm G. 251
London, Westminster Collection, by kind permission of
His Grace the Duke of Westminster DL

380. Young Girl at half-open Door, 1645
Canvas 102 × 84 cm G. 248
Chicago, Art Institute, M.A. Ryerson Collection

381. Ariaentje Hollaer, Wife of Hendrick Martensz. Sorgh, 1647
Panel 74 × 67 cm G. 252
London, Westminster Collection, by kind permission of His Grace the Duke of Westminster DL

382. An Old Man in a Fur Cap, 1647
Panel 25.1 × 22.5 cm G. 259
Rotterdam, Museum Boymans-van Beuningen

383. The Jewish Physician Ephraim Bueno, c. 1647
Panel 19 × 15 cm G. 263
Amsterdam, Rijksmuseum

following pages,
384. Young Girl at a Window, 1651
Canvas 78 × 63 cm G. 285
Stockholm, Nationalmuseum

385. A Girl with a Broom 1651
Canvas 107.5 × 91.5 cm G. 284
Washington D.C., National Gallery of Art.

386. Girl Leaning on a Windowsill, 1645
Canvas 81.6 × 66 cm G. 228
London, Dulwich Picture Gallery

387. Danae, 1636
Canvas 185 × 203 cm G. 270
Leningrad, Hermitage

388. Flora, c. 1654
Canvas 100 × 91.8 cm G. 288
New York, Metropolitan Museum of Art, Gift of Archer M. Huntington

389. Hendrickje Stoffels, 165 (4)
Canvas 72 × 60 cm G. 311
Paris, Musée du Louvre

390 to 392. Woman in Bed, c. 1645
Canvas 80 × 66.5 cm G. 227
Edinburgh, National Gallery of Scotland

393. Hendrickje at an Open Door, 1656-57
Canvas 86 × 65 cm G. 339
Berlin-Dahlem, Gemäldegalerie

394. Hendrickje Stoffels, 1660
Canvas 78.4 × 68.9 cm G. 382
New York, Metropolitan Museum of Art,
Gift of Archer M. Huntington

395. Nicolaes Bruyningh, 1652
Canvas 107.5 × 91.5 cm G. 307
Cassel, Gemäldegalerie

396. Portrait of Jan Six, 1654
Canvas 112 × 102 cm G. 309
Amsterdam, Six Foundation

397. Portrait of a Man, 1650
Canvas 80 × 67.1 cm G. 304
The Hague, Mauritshuis

398. Man Leaning on a Windowsill, 1650
Canvas 82 × 68.5 cm G. 301
Cincinnati, Taft Museum, Bequest of Mrs Louise Taft Semple

399. Portrait of an Old Man, 1651
Canvas 111 × 88 cm G. 299.
Chatsworth, Derbyshire, Devonshire Collection

400. The Polish Rider, c. 1653
Canvas 117 × 135 cm G. 287.
New York, The Frick Collection

401. A Franciscan Monk, c. 1651
Canvas 89 × 66.5 cm G. 300
London, National Gallery

402. An Old Woman Reading, 1655
Canvas 79 × 65 cm G. 292
In the collection of the Duke of Buccleuch and Queensbury, K.T. at
Drumlanrig Castle, Scotland

403. Titus at His Desk, 1655
Canvas 77 × 63 cm G. 325
Rotterdam, Museum Boymans-van Beuningen

404. Titus, c. 1657
Canvas 67 × 55 cm G. 330
London, Wallace Collection

405. Titus Reading, c. 1657
Canvas 70.5 × 64 cm G. 335
Vienna, Kunsthistorisches Museum

406. Titus, c. 1660
Canvas 72 × 56 cm G. 375
Paris, Musée du Louvre

407. Two Negroes, 1661
Canvas 77.8 × 64.4 cm G. 390
The Hague, Mauritshuis

408. Detail of fig. 407

409. Titus in a Monk's Habit, 1660
Canvas 79.5 × 67.7 cm G. 377
Amsterdam, Rijksmuseum

410. Man with a Falcon (Count Floris of Holland?), c. 1661
Canvas 98 × 79 cm G. 370
Gothenburg, Sweden, Konstmuseum

411 to 413. The Sampling Officials of the Drapers' Guild, 1662
Canvas 191 × 279 cm G. 404
Amsterdam, Rijksmuseum

357

414. The Dordrecht Merchant Jacob Trip, c. 1659
Canvas 130.5 × 97 cm G. 383
London, National Gallery

415. Margaretha de Geer, Wife of Jacob Trip, c. 1659
Canvas 130.5 × 97.5 cm G. 384
London, National Gallery

416. A Young Man Seated at a Table, 1662-63
Canvas 110 × 90 cm. G. 405
Washington, D.C., National Gallery of Art, Andrew W. Mellon Collection

417. Portrait of a Lady with a Lap Dog, c. 1665
Canvas 81 × 64.8 cm. G. 398
Toronto, Art Gallery of Ontario

418. A Young Man, perhaps the Artist's Son Titus, c. 1663
Canvas 78.6 × 64.2 cm G. 406
London, Dulwich Picture Gallery

419. Alexander the Great, c. 1655
Canvas 118 × 91.1 cm G. 293
Oeiras, Portugal, Calouste Gulbenkian Foundation

420. A Man in Armour, c. 1655
Canvas 137.5 × 104.4 cm G. 294
Glasgow, Art Gallery and Museum

421-422. Frederick Rihel on Horseback, 1663
Canvas 294.5 × 241 cm G. 410
London, National Gallery

423. Portrait of a Young Woman, c. 1665
Canvas 56 × 47 cm G. 337
Montreal, Museum of Fine Arts, Bequest of Mrs R. Mac D. Paterson 1949

424. Lucretia, 1664
Canvas 120 × 101 cm G. 373
Washington, D.C., National Gallery of Art, Andrew W. Mellon Collection

425. Homer Dictating to a Scribe, 1663
Canvas 108 × 82.4 cm G. 371
The Hague, Mauritshuis

426. Gérard de Lairesse, 1665
Canvas 112.4 × 87.6 cm G. 407
New York, New York, Metropolitan Museum of Art,
Robert Lehman Collection 1975

427. Portrait of a Man, 1667
Canvas 107.5 × 91.5 cm G. 414
Melbourne, National Gallery of Victoria

428. Old Man, 1667
Canvas 81 × 67 cm G. 409
Cowdray Park, Sussex, in the Lord Cowdray Collection

429-430. Portrait of a Lady with an Ostrich-feather Fan, c. 1660
Canvas 99.5 × 83 cm G. 412
Washington, D.C., National Gallery of Art, Widener Collection

431. Portrait of a Gentleman with a Tall Hat and Gloves, c. 1660
Canvas 99.5 × 82.5 cm G. 411
Washington, D.C., National Gallery of Art, Widener Collection

432-433. A Family Group, c. 1669
Canvas 126 × 167 cm G. 416
Brunswick, Herzog Anton Ulrich Museum

434. Adam and Eve, W.B. 28, p. 384

435. Peter and John at the Gate of the Temple, W.B. 95, p. 384

436. St. Paul in Meditation, W.B. 149, p. 384

434 Adam and Eve

Signed and dated: *Rembrandt f 1638*
Etching - 162 × 116 mm
Two states

Second state. The upper outline of the bank on which Adam is half-seated was not continuous in the first state. It has been strengthened here and made continuous.

W.B. 28-II; BB 38-D

Provenance: A. de Peters, 1784

There are two preparatory drawings (Benesch 163-164).

Opinions of Rembrandt's works expressed by those who have catalogued them at different periods are sometimes disconcerting. Concerning this print, for instance, Gersaint wrote in 1751: "As Rembrandt was not at all at his ease when portraying nudes, this piece is rather inaccurate, and the heads are altogether disagreeable; the overall effect is none the less fine, as in every piece by this excellent master." (G 29)

Bartsch, Daulby, Claussin, Wilson and Nagler held similar opinions.

In 1859, however, Charles Blanc challenged this view: "On the contrary, there is not one engraver who would not recognize in this freely treated piece by Rembrandt the work of a master.... What a wonderful vision of Eden is this sun-drenched landscape in which we see... an elephant from Asia; its presence immediately situates the scene presented here and carries us back to the lands of the Bible, the cradle of the world." (Bl. 1)

In 1963, K. G. Boon expressed this view: "In his works dating from 1638, Rembrandt sometimes hesitates between the meticulous rendering of details and rapidly 'getting down' a first impression. His *Adam and Eve*, based on a print by Dürer, is still very descriptive."

But the realistic treatment of Adam and Eve by Rembrandt has nothing to do with Albrecht Dürer's idealized figures, which stemmed from his research into proportions and were worthy of classical antiquity.

435 Peter and John at the Gate of the Temple

Roughly Etched
c. 1629
Etching - 222 × 170 mm
One state only

One of the four known impressions.

Watermarked paper

W.B. 95; BB 29-2

Provenance: J.-L. de Beringhen, 1731

There is a preparatory drawing for the figure of St. Peter in Dresden (Benesch 12, fig. 293).

This is one of Rembrandt's first attempts at etching. The artist had some difficulties with the ground, and the copperplate was incorrectly wiped. Yet the technical flaws in no way alter the powerful composition. The characters are closely related to the beggars the artist had sketched with his point in his earliest works. Their drawing foreshadows the master's great manner.

436 St. Paul in Meditation

c. 1629
Etching - 238 × 200 mm
One state only

This Paris impression has been reduced in height:
232 × 200 mm (formerly 238 × 200).

This is one of the four known impressions.

W.B. 149; BB 27-1

Provenance: Rijksmuseum, Amsterdam

There is a preparatory drawing in Paris (Benesch 15).

Shadow rather than light directs the viewer's gaze towards the eyes of the saint.

437 St. Jerome Kneeling

Large Plate
c. 1629
Etching - 391 × 332 mm
One state only
This is one of the two impressions which have come down to us.

W.B. 106; BB 27-2

Provenance: public sale in Berlin, 1808

438 St. Jerome Kneeling in Prayer, Looking Down

Signed and dated: *Rembrandt f. 1635* (with a reversed *d* and a barely legible *5*)
Etching - 114 × 80 mm
One state only

W.B. 102; BB 35-H

Provenance: J.-L. de Beringhen, 1731

439 Joseph's Coat Brought to Jacob

c. 1633
Signed: *Rembrant van. Ryn. fe*
Etching with touches of drypoint - 107 × 81 mm
Two states

First state. Before the light, close strokes which later strengthened the shading on portions of the seat on which Jacob sits.

W.B. 38-I; BB 37-1

"And they took Joseph's coat, and killed a kid of the goats, and dipped the goat in the blood; and they sent the coat of many colours, and they brought it to their father; and said, This have we found; know now whether it be thy son's coat or no. And he knew it, and said, It is my son's coat; an evil beast hath devoured him; Joseph is without doubt rent to pieces." (Gen. 37. 31-33)

440 The Stoning of St. Stephen

Signed and dated: *Rembrandt. f. 1635*
Etching - 95 × 86 mm
Two states

First state. This state precedes the general reworking of the shadows by very fine hatching and in particular the darkening of the head of the man at the top of the left margin with diagonals.

W.B. 97-I; BB 35-A

Provenance: J.-L. de Beringhen, 1731

441 Joseph and Potiphar's Wife

Signed and dated: *Rembrandt f. 1634.*
Etching - 90 × 115 mm
Two states

Second state. Light parallel strokes accentuate the shading of the pillow above the woman's left knee and on the head of the bed.

W.B. 39-II; BB 34-G

437. St. Jerome Kneeling, W.B. 106, p. 384

438. St. Jerome Kneeling in Prayer, W.B. 102, p. 384

439. Joseph's Coat Brought to Jacob, W.B. 38, p. 384

440. The Stoning of St. Stephen, W.B. 97, p. 384

441. Joseph and Potiphar's Wife, W.B. 39, p. 384

442. **The Return of the Prodigal Son, W.B. 91, p. 392**

443, 444. The Good Samaritan, W.B. 90, p. 392

445. Abraham Caressing Isaac, W.B. 33, p. 392

446. Abraham Casting Out Hagar and Ishmael, W.B. 30, p. 392

442 The Return of the Prodigal Son

Signed and dated: *Rembrandt f 1636*
Etching - 158 × 137 mm
One state only

This is a good impression in which the landscape, lightly sketched to the left, prints very distinctly.

W.B. 91; BB 36-D

Provenance: A. de Peters, 1784

All the figures are inscribed within the same elliptical pattern; this is true of the woman leaning out of the window, and of the father and son group as well: "And the son said unto him, Father, I have sinned against heaven, and in thy sight, and am no more worthy to be called thy son. But the father said to his servants, Bring forth the best robe, and put *it* on him; and put a ring on his hand, and shoes on *his* feet." (Luke 15, 21-22)

443, 444 The Good Samaritan

Signed and dated in the fourth state: *Rembrandt. inventor. et. Feecit. 1633.*

Etching and burin - 258 × 218 mm
Four states

Third state. The wall above the horse's back, unshaded in the former states, has been worked over in drypoint and burin. In the fourth state the plate was reduced to 257 × 208 mm.

W.B. 90-III; BB 33-A (five states)

Provenance: A. de Peters, 1784

Rembrandt often illustrated this subject, with a painting in 1632 (Bredius 545) and drawings from 1641 to 1650. This is, in reverse, a copy of the painting. Much has been written about this print. The following comment by Daniel Daulby, English compiler of De Burgy, Gersaint, and others, is still relevant: "The introduction of a dog towards the right corner, in an attitude in the true *Dutch* style, is an injury to the composition (considered as a piece of sacred history) which otherwise is very fine, and richly picturesque. This is one of the pieces that Rembrandt has finished with the greatest care, producing a wonderful effect, with a fine point and light."

445 Abraham Caressing Isaac

c. 1637
Signed: *Rembrandt. f*
Etching - 116 × 89 mm
Two states

Second state. A slipped stroke is visible above Isaac's left shoulder. Light strokes have been added to Abraham's turban and in other places.

W.B. 33-II; BB 37-2

Provenance: A. de Peters, 1784

One of Rembrandt's most touching works; its treatment is as sensitive as it is light and brilliant. The hands convey a veritable dialogue of tenderness and abandon.

446 Abraham Casting Out Hagar and Ishmael

Signed and dated: *Rembrandt f 1637*
Etching with touches of drypoint - 125 × 95 mm
Only one state

W.B. 30; BB 37-A

Provenance: A. de Peters, 1784

There are approximately ten known copies of this print; its anecdotal aspect must have made it very popular. In treatment it is far from the sober, vigorous quality of the previous print. The architecture in the background is similar to that in *Susanna Surprised by the Elders* (now in The Hague, fig. 608), painted during the same period.

447 The Death of the Virgin

Signed and dated: *Rembrandt f. 1639.*
Etching and drypoint - 410 × 314 mm
Three states

Second state. The chair on the right has been heavily shaded with drypoint lines.

Provenance: A. de Peters, 1784

Third state. This is one of two unusual impressions (the other is in Amsterdam) that show very heavy reworking in drypoint carried out when the additional lines on the lower part of the foremost bedpost had worn away. Not reproduced.

Impression reduced in height - 310 × 299 mm.

W.B. 99-II, III; BB 39-A (four states)

The iconographic sources of this scene are the engravings of the subject by Schongauer and Dürer. Rembrandt, however, has introduced a new duality to his staging of the event. It has a supernatural aspect with angels in the skies, and a realistic one with a doctor feeling the dying woman's pulse, while St. Peter attempts to restore her to life. To the right and left of the plate two curious spectators are peeping at the scene. The young man standing in front of the curtain is inspired by Mantegna.

448 The Beheading of John the Baptist

Signed and dated: *Rembrandt f. 1640*
Etching and drypoint - 129 × 105 mm
Two states

First state. The spears and helmets of the soldiers in the background to the left are barely visible; they were more clearly defined with the burin in the next state.

W.B. 92-I; BB 40-B (three states)

Provenance: J.-L. de Beringhen, 1731

There is a drawing in Bayonne (Benesch 477). Another drawing belonged formerly to the A. W. Mensing Collection (Benesch 478).

449 The Triumph of Mordecai

c. 1641
Etching and drypoint - 174 × 213 mm
Only one state

Two impressions.
One impression on European paper.
A later impression of prepared yellowish paper, whose blond tone suggests a supernatural light.

W.B. 40; BB 41-1

A drawing exists (Benesch 487).

A smaller copy illustrates the book by Thomas Herbert, *Some Years Travel into Africa and Asia the Great*, London, 1677, 4th edition, page 32.

In order to realize how strange this scene is, and how faithful to the Bible, we must go back to the book of Esther. An orphan, she had been raised by her cousin Mordecai, a Jew

447. The Death of the Virgin, W.B. 99, p. 392

448. The Beheading of John the Baptist, W.B. 92 p. 392

449. The Triumph of Mordecai, W.B. 40, p. 392

deported to Persia. King Ahasuerus, charmed by Esther's beauty and intelligence and not knowing who she was, chose her for the house of the women, then made her his queen. With the help of Esther, Mordecai saved the king from a plot against him by his guards. Out of neglect, however, Mordecai received no reward. Later, when the king realized this, he summoned his ambitious prime minister Haman and questioned him: "So Haman came in. And the king said unto him, What shall be done unto the man whom the king delighteth to honour? Now, Haman thought in his heart, To whom would the king delight to do honour more than to myself? And Haman answered the king, For the man whom the king delighteth to honour, let the royal apparel be brought which the king useth to wear, and the horse that the king rideth upon, and the crown royal which is set upon his head: And let this apparel and horse be delivered to the hand of one of the king's most noble princes, that they may array the man withal whom the king delighteth to honour, and bring him on horseback through the street of the city, and proclaim before him, Thus shall it be done to the man whom the king delighteth to honour. Then the king said to Haman, Make haste, and take the apparel and the horse as thou hast said, and do even so to Mordecai the Jew, that sitteth at the king's gate: let nothing fail of all that thou hast spoken. Then took Haman the apparel and the horse, and arrayed Mordecai, and brought him on horseback, through the street of the city, and proclaimed before him, Thus shall it be done unto the man whom the king delighteth to honour." (Esther 6. 6-11)

By flooding two-thirds of the scene with light, Rembrandt celebrates the triumph of Mordecai and the humiliation of Haman, who had intended to annihilate the Jews. Mordecai's dignity as the static central figure contrasts with the agitated movement of the crowd. Rembrandt and Saskia are spectators at the window on the right; though they personify the king and queen, their seventeenth-century apparel gives a timeless quality to this psychological drama. By blending spontaneous sketching, detail and an accurate final touch, Rembrandt gives faces and gestures more impact; they are veritable snapshots. The theatrical impression is heightened by the architectural setting and the round temple in the background.

Lucas van Leyden had made a print of the same subject in a completely different spirit. Rembrandt drew on it for the posture of two men on the right, the one taking off his cap and the one kneeling.

K.G. Boon rightly sees in this composition an analogy with *The Night Watch*: "The scene takes place near a gate... and the groups of figures are arranged about it in the same way. Haman is the 'Banning Cocq' of *The Night Watch*, and his theatrical gesture, reminiscent of that of an actor before the public, is the same as that of the captain of the municipal guards. Likewise the throng of curious onlookers armed with lances, who provide the movement in this scene, crowd the archway."

450 The Baptism of the Eunuch

Signed and dated: *Rembrandt. f 1641*
Etching - 177 × 213 mm
Two states

Second state. The waterfall and the bank on the right have been shaded with burin lines.

W.B. 98-II; BB 41-E

Provenance: A. de Peters, 1784

There is a drawing (Benesch 488).

"But an angel of the Lord said to Philip, 'Rise and go toward the south to the road that goes down from Jerusalem to Gaza.' This is a desert road. And he rose and went. And behold, an Ethiopian, a eunuch, a minister of the Canda'ce, queen of the Ethiopians, in charge of all her treasure, had come to Jerusalem to worship and was returning; seated in his chariot, he was reading the prophet Isaiah... And as they went along the road they came to some water, and the eunuch said, 'See, here is water! What is to prevent my being baptized?'... And he commanded the chariot to stop, and they both went down into the water, Philip and the eunuch, and he baptized him." (Acts 8, 26-28, 36-38)

451 The Angel Departing from the Family of Tobias

Signed and dated: *Rembrandt f 1641*
Etching and drypoint - 103 × 154 mm
Four states

Second state. The back of Tobias's head and the space below his beard have been shaded; crosshatching has been added between young Tobias's head and the edge of a platter held by a servant. In the ensuing states, light shading was added at various places.

W.B. 43-II; BB 41-G (six states; the last two include touches added by Watelet and Basan)

The composition is daring — we see only the lower part of the angel Raphael's body, in one corner, and this gives us a striking sense of the supernaturalism of what is taking place: "Having spake, [the angel] departed from among them and they could see him no longer. Whereupon for three hours they prostrated themselves upon the ground and blessed God" (Tob. 12. 16-20). Rembrandt had already depicted this scene in a vertical painting now in the Louvre. He seems to have drawn inspiration from a woodcut by Maerten van Heemskerck. He made three drawings on the same theme.

452 Three Oriental Figures (Jacob and Laban ?)

Signed and dated (in reverse) : *Rembrandt. f. 1641*
Etching - 143 × 114 mm
Two states

Second state. More foliage has been added to the right of the porch.

W.B. 118-II; BB 41-F

453 Old Man in Meditation, Leaning on a Book

c. 1645
Etching and touches of drypoint - 134 × 107 mm
Two states

Second state. The outline of the forehead, indicated by a series of dots in the first state, is now a single, continuous line in drypoint. The outline of the back has been strengthened, and short intaglios in drypoint have shaded the shoulder.

Impression with a very slight surface tone.

W.B. 147-II; BB 45-4

Provenance : A. de Peters, 1784

450. The Baptism of the Eunuch, W.B. 98, p. 396

454 St. Peter in Penitence

Signed and dated: *Rembrandt f 1645*
Etching - 133 × 114 mm (an impression reduced in width)
One state only

W.B. 96; BB 45-F

Provenance: J.-L. de Beringhen, 1731

455 Abraham Entertaining the Angels

Signed and dated: *Rembrandt f 1656*
Etching and drypoint - 159 × 132 mm
Only one state

W.B. 29; BB 56-B

Provenance: A. de Peters, 1784

Rembrandt etched few biblical scenes (Old Testament), perhaps fifteen at the most; of these, one-third deal with the story of Abraham and Isaac. Human relationships, particularly those between father and son, seem to have held more interest for him than supernatural events. *Abraham Entertaining the Angels* is the last biblical scene that Rembrandt etched. It illustrates Genesis 18. 1-13, in which the birth of Isaac is predicted: "And the Lord appeared unto him in the plains of Mamre; and he sat in the tent door in the heat of the day: ... and lo, three men stood by him.... And they said unto him, Sarah thy wife shall have a son. And Sarah heard it in the tent door, which was behind him... Sarah laughed within herself, saying, After I am waxed old shall I have pleasure, my lord being old also?" Abraham stands humbly on the right and offers the angels his hospitality; the Lord is seated in the middle. Ishmael, son of Hagar, can be identified from Genesis 21. 20: "And God was with the lad, and he grew, and dwelt in the wilderness, and became an archer."

For this composition, Rembrandt drew inspiration from an Indian miniature now at Schönbrunn, near Vienna. He owned several such miniatures; this one enabled him to approach this theme, so often chosen by artists, from a new angle.

456 Abraham and Isaac

Signed and dated: *Rembrandt. 1645.*
Etching and burin - 157 × 130 mm
Only one state

Impression with slight surface tone.

W.B. 34; BB 45-D (two states)

Provenance: A. de Peters, 1784

Eugène Delacroix made a copy of this print in about 1816 (Loys Delteil 3).

457 David in Prayer

Signed and dated: *Rembrandt f. 1652*
Etching with some drypoint - 140 × 93 mm
Three states

First state. A small white space near the left margin, beneath the canopy of the bed, was shaded in the next state.

W.B. 41-I; BB 52-C

Provenance: J.-L. de Beringhen, 1731

Here again we see how endlessly resourceful Rembrandt was: the vigorous play of parallel strokes (horizontal, diagonal or vertical), which stand out clearly from the crosshatching; the extraordinarily simple, and therefore singular, treatment of King David's head and hands.

458 The Blindness of Tobit

The Larger Plate
Signed and dated twice: *Rembrandt f 1651*
Etching with a few touches of drypoint - 161 × 129 mm
Two states

First state. At the bottom of the print, above the signature, is a partly burnished space; it was shaded with horizontal lines in the next state. This impression is crossed by a horizontal line, and retouched by pen and brown ink along the lower margin.

Single impression retouched with a pen.

W.B. 42-I; BB 51-D

By using very sober means — a great many widely spaced parallel strokes and extensive white spaces — Rembrandt bathes his central figure in light; Tobit's shadow falls on the wall. As a result, our attention is focused entirely on the blind man, who gropes before him; in his haste to welcome his son, he knocks over the spinning wheel and has trouble finding his way. Like several other artists before him (Van Orley, Massys, Elsheimer, Lastman, Brill), Rembrandt was inspired by the story of Tobit, from one of the Apocryphal books of the Bible. He depicted several episodes from it in five paintings, thirty drawings and three etchings.

459, 460, 461, 462 Four Illustrations to a Spanish Book

A. The image seen by Nebuchadnezzar
B. Jacob's ladder
C. David and Goliath
D. Daniel's vision of the four beasts
Signed and dated beginning with the second state:
Rembrandt f 1655.
Etching, burin and drypoint
Trimmed impression of the entire plate on Japanese paper
243 × 162 mm.

W.B. 36; BB 55-C

These four prints were made to illustrate the book by Samuel Manasseh Ben Israel, *Piedra gloriosa o de la estatua de Nebuchadnezar, con muchas y diversas authoridades de la S.S. y antiguos sabios. (Glorious stone or stone of the statue of Nebuchadnezzar, with several and divers authorities of the Holy Gospel and the ancient wise men)*, Amsterdam, 1655. They were engraved on a single plate which was divided into four almost immediately afterward. Rembrandt printed a very few impressions of the entire plate, and most of them in turn were divided.

A. The image seen by Nebuchadnezzar

First state. The legs are broken above and below the knees. Unique impression of the entire plate, later cut down. It is trimmed, 95 × 67 mm (W.B. 36-A, I)

Second state. The background all around the statue has been reworked. Signed and dated: *Rembrandt f. 1655*
Impression on vellum, 110 × 70 mm (W.B. 36-A, II)

Third state. Legs of the statue now straight, broken only at the ankles. Jacob's stone and globe engraved on the right; an arch has been added above Nebuchadnezzar's head.

(W.B. 36-A, III). Impression of the entire plate on Japanese paper.

The other three etchings (B,C,D) are second states (W.B. 36, III).

Fourth state. Differs from the third state only in that it was made after the plate was divided. Unique trial proof, on Japanese paper, with the names of the nations added in brown ink on the arms, legs and forehead, 112 × 70 mm. (W.B. 36-A, IV)

Fifth state. State made after the plate was divided. Names of the nations inserted. The turban on the statue's forehead comes down to the eyebrows. The shadow around the head is burnished away, 112 × 70 mm (W.B. 36-A, V)

B. Jacob's ladder

First state. Only the upper portion of the ladder is visible. Impression on vellum made from the entire plate and later cut down, 110 × 71 mm (W.B. 36-B, I)

Second state. The vertical parts of the ladder have been burnished in. Impression on Japanese paper of the entire plate. (W.B. 36-B, II)

Third state. The lower rungs of the ladder visible. Impression of the divided plate, 112 × 71 mm (W.B. 36-B, III)

C. David and Goliath

Second state. The contour of the hill on the right has been filled in, 106 × 74 mm.
Impression on Japanese paper of the entire plate.
(W.B. 36-C, II)
Impression used as illustration for the book (W.B. 36-C, II).

D. Daniel's vision of the four beasts

First state. The two diagonal lines in the top left corner do not reach the border. Not reproduced.
Impression on vellum 106 × 79 mm at the border (W.B. 36-D, I)

Second state. The two diagonal lines now reach the border. Impression on Japanese paper of the entire plate.
(W.B. 36-D, II)
This book refers to the Dream of Nebuchadnezzar, as interpreted by the prophet Daniel: "Thou, O king, sawest, and behold, a great image. This great image, whose brightness was excellent, stood before thee, and the form thereof was terrible. This image's head was of fine gold, his breast and his arms of silver, and his belly and his thighs of brass, His legs of iron, his feet part of iron and part of clay. Thou sawest till that a stone was cut off without hands, which smote the image upon his feet that were of iron and clay, and brake them to pieces. Then was the iron, the clay, the brass, the silver, and the gold broken to pieces together, and became like the chaff of the summer threshing floors; and the wind carried them away, that no place was found for them; and the stone that smote the image became a great mountain, and filled the whole earth. This is the dream, and we will tell the interpretation thereof before the king. Thou, O king, art a king of kings: for the God of heaven hath given thee a kingdom, power, and strength, and glory. And wheresoever the children of men dwell, the beasts of the field, and the fowls of the heaven, hath he given into thine hand, and hath made thee ruler over them all. Thou art this head of gold. And after thee shall arise another kingdom inferior to thee, and another third kingdom of brass, which shall bear rule over all the earth. And the fourth kingdom shall be strong as iron: forasmuch as iron breaketh in pieces and subdueth all things; and as iron that breaketh all

these, shall it break in pieces and bruise. And whereas thou sawest the feet and toes of potters' clay and part of iron, the kingdom shall be divided; but there shall be in it of the strength of the iron, forasmuch as thou sawest the iron mixed with miry clay. And as the toes of the feet were part of iron and part of clay, so the kingdom shall be partly strong and partly broken. And whereas thou sawest iron mixed with miry clay, they shall mingle themselves with the seed of men; but they shall not cleave one to another, even as iron is not mixed with clay. And in the days of these kings shall the God of heaven set up a kingdom which shall never be destroyed; and the kingdom shall not be left to other people, but it shall break in pieces and consume all these kingdoms, and it shall stand for ever. Forasmuch as thou sawest that the stone was cut out of the mountain without hands, and that it brake in pieces the iron, the brass, the clay, the silver and the gold; the great God hath made known to the king what shall come to pass hereafter; and the dream is certain, and the interpretation thereof sure. Then the king Nebuchadnezzar fell upon his face, and worshipped Daniel, and commanded that they should offer an oblation and sweet odours unto him." (Dan. 2. 31-46)

Manasseh commented as follows upon Daniel's prophecy in favor of the Jews: "There can be no doubt that the statue of Nebuchadnezzar symbolizes the four greatest monarchies or the four most flourishing empires which the world was to know, namely, the Babylonian, the Persian, the Greek and the Roman... (that is, a kingdom of gold, another of silver, another of brass, and a fourth of iron).... The stone is the Messiah, and it shall emerge from a great mountain without being touched by the hand of man and it shall fill the whole earth; for from that sublime and lofty mountain, which is the sovereign majesty of God, as it is said in the Psalm, 'Who shall rise from the mountain of the Lord?' shall come forth, by the workings of his divine Providence, a Prince, the Messiah who without need of weapons nor human force nor industry shall conquer and submit to his obedience the entire world. And as the kingdoms lasted each one a certain time, governed by divers princes and composed of different nations dwelling in different territories—Babylonians, Persians, Greeks and Romans—so the fifth kingdom shall be composed of divers nations and divers territories, and hence of the people of Israel, which possesses Judea as a gift from God. And just so also shall the Messiah (that is to say, the stone) destroy all of the other kingdoms with their temporal and earthly empire. And in the same way as the Persians destroyed the Babylonians and conquered their territory, as the Greeks destroyed the Persians and as the Romans destroyed the Greeks, just so shall the Messiah and the people of Israel enclosed within the latter kingdom (in which the others are encompassed) be the temporal, earthly and eternal masters of the universe, according to the infallible interpretation of Daniel." (Bl. 8)

464 Abraham's Sacrifice

Signed and dated: *Rembrandt f. 1655* (the *d* and the *6* reversed)
Etching and drypoint - 156 × 131 mm
Only one state

W.B. 35; BB 55-B

Provenance: J.-L. de Beringhen, 1731

The figures are carved, so to speak, out of one and the same block of light, which is what bestows such intensity on the simultaneous gestures of the angel and Abraham.

451. The Angel Departing from the Family of Tobias, W.B. 43, p. 396

452. Three Oriental Figures (Jacob and Laban?), W.B. 118, p. 396

453. Old Man in Meditation, Leaning on a Book, W.B. 147, p. 398

454. St. Peter in Penitence, W.B. 96, p. 398

455. Abraham Entertaining the Angels, W.B. 29, p. 398

456. Abraham and Isaac, W.B. 34, p. 398

457. David in Prayer, W.B. 41, p. 398

458. The Blindness of Tobit, W.B. 42, p. 398

459. The Image Seen by Nebuchadnezzar, W.B. 36-I, p. 399

460. The Image Seen by Nebuchadnezzar, W.B. 36-III, p. 399

461. Jacob's Ladder, W.B. 36-I, p. 399

462. Four Illustrations to a Spanish Book, W.B. 36, p. 398

gigante, cuyo nombre, era גלית Goliat, de la ciudad de גת Gat: dos circunstancias, que siendo al parecer superfluas, quedan necessarias para mayor declaracion del intento.

I. Este gigante representaua en la altura del cuerpo, la Estatua, y al mismo passo los 4. captiverios. Conviene con el nombre: por que גלית, es lo mismo que גלות *captiverio.*

II. Era de גת, significa *lagar,* lo mismo que dize Jesayas, tratando de la vengança que Dios hara en Edom, *por que son bermejos tus vestidos? y tus paños como el que pisa en lagar.* Joel, *venid y baxad que se lleno el lagar,* y Hachamim, que Asaph y Dauid, quando en sus Psalmos dizen, על הגיתית significan, la destruició desta quarta

Reinbrant. f. 1655.

463. Piedra gloriosa o de la estatua de Nebuchadnezzar, p. 398
Book for Samuel Manasseh Ben Israel
Amsterdam, 1655

464. Abraham's Sacrifice, W.B. 35, p. 410

465 St. Jerome Beside a Pollard Willow

Signed and dated (in the second state only): *Rembrandt f. 1648*
Etching and drypoint - 179 × 130 mm
Two states

First state. Before the signature and date and additional work in drypoint on the lion's face and the reeds in the foreground.

Impression on Japanese paper.

W.B. 103-I; BB 48-B

Provenance: Dufresne

There is a preliminary study of the tree in Turin (Benesch 852A).

The contrasting manners, the sketchy and the highly finished, so often used together by Rembrandt, are most effective in this print. Rembrandt made seven etchings of St. Jerome, the only doctor of the Church who really fired the artist's imagination. In all Rembrandt's representations of St. Jerome, the saint is engrossed in his reading of the Scriptures.

466, 467 St. Francis Beneath a Tree Praying

Signed and dated: *Rembrandt f. 1657* (with *d* reversed)
Drypoint (completed in etching in the second state)
183 × 247 mm
Two states

First state. Unfinished drypoint sketch, without the landscape at the right and with a white area between the saint's head and the tree trunk. This is one of the five known impressions of the first state.

Proof on Indian paper with surface tone to the left.

Second state. The sketch has been completed in etching. A landscape has been added on the right. The background has been reworked in etching and the details can be clearly made out. A second signature and date have been superimposed on the former ones.

W.B. 107-I, II; BB 57-A

Provenance: J.-L. de Beringhen, 1731

Rembrandt has represented St. Francis during his 1224 spiritual retreat at Monte della Verna, near Borgo San Sepolcro in Tuscany. Brother Leo, to the right of the plate, remained alone with the saint from the feast of the Assumption to that of St. Michael. It was on this very spot that the saint had his visions. Count Catanio had a monastery and a chapel built there for him.

Rembrandt's version shows no vision. In it the saint, who died at the age of thirty-eight, has the features of an elderly man. Here again, the artist has intensified contrasts by opposing the deep, thick black of the drypoint lines to the natural color of the Indian paper in the first state; in the second state, he has covered the plate with silvery hues. One passes from a sense of stress in the first state to a sense of peace in the second.

468 Peter and John Healing the Cripple at the Gate of the Temple

Signed and dated: *Rembrandt f. 1659.*
Etching, drypoint and burin - 180 × 215 mm
Four states

Second state. The falling fold of St. Peter's cloak hides his elbow; the right side of Peter's body, concave in the previous state, is now straight. In the next state, reworked in drypoint, several areas of the plate were altered. Impression on Japanese paper with a light surface tone.

W.B. 94-II; BB 59-A

Provenance: A. de Peters, 1784

This is the last of Rembrandt's biblical illustrations. With this scene, his activity as an etcher was also about to end. Only three more plates would follow. The artist had broached the same subject in his earliest prints, but in a very different manner (W.B. 95, fig. 433). The miracle takes place in the foreground, at the gate of the temple of Jerusalem, the architectural gigantism of which develops in the background. In spite of the animated scene, two passers-by alone balance the group of the apostles, whose action has not been premeditated. John, about to go on his way, turns his head towards the beggar. Rembrandt follows the Bible very closely: "Now Peter and John were going up to the temple at the hour of prayer, the ninth hour. And a man lame from birth was being carried, whom they laid daily at that gate of the temple which is called Beautiful to ask alms of those who entered the temple. Seeing Peter and John about to go into the temple, he asked for alms. And Peter directed his gaze at him, with John, and said, 'Look at us.' And he fixed his attention upon them, expecting to receive something from them. But Peter said, 'I have no silver and gold, but I give you what I have; in the name of Jesus Christ of Nazareth, walk'." (Acts 3, 1-6)

469 Virgin and Child in the Clouds

Signed and dated: *Rembrandt f. 1641*
Etching and drypoint - 168 × 105 mm
Only one state

W.B. 61; BB 41-4

Provenance: A. de Peters, 1784

A head visible in the clouds is undoubtedly an abandoned attempt.

470 The Holy Family

c. 1632
Signed: *RHL* (in monogram)
Etching - 96 × 72 mm
Only one state

W.B. 62; BB 32-3

Provenance: A. de Peters, 1784

This print is based on an etching by Annibale Carracci. Rembrandt owned prints by the Bolognese masters that are included in his posthumous inventory, n° 209: a portfolio of Hanibal, Augustijn and Loduwijck Crats (Carracci), Guwido the Bolognese (Guido Reni) and Spanjolette (Ribera).

465. St. Jerome Beside a Pollard Willow, W.B. 103, p. 412

466. St. Francis Beneath a Tree Praying, W.B. 107-I, p. 412

467. St. Francis Beneath a Tree Praying, W.B. 107-II, p. 412

468. Peter and John Healing the Cripple at the Gate of the Temple, W.B. 94, p. 412

469. Virgin and Child in the Clouds, W.B. 61, p. 412

470. The Holy Family, W.B. 62, p. 412

471. The Virgin and Child with the Cat and Snake, W.B. 63, p. 419

471 The Virgin and Child with the Cat and Snake

Signed and dated: *Rembrandt f. 1654*
Etching - 95 × 145 mm
Two states

First state. Two white spaces at upper right were shaded with the burin in the second state.

W.B. 63-I; BB 54-C

Provenance: A. de Peters, 1784

It is customary to refer to Mantegna's *Madonna with Child* (Hind V, 10, 1) in connection with this etching. Indeed, Rembrandt did base the Virgin's pose on the one used by Mantegna. He owned "The precious work of André de Montaingie" (posthumous inventory, nº 200). And yet nothing could be more different than these two interpretations of the subject. Mantegna's Madonna is powerful and sculptural, reminiscent of monumental art; Rembrandt's is a hymn to motherhood, a delicate genre scene. Along with *Jesus Returning from the Temple with His Parents* (W.B. 60, fig. 500), this is one of Rembrandt's most subtle and most natural depictions of the Holy Family.

472 The Angel Appearing to the Shepherds

Signed and dated beginning with the second state: *Rembrandt. f. 1634*
Etching, burin and drypoint - 262 × 218 mm
Three states

Third state. In the first state, the sky and foreground were largely unfinished; in the second, they were completed. The tree trunk in the middle, part of which had been left light, is now completely shaded. Shading has been added to the face of the second man from the left, to the ground about him, to the two cows on his right, and to the angel's wings.

W.B. 44-III; BB 34-J

Provenance: A. de Peters, 1784

This is Rembrandt's first night scene.

The luminous circle of angels is reflected on earth; there is thus an almost symmetrical correspondence between the light-projecting celestial scene and the earthly scene: between the angel and the upright shepherd, between the excited little angels and the panic-strickenered. Rembrandt based his etching on Luke 2. 8-14, which is the only description in the Bible of this scene: "And there were in the same country shepherds abiding in the field, keeping watch over their block by night. And, lo, the angel of the Lord came upon them, and the glory of the Lord shone round about them; and they were sore afraid. And the angel said unto them, Fear not: for, behold, I bring you good tidings of great joy, which shall be to all people. For unto you is born this day, in the city of David, a Saviour, which is Christ the Lord. And this shall be a sign unto you: Ye shall find the babe wrapped in swaddling clothes, lying in a manger. And suddenly there was with the angel a multitude of the heavenly host, praising God, and saying, Glory to God in the highest, and on earth peace, good will toward men."

Rembrandt has added a dove.

473 The Circumcision

Small Plate
c. 1630

Etching with some drypoint - 88 × 64 mm
Only one state

W.B. 48; BB 30-8

This small etching is one of Rembrandt's first to illustrate a subject from the New Testament. It shows his new concern with light: he draws our attention to the central group by bathing it in light while leaving the rest of the scene in shadow.

474 The Circumcision in the Stable

Signed and dated twice: *Rembrandt f 1654* (the *d* of the signature top left is reversed)
Etching - 96 × 145 mm
Two states

First state. Two white spaces caused by faulty biting: one below the signature, top left, the other towards the middle of the upper edge. They were shaded with the burin in the second state.

W.B. 47-I; BB 54-B

This scene is part of a series on the childhood of Christ (W.B. 98, 100, 102, 103, figs. 450, 438, 465), all of equal size, all of them peaceful, all given simple and spontaneous treatment. There are, however, occasional special effects, such as the figures on the right in this scene, visible behind a screen of strokes.

475 The Star of the Kings: A Night Piece

c. 1651
Etching with a few touches of drypoint - 94 × 143 mm
One state only
W.B. 113; BB 51-1 (two states)
Provenance: A. de Peters, 1784

The best comment on this plate is again Gersaint's, which so aptly describes how the nocturnal effect is appropriate to the subject (G. 112): "It is a common custom in Holland, among low people, on the Day of Epiphany, to carry about town a big lantern in the form of a bright star, at the end of a stick. The man who carries it is ridiculously clad in kingly clothes and followed by others in the same disguise: together these people form a masquerade and go at night about the streets, accompanied by assorted minstrels. They knock on all doors, hoping to grasp some money from the burghers."

Bernard Picart, in his *Cérémonies religieuses*, engraved a similar scene entitled *The Star of the Kings Taken About Amsterdam.*

476, 477, 478 The Adoration of the Shepherds: A Night Piece

c. 1652
Etching, drypoint and burin - 148 × 198 mm
Eight states

Third state. The figures who stood out fairly distinctly in the first and second states now fade into the shadow. We can make out two faces, the hand holding the lantern, and the group formed by the Holy Family. A narrow white band is visible on the Virgin's forehead. Joseph's head and hat have been retouched and shading has been added to the pillow between the Virgin and Child.

Impression on Japanese paper.

Provenance: A. de Peters, 1784

Fifth state. The reeds which had stood behind the Virgin and the Child were reworked in the fourth state into a halo by touches of drypoint; in the sixth state, they became very close and thick, enclosing the mother and infant in a halo of velvety shadow. The lantern in the center projects two symmetrical beams of light which pick out the figures in this scene. Shading models the Virgin's nose; a double outline separates her hand from her sleeve.

Seventh state. The darkness is not so dense. The planks and nails of the partition behind the Virgin and Child, added in the sixth state, appear more clearly and have been burnished lighter.

Impression on Japanese paper.

Eight state. Joseph's hat has been reworked and the shadow around his head has been burnished lighter.

W.B. 46-III, V, VII, VIII; BB 52-1

By having the shepherds come upon the Virgin and Child asleep while Joseph reads, Rembrandt found a new way to treat this scene. Eight times he reworked his copperplate; and each impression, even of one and the same state, offers a different vision of darkness. Our eyes adapt to the shadows and to the gleams from the lantern, and reconstitute the nocturnal scene. The effect is altogether different from that of *The Adoration of the Shepherds: With the Lamp.*

The old shepherd holding a lantern is also found in the small *Adoration of the Shepherds* in the National Gallery, London.

479 The Adoration of the Shepherds: With the Lamp

c. 1654
Signed: *Rembrandt f.*
Etching - 105 × 129 mm
Two states

First state. Near the upper edge of the plate, on the right, a horizontal white strip, caused by faulty biting. It was shaded in the second state.

Impression on thin Japanese paper with partial surface tone.

W.B. 45-I; BB 54-1

Provenance: P.-J. Mariette, 1775; A. de Peters, 1784

Rembrandt did not strive for striking effect in his depiction of this peaceful scene. For the most part he used simple strokes and the Virgin and Child, the main figures, are merely sketched. But they stand out because the central portion of the plate has been wiped, a technique which creates the aura around the real source of light, the oil lamp. The secondary figures are left in shadow. The traditional ass has been replaced by a cow. Nicolas Maes, Benjamin Cuyp and Pieter Potter all borrowed this detail and incorporated it into their own paintings.

480, 481, 482 The Flight into Egypt

A Sketch
c. 1627
Etching - 149 × 122 mm
Six states

First state. Impression of the entire plate retouched with pen and brown ink by the artist at lower right, thus adding detail to the ass's hind legs, its hooves and the ground. The plate has not been wiped.

A single impression, retouched.

Provenance: J.-L. de Beringhen, 1731

Second state. The plate has been cut down and arched at the top; only Joseph and the ass's head remain. It now measures 79 × 51 mm.

Sixth state. The tall hat has been replaced by a flat one. Two corner pieces have been added at the top.

W.B. 54-I, II, VI; BB 29-4

That part of the plate which was cut off was used to etch the *Self-Portrait Leaning Forward* (W.B. 5, fig. 675).

483, 484, 485 The Flight into Egypt

A Night Piece
Signed and dated: *Rembrandt f. 1651* (the *6* is reversed)
Etching, burin and drypoint - 128 × 110 mm
Six states

First state. The figures are lighted by the lantern and by moonlight; there are only a few parallel strokes on their white garments. To a large extent, the ass too is modeled by parallel strokes. The lantern throws pools of light on the ground. Joseph's right hand is not shaded.

Provenance: J.-L. de Beringhen, 1731

Third state. The clothing and the white spaces have been extensively shaded. Part of the sky has also been darkened. The lantern sheds a little light on Joseph, the ass's head, and the Virgin's hood.

Provenance: A. de Peters, 1784

Sixth state. Further shading added in the fourth and fifth states has darkened the background completely, and the sky is indistinguishable from the landscape. Figures can be made out in the shadow, and a pale light shows the outline of the ass. Joseph's right hand and the ass's nose are covered with light crosshatching.

W.B. 53-I, III, VI; BB 51-E (five states)

Provenance: A. de Peters, 1784

For the first time Rembrandt uses successive states to suggest the development of an action or a change in a state of nature or in a place. Here, as the Holy Family flees, there is a shift from moonlight to increasing darkness.

486 The Flight into Egypt: Altered from Seghers

c. 1653
Etching, burin and drypoint - 212 × 280 mm
Seven states

Seventh state. The first state is the impression of the copperplate etching by Hercules Seghers, *Tobias and the Angel.*

Rembrandt burnished out the right-hand part of the plate, where figures were visible, and replaced them with the Holy Family before a group of trees. In this second state, the figures and the ass were fairly indistinct. The landscape in the background was slightly different; the river was much nearer. After some retouching and after parts had been lightened by burnishing, the figures and the ass became quite distinct. In the fifth state, Rembrandt added a third tower in the background. The scene as a whole has been lightened by burnishing, which gives it an entirely different effect. The nocturnal, oppressively dark landscape of the second state has become a peaceful landscape, bathed in the light of dawn over the countryside. Even the sky, still somewhat dirty in the sixth state, has been burnished clean in the seventh. Impression

472. The Angel Appearing to the Shepherds, W.B. 44, p. 419

473. The Circumcision, W.B. 48, p. 419

474. The Circumcision in the Stable, W.B. 47, p. 419

475. The Star of the Kings, W.B. 113, p. 419

476. The Adoration of the Shepherds: A Night Piece, W.B. 46-I, p. 419

477, 478. The Adoration of the Shepherds: A Night Piece, W.B. 46-III, II, p. 419

479. The Adoration of the Shepherds: With the Lamp, W.B. 45, p. 420

with slight highlights of wash on the Virgin's veil, her face, and the edge of the group of trees.

W.B. 56-VII; BB 53-2

Provenance: A. de Peters, 1784

487 The Flight into Egypt

Small Plate
Signed and dated: *Rembrandt. inventor et fecit. 1633*
Etching - 89 × 62 mm
Two states

First state. The gray background is due to faulty biting; it was burnished lighter in the next state.

W.B. 52-I; BB 33-D

Provenance: A. de Peters, 1784

The Flight into Egypt was one of Rembrandt's favorite subjects throughout his active life. The first version he etched dates from 1627; the fifth and last, from 1654. Both this print and the *Good Samaritan* are signed in the same way: *Rembrandt. inventor et fecit.*

A painting now in the Musée des Beaux-Arts in Tours is similar to this etching in its intimate atmosphere.

488 The Flight into Egypt: Crossing a Brook

Signed and dated: *Rembrandt f. 1654*
Etching and drypoint - 94 × 143 mm
Only one state

W.B. 55; BB 54-D

Provenance: Leblond

490 The Rest on the Flight

A Night Piece
c. 1644
Etching and drypoint - 92 × 59 mm
Four states

Third state. The ass's head, halfway up on the right, has been added.

W.B. 57-III; BB 44-2

491 The Rest on the Flight

Lightly Etched
Signed and dated: *Rembrandt f. 1645*
Etching with some drypoint - 131 × 114 mm
Only one state

W.B. 58; BB 45-E

Provenance: J.-L. de Beringhen

492 Presentation in the Temple with the Angel

Small Plate
Signed and dated: *RHL (in monogram) 1630*
Etching - 103 × 78 mm
Two states

Second state. The plate has been cut down from its original 120 × 78 mm, thus eliminating the blank space at the top.

W.B. 51-II; BB 30-C

The left half of the scene is bathed in strong light, which stops at the door to the Temple. Our attention is distracted by surprising details: the crippled beggar stepping out of the plate, the little girl looking at him, the theatrical setting provided by the Temple.

493 The Presentation in the Temple

Oblong Plate
c. 1639
Etching and drypoint - 215 × 292 mm
Three states

Second state. Simeon now wears a skullcap. Drypoint shading has been added to his clothing and that of the Virgin. Joseph's beard has been shortened by burnishing.

W.B. 49-II; BB 40-1

Provenance: J.-L. de Beringhen, 1731

494 The Presentation in the Temple in the Dark Manner

c. 1654
Etching, drypoint and burin - 210 × 162 mm
Only one state
Two impressions: one lightly inked; one heavily inked with surface tone.

W.B. 50; BB 57-1

A sketch exists (Benesch 1032).

Rembrandt did three etchings of this subject (W.B. 49, 50, 51, figs. 492, 493, 494), each time in a different manner. This one can be compared to a series of etchings that are similar in format, style, technique and dating (W.B. 83, 86, 87, figs. 562, 563, 564, 511).

There are five known impressions; their heavy inking endows the scene with a theatrical, visionary effect. Attention is focused on Simeon, who is holding the Child; on the high priest, seated; and on the man who bears the torch aloft. Christ's parents kneel in the shadow, and Anna, the prophetess, is in the right background.

The stark contrast between whites and deep blacks against a strongly shadowed background intensifies the light and causes the precious fabrics, brocades and orphreys to scintillate. Our gaze is guided by the light glimpsed through the parted curtains on the left, in the same perspective as the torch. Each of the known impressions differs from the others because of the inking and paper used, and this gives a fresh aspect each time to the nocturnal effect.

495, 496 Christ Disputing with the Doctors

Small Plate
Signed and dated in the first and second states only: *RHL (in monogram) 1630*
Etching - 106 × 79 mm
Three states

Second state. The two seated figures near the left edge of the plate who had been light in the first state are now covered with shading. In this trimmed impression, only part of the signature remains, lower center.

Third state. Three sides of the plate have been cut down; it is now only 89 × 68 mm, and, as a result, two figures on the left and the signature at the bottom have disappeared. Two male figures have been added to the right of the seated man reading.

W.B. 66-II, III; BB 30-D

497 Joseph Telling His Dreams

Signed and dated: *Rembrant f 1638*
Etching - 110 × 83 mm
Three states

Second state. In the first state the space between Joseph's left arm and the profile of the young woman sitting on the right was shaded. Here it has been burnished white, making the profile stand out more clearly. This impression shows slight highlights of wash on the curtain on the left and on several shaded parts.

W.B. 37-II; BB 38-E

Provenance: A. de Peters, 1784

There is a drawing of Jacob, Joseph's father (Benesch 20), as well as a grisaille painting in which the composition is reversed (Bredius 504). This composition, which manages to include thirteen figures in a very small space, is a sheet of studies showing different types of facial expression. On the faces of Joseph's jealous brothers, on the face of his incredulous father, and on that of his attentive stepmother Lea, who is lying down in the background, are portrayed all of the feelings aroused by Joseph's recital.

498 Christ Seated Disputing with the Doctors

Signed and dated: *Rembrandt. f. 1654*
Etching - 95 × 144 mm
Only one state

Impression with light surface tone.

W.B. 64; BB 54-E

499 Christ Disputing with the Doctors

A Sketch
Signed and dated: *Rembrandt. f. 1652*
Etching and drypoint - 127 × 214 mm
Three states

First state. Spots, caused perhaps by corrosion of the copper, appeared in the next state.

W.B. 65-I; BB 52-B

Provenance: A. de Peters, 1784

There is a drawing (Benesch 885).

500 Christ Returning from the Temple with His Parents

Signed and dated: *Rembrandt f. 1654*
Etching and drypoint - 97 × 145 mm
Only one state

W.B. 60; BB 54-F

Provenance: A. de Peters, 1784

This etching is one of many to have been variously interpretated by Rembrandt's cataloguers. Gersaint relates it to the Flight into Egypt. Daulby, Bartsch and Claussin call it the "Return from Egypt". It was Wilson who in 1836 gave it the title used here, which, considering Jesus's age, seems more appropriate. It illustrates the passage in Luke in which Mary and Joseph have taken the twelve-year-old Jesus with them to Jerusalem for the Passover feast; there they loose him and look for him for three days. They find him in the Temple, sitting in the midst of the doctors. "And he said unto them, How is it they ye sought me? Wist ye not that I must be about my father's business? And they understood not the saying that he spake unto them. And he went down with them, and came to Nazareth." (Luke 2. 49-51)

480, 481, 482. The Flight into Egypt (A Sketch), W.B. 54-I, II, IV, p. 420

483, 484, 485. The Flight into Egypt (A Night Piece), W.B. 53-I, III, VI, p. 420

486. The Flight into Egypt, W.B. 56, p. 420

7. The Flight into Egypt (Small Plate), W.B. 52, p. 427

488. The Flight into Egypt: Crossing a Brook, W.B. 55, p. 427

Night Piece), W.B. 57, p. 427

491. The Rest on the Flight (L

494. The Presentation in the Temple in the Dark Manner, W.B. 50, p. 427

495, 496. Christ Disputing with the Doctors, W.B. 66, p. 427

497. Joseph Telling His Dreams, W.B. 37, p. 428

498. Christ Seated Disputing with the Doctors, W.B. 64, p. 428

499. Christ Disputing with the Doctors, W.B. 65, p. 428

501 Christ Preaching ("La Petite Tombe")

c. 1652
Etching, burin and drypoint - 155 × 208 mm
Only one state

Two impressions.

So-called *black-sleeve* impression (not reproduced), i.e., the first impressions made, with abundant burr, especially on the right sleeve of the turbaned man in the left foreground.

Impression with some wash highlights, accentuating the effect of the drypoint.

Provenance: A. de Peters, 1784

The so-called *white-sleeve* impression is one of the later impressions, made from a plate without burr, so that the sleeve appears white. The inking of this impression darkens the foreground and thus focuses the light on the scene in the center. Christ's halo becomes a miter of light.

Watermark

These differences in printing have led to statements that there are actually different states, and to falsifications (see Bartsch 67, Claussin 71, Blanc 39).

W.B. 67; BB 52-2

The customary title, "La Petite Tombe," used by Gersaint, was challenged by Pierre Yver as early as 1756: "I do not believe, as does M. Gersaint, that Our Lord is shown standing on a sort of Tomb in this print and that it is because of that that it has been titled 'La Petite Tombe'; rather, it appears to me that he is placed on a step or amphitheater, and that the reason which may have caused the print to be given that title is that the owner of the plate was one la Tombe" (Yver 66). Pieter de la Tombe, a draftsman and art dealer, was a friend of Rembrandt's. Clement de Jonghe's inventory, dated 1697, includes *"La petite estampe de La Tombe"*; it is also mentioned in the catalogue of the Amadée de Burgy collection, dating from 1755. Standing on a step, Christ is preaching, and captures the attention of his audience all along a band of light which crosses the entire print. The variety of expressions and gestures that his words arouse are more significant than the figure of Christ himself.

502 The Raising of Lazarus

Small Plate
Signed and dated: *Rembrandt f 1642* (the *2* reversed)
Etching - 150 × 114 mm
Two states

Second state. Lazarus's forehead is shaded with very light diagonal lines.

Watermark

W.B. 72-II; BB 42-B

There is a drawing (Benesch 518).

Ten years earlier, Rembrandt etched *The Raising of Lazarus: The Larger Plate* in the manner of the Baroque. The small plate gives a completely different version of the subject, vividly lighted, imbued with spirituality; the miracle takes place naturally, requiring no mise-en-scène. Lazarus is alone; Christ is surrounded by two groups of figures arranged more or less symmetrically. At the Exposition Universelle in Paris, 1855, Eugène Delacroix showed a *Résurrection de Lazare* based to a very large extent on this etching.

503, 504 The Raising of Lazarus

The Larger Plate
c. 1632
Signed: *RHL* (in monogram) *v. Ryn f.* (the *f* was added in the fifth state)
Etching and burin - 369 × 258 mm
Ten states

Fourth state. A number of changes were made in the ensuing states. Here the image is still very similar to that in earlier states, except that the outline of Christ's right leg above his foot has been completed and the shading of the right background continued down to the affrighted man. The only change in this state has to do with the arched frame, more heavily shaded with crosshatching. This impression was restored for purposes of the exhibition; in the process, it was found that the border and margin had been added. The paper is different from that used for the main sheet; a thick glue, similar to wood pulp, was used to hold the edges together, then polished down. This unique impression of the fourth state, which, according to White and Boon, differs from the others only with regard to the border, is merely a falsified or clumsily rebordered impression. Thus, the number of states listed by White and Boon can be reduced to nine.

Watermark

Eighth state. The significant changes made in the three previous states are these:
In the fifth state, the position of the woman in the lower right corner was changed so that she appeared in profile.
In the sixth, the affrighted man was given a cap (not reproduced).
In the seventh state, the old man in the right background was given a turban and the man on his left, a cap. The two faces below the man's outstretched right arm were shaded. The face of the woman with upraised arms was changed : her mouth is closed and her headgear different. Lastly, in the eighth state, the right leg of the affrighted man was etched more accurately.

Trimmed impression, 370 × 244 mm.

Watermark

Provenance : A. de Peters, 1784

Tenth state. The shading, already reworked in the ninth state, has been darkened with crosshatching. The face of the woman in the lower right and the heads of the two small figures below the arm of the affrighted man are more heavily shaded.

W.B. 73-IV, VIII, X; BB 32-4 (nine states)

These three states enable us to see how the plate developed; it is one of Rembrandt's first large pieces, much influenced by Baroque painting, the Bolognese school and Rubens. The dramatic effect, the setting and the theatrical stance of the various figures are enhanced by the drapery of the curtain, the unexpected still life and the dazzling, overwhelming lighting of the portion on the right. Christ's static position, as he stands with hand on hip and left arm upraised, is emphatically vertical and brings out the dimensions of the figure while contrasting with the amazed and agitated witnesses to the scene: "Could not this man, which opened the eyes of the blind, have caused that even this man should not have died? Jesus therefore, again groaning in himself, cometh to the grave" (John 11. 37-38). Imperceptibly, Jesus's raised hand raises Lazarus; the lighting of the widely spaced strokes on the right suggests a divine shape. An ecstatic correspondence.

This is one of the plates which has aroused much contradictory comment. Seymour Haden ascribes it to Bol and to Lievens; Middleton finds that only the figure of Christ and the curtain are by Rembrandt's hand. Dutuit believes that the plate was partially etched by Vliet. Blanc claims that "it is a magnificent piece, beyond any doubt Rembrandt's work" (Bl. 48), and Rovinski thinks that "it betrays the hand of a great master" (R. 73). The impressions made before the caps or hats were added were once much sought after and commanded very high prices.

About 1816, Eugène Delacroix made an interpretive copy of the lower right portion of this scene (Loys Delteil 4).

Van Gogh painted Lazarus, the two women and a sun in the background.

505 Christ and the Woman of Samaria Among Ruins

Signed and dated: *Rembrandt f. 1634*
Etching - 123 × 106 mm
Two states

First state. The two parallel lines at the top and the line at the bottom were removed from the next state.

W.B. 71; BB 34-L

Provenance: A. de Peters, 1784

506, 507 Christ and the Woman of Samaria

An Arched Print
Signed and dated: *Rembrandt f. 1658*
Etching and drypoint - 125 × 160 mm
Three states

Third state. The height of the plate, measuring 205 mm, in the first state, has been reduced.

The shadow that the woman had cast on the wall, and the window have been burnished out; the shadow at top left has been burnished lighter and redrawn. Shadow extends beyond the woman's profile and bust. The shadows on the wall and in the left foreground have been darkened. The date of the first state, 1657, has been changed.

Impression on Japanese paper.

W.B. 70-III; BB 57-B

Provenance: J.-L. de Beringhen, 1731

Rembrandt made two etchings of this subject; this one is infused with a spiritual quality, while the other remains merely anecdotal (cf. W.B. 71, fig. 505).

508 Christ Driving the Money Changers from the Temple

Signed and dated: *Rembrandt. f. 1635*
Etching - 137 × 167 mm
Two states

Second state. The shadow in the foreground is darkened by very fine strokes. The sole of the man being dragged by the cow is stained, and his mouth is very large.

W.B. 69-II; BB 35-B (three states)

Provenance: A. de Peters, 1784

Christ's face is based on a woodcut by Dürer (Bartsch 23). The rays denoting a supernatural presence surround, not Christ's head, but the hand that chastises. "And Jesus went into the temple of God, and cast out all them that sold and bought in the temple, and overthrew the tables of the moneychangers, and the seats of them that sold doves; And said unto them, It is written, My house shall be called the house of prayer; but ye have made it a den of thieves." (Matt. 21. 12-13)

509 The Tribute Money

c. 1635
Etching - 73 × 103 mm
Two states

First state. In the next state, the shadows were lightly reworked with the burin and drypoint, and very fine parallel lines appeared on Christ's head.

W.B. 68-I; BB 35-2

Provenance: A. de Peters, 1784

"Is it lawful to give tribute to Caesar, or not? Shall we give or shall we not give? But he, knowing their hypocrisy, said unto them, Why tempt ye me? Bring me a penny, that I may see it. And they brought it. And he saith unto them, Whose is this image and superscription? And they said unto him, Caesar's. And Jesus, answering, said unto them, Render to Caesar the things that are Caesar's, and to God the things that are God's. And they marvelled at him." (Mark 12. 14-17)

510 Christ at Emmaus

The Smaller Plate
Signed and dated: *Rembrandt f. 1634*
Etching with touches of drypoint - 102 × 73 mm
One state only

W.B. 88; BB 34-K

511 Christ at Emmaus

The Larger Plate
Signed and dated: *Rembrandt f. 1654*
Etching, burin and drypoint - 211 × 160 mm
Three states

Third state. Simply etched in the first state, the plate was completed in drypoint in the second. The rays encircling Christ's head and the broken outline on the back and hat of the disciple to the right have been more precisely defined. Some shadows have been made darker still. Impression with heavy inking around the figures.

W.B. 87-III; BB 54-H

Provenance: Don Eugène Béjot, 1931

There is a preparatory drawing in Amsterdam (Benesch A 66).

Inking has contributed to the intensity of Christ's radiance and emphasized the sense of an apparition.

512 to 547, 548, 549 The Hundred Guilder Print

c. 1649
Etching, drypoint and burin - 281 × 394 mm
Two states

First state. Before parallel lines were added to the neck of the ass on the right.

Impression on Chinese paper.

Second state. Diagonal parallel lines added to the ass's neck. The burr of the drypoint is worn down.

W.B. 74-I, II; BB 49-1

There has been abundant commentary on this masterpiece, this key to Rembrandt's universe. It can be approached in two ways: through silent contemplation, or more indirectly, through the many technical considerations and through the inevitable legend that clings to famous works.

Christ preaching was not a subject commonly treated in art at this time. Jesus stands among the crowd, as Matthew describes him, and his entire doctrine is revealed in this scene: "And great multitudes followed him; and he healed them there" (Matt. 19. 2). The healing of the cripple; the blessing of the children; the protestations of the disciples; the conversation with Peter; the discussion with the Pharisees who, on the left, mock Christ's words; the parable of the rich young man and the camel, in the archway on the right — it is all there: "And again I say unto you, It is easier for a camel to go through the eye of a needle, than for a rich man to enter into the kingdom of God" (Matt. 19. 24). Holfstede de Groot, the Dutch art historian, has pointed out that Saint Peter is shown here with Socrates' features and that the disciple behind him, wearing the tall hat, has those of Erasmus, who at that time was still very influential. Rembrandt has brought the wisdom of antiquity and that of the Renaissance together before Christ, who instructs Socrates in Christian doctrine. The Christ we see here — an immaterial being, his face modeled by light, with no definite outline but delicate touches of drypoint — recalls the portrait of Jan Six in technique, as do the weightless, velvety shadows of the darker portions. In this etching we find several of Rembrandt's different "manners," from the relatively sketchily outlined figures in the light on the left, to the very closely detailed, finished figures in the shadowy area. Every degree of shading, from ash gray to deepest black, is used, as is every density, every resource that light has to offer.

This etching is neither dated nor signed. Rembrandt appears to have worked on it for a number of years; it may have been begun in 1639 and completed in 1649, after many studies. All of the right side underwent alteration. Christ was originally taller: we can still make out the first outline of the head and shoulders; his left hand, now raised, was lowered. There are several preparatory drawings (White, 1969, pp. 58-61).

Prints of this scene vary depending on the paper used (Holland, Japanese or Chinese) and the inking. Already, in the seventeenth century, the etching was considered one of Rembrandt's greatest masterpieces — one of the greatest masterpieces of etching in general. Its title, far from expressing the meaning of the scene, is testimony to the esteem in which it was held. The title goes back at least to 1718, when it was used by Houbraken (vol. I, p. 259). The story has it that the etching was sold for one hundred guilders during Rembrandt's lifetime. Says Gersaint: "Here is what I learned of it, in that country. It is said that one day a picture-dealer from Rome proposed to Rembrandt several prints of Marc-Antony on which he put a price of one hundred guilders; that Rembrandt offered this work in exchange for the prints and that the dealer accepted, either because he wished to do Rembrandt a service or because he was genuinely content to take the work in exchange. I have moreover seen, in the museum in Amsterdam, a magnificent first impression of the Hundred Guilder Print on the back of which is written, in old Dutch, Given by my worthy friend Rembrandt, in exchange for a print of Marc-Antony. Signed, Z.P. Hoomer." Gersaint adds: "Seeing the prices for which Rembrandt's prints sell, there is every reason to believe that in time, the name Hundred Guilder Print will be justified." The price rose continually, from one sale to the next. The print by Marc-Antony (Marcantonio Raimondi) referred to here was *The Plague*, an engraving which was long renowned. According to Mariette, Rembrandt, at a sale, bought his own etching for one hundred guilders: hence, another explanation of its title.

So famous did this print become that ultimately it fell victim to its own success. The copperplate was bought by William Baillie from an English engraver named Greenwood, who had found it in Holland. Baillie very skilfully retouched the plate and sold impressions made from it, charging five guineas for those on ordinary paper, five and a half for those on Chinese paper. After he had made one hundred impressions, he cut the plate into four pieces and made separate impressions from each of them.

550 The Agony in the Garden

Signed and dated: *Rembrandt f. 165* (last digit missing)
c. 1657
Etching and drypoint - 111 × 84 mm
Only one state

W.B. 75; BB 57-3

There are three drawings (Benesch 626, 898 and 899).

The treatment is astonisghingly modern: space is constructed, and divided into nearer and farther planes, by vigorous, widely spaced parallel lines; clouds gradually move to cover the moon.

551 Christ Before Pilate

Large Plate
Signed and dated: *Rembrandt f. 1636 cum privile.*
Etching - 549 × 447 mm
Five states

Second state. The central group of figures (Pilate and the Jews facing him), which had been left unfinished in the first state, has been completed. Several areas of the plate have been reworked. The date, 1635, has also been modified.

W.B. 77-II; BB 35-K

There is a preparatory grisaille (Bredius 546) in London.

Twenty years or so separate these two *Ecce Homo*'s by Rembrandt. A comparison of the prints eloquently demonstrates the artist's evolution.

Recently, Martin Royalton-Kisch and Peter Schatborn attributed this etching, along with another, *The Descent from the Cross* (W.B. 81, fig. 560), to an etcher of reproductions, Jan van Vliet. They believe Rembrandt merely did the drawing for the plate and retouched it with drypoint (*Apollo,* February 1984, pp. 130-32).

500. Christ Returning from the Temple with His Parents, W.B. 60, p. 428

501. Christ Preaching, W.B. 67, p. 438

502. The Raising of Lazarus, W.B. 72, p. 438

503. The Raising of Lazarus, W.B. 73-IV, p. 438

444

504. The Raising of Lazarus, W.B. 73-VIII, p. 438

445

505. Christ and the Woman of Samaria Among Ruins, W.B. 71, p. 439

506. Christ and the Woman of Samaria, W.B. 70, p. 439

507. Detail of fig. 506

508. Christ Driving the Money Changers from the Temple W.B. 69, p. 439

509. The Tribute Money, W.B. 68, p. 439

510. Christ at Emmaus, W.B. 88, p. 439

548. The Hundred Guilder Print, W.B. 74-I, p. 440

550. The Agony in the Garden, W.B. 75, p. 440

551. Christ Before Pilate, W.B. 77, p. 459

552, 553 Christ Presented to the People; Ecce Homo

Oblong Plate
Signed and dated (from the seventh state onwards):
Rembrandt f. 1655
Drypoint - 383 × 455 mm
Eight states

Third state. Crosshatching has been added to the thigh of the man on the extreme left of the tribune. This is the last state in which the plate is entirely visible, with the architrave above the statues. The engraved copperplate was so tall that it required the printing of an additional strip of paper, since the standard sheets of Chinese, Japanese and vellum paper used by Rembrandt at that time were not large enough. Two known impressions of this state lack this additional strip. The artist finally gave up the architrave and reduced the plate.

Impression on Chinese paper. Not reproduced. The restoration of the etching has enabled us to see that this impression was originally printed on a large sheet of Chinese paper without further work.

Provenance: A. de Peters, 1784

Fourth state. The dimensions of the plate have been reduced to 358 × 455 mm. The group immediately to the left of Pilate has been shaded. Further intaglios have been added to Christ's loincloth and various areas of the plate.

Impression on vellum with slightly smaller dimensions: 353 × 448 mm.

Provenance: J.-L. de Beringhen, 1731

Eighth state. The plate has been extensively reworked in the preceding states. Alterations involved burnishing out and scraping of the copperplate. In the sixth state, the crowd gathered in front of the tribune was burnished out; traces of it can still be made out. In the seventh state two dark arches separated by a statue (bust) of Neptune were introduced at the bottom of the tribune. The statue was ultimately covered with a screen of horizontal hatching but it has remained clearly visible. The figures on the tribune have been redrawn in drypoint. The design of the two upper windows on the right has been altered: the openings have become higher and arch-shaped. Three figures have been added to the left in the doorway. The top of the central doorway has been altered.

Provenance: J.-P. Mariette, 1775; A. de Peters, 1784

W.B. 76-III, IV, VIII; BB 55-A (seven states)

Comments on this print are usually matched with comments on a similar subject by Lucas van Leyden. Although parallels of this sort are generally of little value, since a comparison with Rembrandt is always detrimental to the other artist, yet the central tribune, the various architectural elements, and the crowd below invite such a comparison. This type of "presentation to the people" was probably inspired by contemporary Passion plays.

The agitation of the inquisitive crowd is contrasted with the awkward rigidity of the figures standing on the tribune; this statuesque rigidity is emphasized by the imposing façade accented by rhythmical structural elements.

The composition also recalls the engraving by Marcantonio Raimondi (c. 1480 - before 1534): *The Martyrdom of St. Lawrence* after a drawing by Bandinelli. Rembrandt, though he never visited Italy, was imbued with the Italianate and owned portfolios of the entire production of Michaelangelo and many other masters. Mantegna, Raphael, Vanni, Titian, the Carracci, Barocci, Tempesta, Bonasone, Guido da Como and Guido da Siena are mentioned in the inventory of his possessions. The two statues on this façade, blindfolded Justice with scales, and Force with a club, symbolize the two groups of people below and sum up the drama. By finally removing the mob and darkening the shadow that pervades the lateral and bottom parts of the print, the artist has focused the viewer's attention on the main subject. Rembrandt proceeds from analysis to synthesis his grand manner. However, the crowd is still present, its bulk, indistinct yet threatening, moves against the wall. Rembrandt intensifies the drama by simplifying the composition and brings to life a visionary world.

Picasso adopted the general composition of this engraving for a plate executed in 1970.

554 The Crucifixion

Small Plate
Signed; *Rembrandt f.*
c. 1635
Etching - 95 × 67 mm
One state only

W.B. 80; BB 35-1

An existing sketch (Benesch 17, fig. 582) was possibly the source used for this print.

The *Crucifixion* by Prud'hon (Paris, Musée du Louvre) was inspired by this small etching.

555 Christ Crucified Between the Two Thieves

An Oval Plate
c. 1641
Etching and drypoint - 136 × 140 mm
Two states

First state. The left arm of the nearest cross has a square end, touching the border of the plate.

W.B. 79-1; BB 41-2

The light radiating from Christ's body broadens upwards. Dominating the other two, the divine cross suggests triumph rather than death.

552. Christ Presented to the People, W.B. 76-III, p. 459

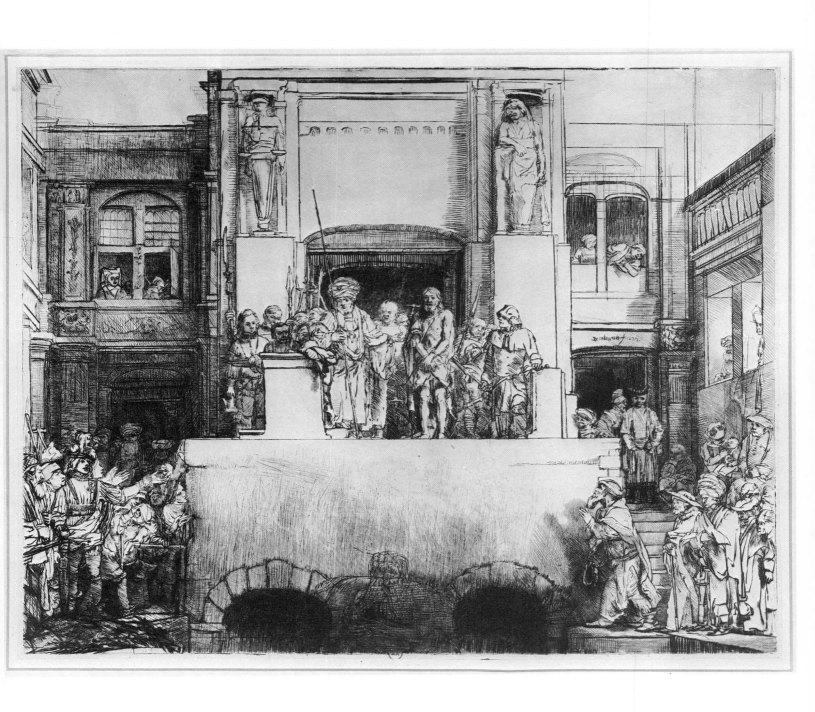

553. Christ Presented to the People, W.B. 76-VII, p. 459

554. The Crucifixion, W.B. 80, p. 459

555. Christ Crucified Between the Two Thieves, W.B. 79, p. 459

556. The Three Crosses, W.B. 78-I, p. 466

557. The Three Crosses, W.B. 78-III, p. 466

556, 557, 558 The Three Crosses

Signed and dated (on the impression of the third state only): *Rembrandt. f. 1653*
The fourth state is dated c. 1660
Drypoint and burin - 385 × 450 mm
Five states

First state. The face of the man in the left foreground (Simon of Cyrene?), who is being led away by two other figures, was left unshaded. Light falls obliquely from the upper center down to the lower corners.

Impression on vellum with surface tone - 373 × 428 mm.

The light inking of the support has imparted a great softness to the outlines and considerable airiness to the intense darks in drypoint lines.

Second state. The face of the man behind the bush on the extreme right has been defined and shaded with parallel intaglios. Impression with light surface tone. This state has much more light than the preceding ones. Not reproduced.

Third state. The upper background has become lighter through burnishing out. The left side of the foreground has been heavily shaded in drypoint, particularly the three figures mentioned in the first state. The face of Simon of Cyrene has been shaded with fine parallel intaglios. A dazzling light pervades the picture.

Provenance: J.-L. de Beringhen, 1731

Fourth state. The plate has been completely altered. The scene takes place in deep shadow penetrated by a gloomy light. Certain areas of the plate have been burnished out; others have been altered. In order to make these alterations, Rembrandt used the scraper and the burnisher. Most of the figures that remain have either been redrawn in drypoint or dissolve into the shadows. The third cross to the right is hardly visible. The horse without a rider, in front of the left-hand cross, has been reversed in this state; a rider inspired by Pisanello sits on the horse. The horse that faced it now rears; the horse in profile near Christ's cross is unbridled.

This state must have been completed around 1660-61. The print was then finished. The fifth state indicates at bottom the address of a printer: *Frans Carelse excudit.*

Two impressions, one on a bluish paper. From top to bottom the plate has been slashed by vigorous intaglios in drypoint and burin.

W.B. 78-I, II, III, IV; BB 53-A

This is the last of the three etchings by Rembrandt dealing with this subject and, together with *Christ Presented to the People* (W.B. 76, figs. 552, 553) it is one of the largest of his monumental prints. This supernatural composition, which became really popular only from the Romantic period onwards, defies comment. In this context, only the Bible merits quotation: "Now from the sixth hour there was darkness over all the land unto the ninth hour.... And, behold, the veil of the temple was rent in twain from the top to the bottom; and the earth did quake, and the rocks rent.... Now when the centurion, and they that were with him, watching Jesus, saw the earthquake, and those things that were done, they feared greatly, saying, Truly this was the Son of God." (Matthew, 27, 45-51-54)

559 The Descent from the Cross

The First Plate
Signed and dated: *Rembrandt. Ft. 1633.*

Etching - 520 × 400 mm (the width of this impression has been reduced)
One state only

W.B. 81-I; BB 33-B

Provenance: J.-L. de Beringhen, 1731

This and the next plate are Rembrandt's largest copperplates. There are only four impressions of the present one. As the plate failed in biting, Rembrandt attempted to rub it down (with stone probably), then used another, slightly larger support (530 × 410 mm).

560 The Descent from the Cross

The Second Plate
Signed and dated: *Rembrandt. f. cum pryvl°. 1633*
Etching and burin - 527 × 450 mm. (The height of this impression has been reduced).
Five states

Second state. Horizontal hatching has darkened the legs of the two men taking hold of Christ's body. The next two states have had the publisher's inscription added. The inscription was ultimately burnished out in the fifth state.

W.B. 81-II; BB 53-C

The present composition resembles that of the preceding work. It was inspired by a painting by Rubens, then circulating in the form of a print by Lucas Vorsterman. But, above all, it is the etched replica of a painting by Rembrandt himself, executed the same year for the prince of Orange-Nassau, Frederick Henry (Bredius 550). Here the artist was, for the second time, reproducing one of his own paintings. Rembrandt has portrayed himself on the ladder to the right. The art dealer signing *Amstelodami Hendrickus Vlenburgensis* in the margin of the third state was Saskia's cousin. Rembrandt lived at this cousin's house for a while and there probably met his future wife.

561 The Descent from the Cross

A Sketch
Signed and dated: *Rembrandt. f. 1642*
Etching and drypoint - 149 × 116 mm
One state only

W.B. 82; BB 42-C

Provenance: A. de Peters, 1784

The two lines rising obliquely from the foot of the cross, together with the part of the ladder on which a figure stands, seem to be a projection of the cross itself. As always, the viewer is invited to complete the composition mentally.

562 The Descent from the Cross by Torchlight

Signed and dated: *Rembrandt. f. 1654* (the *a* reversed)
Etching and drypoint - 210 × 160 mm
One state only
Impression on Japanese paper.

W.B. 83; BB 54-G (two states)

Provenance: J.-L. de Beringhen, 1731

The effect of night is adroitly enhanced by the composition itself. The figures follow one another along an oblique line which divides the print into two triangles, one light and one dark. Christ's body hangs parallel to the shroud Joseph of Arimathaea is spreading in the tomb; the hand emerging from the shadow reflects the torchlight.

558. The Three Crosses, W.B. 78-IV, p. 466

559. The Descent from the Cross, W.B. 81-I, p. 466

560. The Descent from the Cross, W.B. 81-II, p. 466

561. The Descent from the Cross (A Sketch), W.B. 82, p. 466

562. The Descent from the Cross by Torchlight, W.B. 83, p. 466

563. The Entombment, W.B. 86-II, p. 476

564. The Entombment, W.B. 86-III, p. 476

565. Christ Carried to the Tomb, W.B. 84, p. 476

566. Christ Appearing to the Apostles, W.B. 89, p. 476

563, 564 The Entombment

c. 1654
Etching, drypoint and burin - 211 × 161 mm
Four states

First state. Etching only, apart from a few drypoint lines on the Virgin's left elbow and the side of the tomb. The technique is here reminiscent of Mantegna's.

Second state. In order to achieve an effect of night, the whole plate has been worked over and darkened. The parallel shading added on the figures and up to the border of the plate is clearly visible. Christ and the two figures behind him have been shaded by closer parallel hatching and some crosshatching. Not reproduced.

Impression on vellum.

Provenance: P.-J. Mariette, 1775; A. de Peters, 1784

Third state. The lower part of the wall halfway down the right margin has been covered with diagonal shading. Burnishing out has lightened the background. Impression printed with very heavy surface tone.

Fourth state. The diagonal lines have been continued so as to reach the right upper border of the plate.

W.B. 86-I, II, III, IV; BB 54-2 (five states)

There are four preparatory drawings, two of them after Perino del Vaga (Benesch 938, 939, 1208 and 1209).

Compared with Rembrandt's treatment of the subject, the description of the different changes occurring from one state to the next seems irrelevant and meaningless. The composition is organized around an oval structure: the figures are on the lower curve, the vault of the tomb closes the oval. The source of light is Christ himself. The daylight in the first state has been reduced in the second, where shapes seem to dissolve into the darkness of the tomb. Only faces and hands, given form by some pale golden light, animate the darkness. The heavy inking of the plate in the third state has unified the shadows, deepening the sense of meditation. In this state Christ's body and the figures behind him are still faintly glowing. In the fourth state darkness and light have become more contrasted; the white appearing between the intaglios and the increased definition of the background lighten the atmosphere of deep mourning. The present state offers a single vision of the scene, rendered different with each inking of the plate, with the kind of paper used, and with the printing itself.

565 Christ Carried to the Tomb

c. 1645
Signed: *Rembrandt.*
Etching, with touches of drypoint - 131 × 109 mm
One state only

W.B. 84; BB 45-3

Provenance: J.-L. de Beringhen, 1731

This funeral procession, lightly accented by the interplay of shading modulated by small intaglios, is a new theme in Christian iconography, foreshadowing the Entombment.

566 Christ Appearing to the Apostles

Signed and dated: *Rembrandt f. 1656*
Etching - 163 × 210 mm
One state only

An excellent impression, as is often the case with this etching.

W.B. 89; BB 56-A

Provenance: A. de Peters, 1784

The phenomenon of Christ's apparition is even better rendered in this plate than in the previous *Christ at Emmaus* (W.B. 87, fig. 511), of 1654. The simple etching, with discontinuous hatched lines (perhaps Rembrandt used the burnisher to cut down his lines), and the brilliant rays of light beautifully render the supernatural character of the event. The lack of definition, the incompleteness, the radiance of Christ suggest the transient quality of the event. The image imparts the feeling that all the figures are likely to vanish into thin air.

567 The Virgin with the Instruments of the Passion

c. 1652
Etching and drypoint - 110 × 89 mm
One state only

This Paris print is one of the early impressions presenting drypoint burr under the Virgin's arms, on her veil, and on her neck.

W.B. 85; BB 41-5

Provenance: J.-L. de Beringhen, 1731

According to Rovinski, the model for the Virgin also sat for *The Spanish Gypsy "Preciosa"* (W.B. 120, fig. 186).

567. The Virgin with the Instruments of the Passion, W.B. 85, p. 476

568. Isaac Blessing Jacob, c. 1652
Pen and bistre 176 × 197 mm Ben. 891
Chatsworth, Derbyshire, Devonshire Collection (1015)

569. The Presentation in the Temple, 1661
Pen and brush in bistre with white 120 × 89 mm Ben. 1057
The Hague, Royal Library

570. Study for the Drunkenness of Lot, 1633
Black chalk 251 × 189 mm Ben. 82
Frankfurt, Städelsches Kunstinstitut

571. Jacob and Rachel Listening to the Account of the Dreams of Joseph, c. 1642-43
Pen and bistre, wash heightened with white 180 × 163 mm Ben. 528
London, British Museum

**572. Preparatory Drawing for the Etching St. Jerome Reading
in an Italian Landscape, c. 1653-54**
Pen, wash 250 × 207 mm Ben. 886
Hamburg, Kunsthalle

573. The Good Samaritan Arriving at the Inn, c. 1641-43
Pen, bistre, wash, corrected in white 184 × 287 mm Ben. 518a
London, British Museum

574. The Star of the Kings, c. 1641-42
Pen and bistre, wash 204 × 323 mm Ben. 736
London, British Museum

575. Rebecca Taking Leave of Her Family, c. 1637
Pen and bistre, wash 185 × 306 mm Ben. 147
Stuttgart, Staatsgalerie

485

576. The Holy Family in the Carpenter's Workshop, c. 1648-49
Pen and brown ink 173 × 227 mm Ben. 620
Rotterdam, Boymans-van Beuningen Museum

577. The Holy Family, c. 1652
Pen and bistre with brown wash 220 × 191 mm Ben. 888
Vienna, Albertina

578. Jesus Washing the Feet of His Disciples, c. 1653-55
Pen and bistre 156 × 220 mm Ben. 931
Amsterdam, Rijksprentenkabinet

579. Jesus and His Disciples, 1634
Red and black chalk, pen and bistre, washes in different tones,
heightened in white 335 × 476 mm Ben. 89
Haarlem, Teylers Museum

580. Sketch After Leonardo's Last Supper, c. 1635
Red chalk 365 × 475 mm Ben. 443
New York, Metropolitan Museum of Art, Lehman Collection

581. Christ Crowned with Thorns
Pen and bistre, wash 196 × 200 mm Ben. A 82
Chatsworth, Derbyshire, Devonshire Collection (1017)

582. The Entombment of Christ, 1630
Red chalk heightened with white 280 × 203 mm Ben. 17
London, British Museum

583. Jesus Appearing to Mary Magdalene as a Gardener, c. 1638
Pen and brown ink 154 × 146 mm Ben. 538
Amsterdam, Rijksprentenkabinet

584. Tobit Asleep, 1651
Pen and bistre heightened with white 170 × 190 mm Ben. 872
Rotterdam, Boymans-van Beuningen Museum

585. The Stoning of Saint Stephen, 1625 Panel 89.5 × 123.6 cm G. 2 Lyons, Musée des Beaux-Arts

586. David Presenting the Head of Goliath to Saul, 1627 Panel 27.5 × 39.5 cm G. 3 Basel, Oeffentliche Kunstsammlung

▲587. **The Denial of St. Peter, 1628**
Copper 21.5 × 16.5 cm G. 7
Tokyo, Bridgestone Museum of Art

588. Anna Accused by Tobit of Stealing the Kid, 1626
Panel 39.5 × 30 cm G. 4
Amsterdam, Rijksmuseum (on loan from Baroness Bentinck-Thyssen)

589. Samson Betrayed by Delilah, 1628
Panel 59.5 × 49.5 cm G. 9
Berlin-Dahlem, Gemäldegalerie

590. Two Scholars Disputing, 1628
Panel 71 × 58.5 cm G. 11
Melbourne, National Gallery of Victoria

591. The Apostle Paul at His Desk (Rembrandt's Father), c. 1627
Panel 47 × 39 cm G. 23
Nuremberg, Germanisches Nationalmuseum

592. The Prophet Jeremiah Lamenting the Destruction of Jerusalem (Rembrandt's Father), 1630
Panel 58 × 46 cm G. 24
Amsterdam, Rijksmuseum

▲ 593A. Scholar Meditating, c. 1632
Panel 29 × 33 cm G. 91
Paris, Musée du Louvre

▲ 593. Rembrandt's Father, 1625-31
Panel 24.1 × 20.5 cm G. 29
Wassenaar, Holland, Collection of Mr. S.J. van den Bergh

▲ 594. A Scholar in a Lofty Room ("Saint Anastasius"), 1631
Panel 60 × 48 cm G. 26
Stockholm, Nationalmuseum

595, 596. Esther Preparing to Intercede with Ahasuerus, 1633
Panel 109 × 93 cm G. 58
Ottawa, National Gallery of Canada

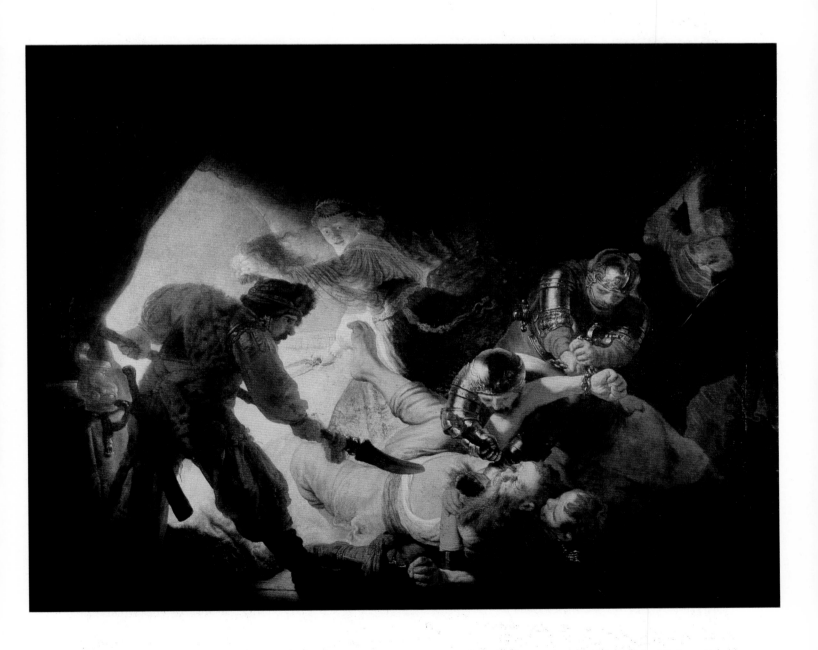

597. Tobias Healing His Father's Blindness, 1636
Panel 47.2 × 38.8 cm G. 75
Stuttgart, Staatsgalerie

598. The Blinding of Samson by the Philistines, 1636
Canvas 236 × 302 cm G. 76
Frankfurt, Städelsches Kunstinstitut

507

599. King Uzziah Stricken with Leprosy, 1635
Panel 101 × 77 cm G. 70
Chatsworth, Derbyshire, Devonshire Collection

600. Samson Threatening His Father-in-Law, 1635
Canvas 156 × 129 cm G. 78
Berlin-Dahlem, Gemäldegalerie

601. Belshazzar Sees the Writing on the Wall, c. 1636
Canvas 167 × 209.5 cm G. 77
London, National Gallery

602, 603. Details

604, 605. Samson Posing the Riddle to the Wedding Guests, 1638 Canvas 126 × 175 cm G. 85 Dresden, Gemäldegalerie

606. Joseph Telling His Dreams, c. 1638
Paper on panel 51 × 39 cm G. 86
Amsterdam, Rijksmuseum

607. The Visitation, 1640
Panel 57 × 48 cm G. 203
Detroit, Michigan, Institute of Arts

608. Susanna Surprised by the Elders, 1637
Panel 47.5 × 39 cm G. 84
The Hague, Mauritshuis

609. Susanna Surprised by the Elders, 1647
Panel 76 × 91 cm G. 221
Berlin-Dahlem, Gemäldegalerie

610. Bathsheba with King David's Letter, 1654
Canvas 142 × 142 cm G. 271
Paris, Musée du Louvre

611. Jacob Blessing the Sons of Joseph, 1656
Canvas 175.5 × 210.5 cm G. 277
Cassel, Gemäldegalerie

612. Jacob Wrestling with the Angel, 1659-69 Canvas 137 × 116 cm G. 346 Berlin-Dahlem, Gemäldegalerie

613. David and Saul, 1657 Canvas 130.5 × 164 cm The Hague, Mauritshuis

614. Moses with the Tables of the Law, 1659
Canvas 167 × 135 cm G. 347
Berlin-Dahlem, Gemäldegalerie

528

615. The Apostle Paul, c. 1657
Canvas 129 × 102 cm G. 295
Washington, D.C., National Gallery of Art, Widener Collection

616. The Evangelist Matthew Inspired by the Angel, 1661
Canvas 96 × 81 cm G. 359
Paris, Musée du Louvre

617. The Apostle Simon, 1661
Canvas 98.3 × 79 cm G. 362
Zurich, Kunsthaus (Ruzicka Foundation)

618. Old Man in an Armchair (The Patriarch Jacob?), c. 1650-58
Canvas 51 × 37 cm G. 283
Berlin-Dahlem, Gemäldegalerie

619. The Return of the Prodigal Son, c. 1659-69
Canvas 262 × 206 cm G. 355
Leningrad, Hermitage

620. An Evangelist Writing, c. 1661
Canvas 102 × 80 cm G. 363
Rotterdam, Boymans-van Beuningen Museum

621. Old Man Praying, c. 1661
Canvas 87.6 × 72.4 cm G. 365
Cleveland, Ohio, Museum of Art, Bequest of Leonard C. Hanna, Jr.

622. Isaac and Rebecca ("The Jewish Bride"), c. 1660
Canvas 121.5 × 166.5 cm G. 356
Amsterdam, Rijksmuseum

623. Detail

624. Head of Christ, c. 1648-52
Panel 25.5 × 19.9 cm G. 322
Cambridge, Massachusetts, Fogg Art Museum

625. The Risen Christ, 1661
Canvas 78.5 × 63 cm G. 360
Munich, Alte Pinakothek

626. Head of Christ, 1650
Canvas 47.5 × 37.1 cm G. 258
New York, Metropolitan Museum of Art,
Bequest of Isaac D. Fletcher, 1917

627. Head of Christ, c. 1640-49
Panel 25 × 23 cm G. 257
Detroit, Michigan, Institute of Arts

628. Christ, c. 1659-69
Canvas 108 × 89 cm G. 368
Glens Falls, New York, The Hyde Collection

629. The Adoration of the Shepherds, 1646
Canvas 97 × 71.3 cm G. 215
Munich, Alte Pinakothek

630. The Holy Family with Angels, 1645
Canvas 117 × 91 cm G. 211
Leningrad, Hermitage

631. Detail
632. The Holy Family (with Painted Frame and Curtain), 1646
Panel 46.5 × 68.8 cm G. 212 Cassel, Gemäldegalerie

633. Detail

634. Rest on the Flight into Egypt, 1647
Panel 34 × 48 cm G. 220
Dublin, National Gallery of Ireland

635. The Adoration of the Shepherds, 1646
Canvas 63 × 55 cm G. 216
London, National Gallery

636. Detail

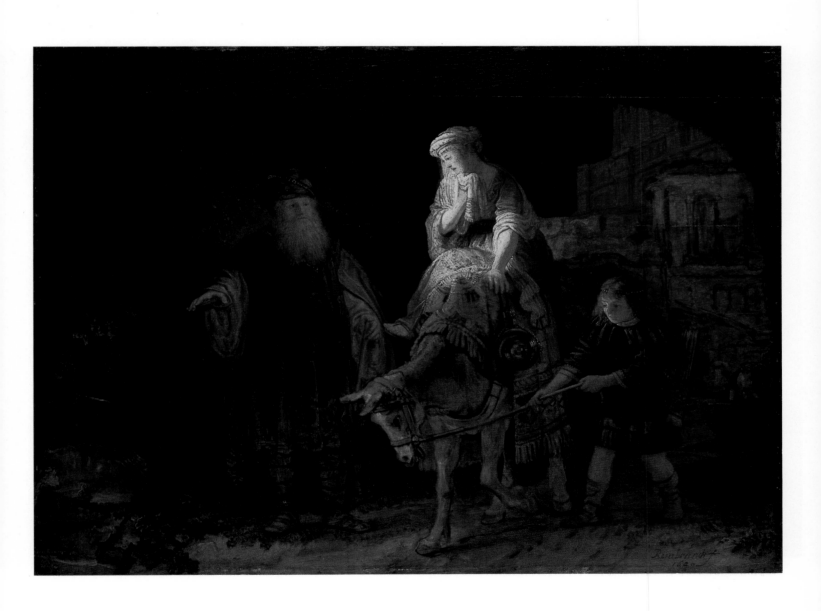

▲ **637. The Flight into Egypt, 1627**
Panel 26.4 × 24.2 cm G. 8
Tours, Musée des Beaux-Arts

638. The Departure of the Shunamite Wife, 1640
Panel 39 × 53 cm G. 202
London, Victoria and Albert Museum

639. Judas Returning the Thirty Pieces of Silver, 1629
Panel 76 × 101 cm G. 12
England, Private Collection

640. The Presentation in the Temple, c. 1628
Panel 55.5 × 44 cm G.10
Hamburg, Kunsthalle

641. The Circumcision, 1661
Canvas 56.5 × 75 cm G. 350
Washington, D.C., National Gallery of Art, Widener Collection

642. Detail

643. The Presentation in the Temple, 1631
Panel 61 × 48 cm G. 17
The Hague, Mauritshuis

644. Christ and the Woman Taken in Adultery, 1644
Panel 83.8 × 65.4 cm G. 208
London, National Gallery

645. Detail

646. **Christ and the Woman of Samaria, 1655**
Panel 46.5 × 39 cm G. 272
Berlin-Dahlem, Gemäldegalerie

647. Christ and the Woman of Samaria, 1655
Panel 63.5 × 48.9 cm G. 273
New York, Metropolitan Museum of Art, Bequest of Lillian S. Timken, 1959

561

648. The Storm on the Sea of Galilee, 1633
Canvas 159.5 × 127.5 cm G. 60
Boston, Isabella Stewart Gardner Museum

▲ 649. The Tribute Money, 1629
Panel 41 × 33 cm G. 15
Ottawa, National Gallery, Canada

650. St. John the Baptist Preaching, c. 1634
Panel 62 × 80 cm G. 71
Berlin-Dahlem, Gemäldegalerie

651. The Raising of Lazarus, c. 1630
Panel 96.3 × 81.3 cm G. 16
Los Angeles Museum of Art, Gift of H.F. Ahmanson and Co.,
in Memory of Howard F. Ahmanson

652. The Supper at Emmaus, 1648
Canvas 89.5 × 111.5 cm G. 219
Copenhagen, Statens Museum for Kunst

653. The Risen Christ at Emmaus, c. 1629
Paper on panel 39 × 42 cm G. 14
Paris, Musée Jacquemart-André

654. Philemon and Baucis, 1658
Panel 54.5 × 68.5 cm G. 278
Washington, D.C., National Gallery of Art, Widener Collection

655. The Risen Christ at Emmaus, 1648
Panel 68 × 65 cm G. 218
Paris, Musée du Louvre

656. Christ Before Pilate and the People, 1634
Paper on canvas 54.5 × 44.5 cm G. 72
London, National Gallery

657, 659. Details
658. Christ on the Cross, 1631
Canvas 100 × 73 mm G. 56
Le Mas d'Agenais, France, Parish Church

660. The Raising of the Cross, c. 1632-39
Canvas 96.2 × 72.2 cm G. 64
Munich, Alte Pinakothek

661. **The Descent from the Cross, c. 1632-39**
Panel 89.4 × 65.2 cm G. 65
Munich, Alte Pinakothek

662. The Lamentation over the Dead Christ, c. 1632-39
Paper and canvas stuck on panel 32 × 26.5 cm G. 89
London, National Gallery

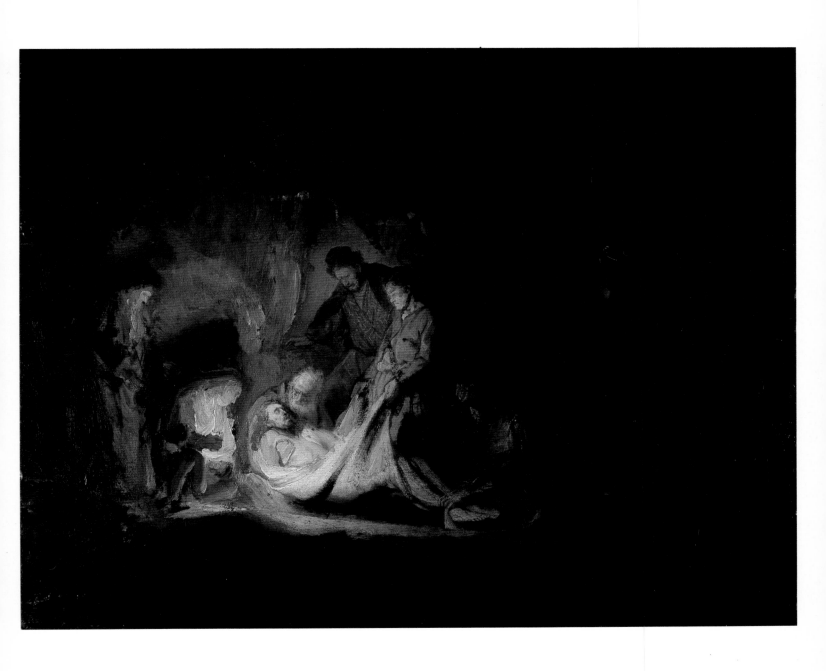

663. The Entombment of Christ, c. 1646
Panel 32.2 × 40.5 cm G. 217
Glasgow, Hunterian Museum

668. Self-Portrait, 1629
Panel 15.5 × 12.7 cm G. 32
Munich, Alte Pinakothek

589

669. Self-Portrait, 1629
Panel 22.6 × 18.7 cm
Amsterdam, Rijksmuseum

670. Self-Portrait, 1625-31
Panel 23.4 × 17.2 cm G. 30
Cassel, Gemäldegalerie

671. Self-Portrait, c. 1628-29
Pen and bistre, brush and India ink 127 × 95 mm Ben. 54
Amsterdam, Rijksmuseum

▲ **672. Self-Portrait, 1625-31**
Panel 41.2 × 33.8 cm G. 33
Amsterdam, Rijksmuseum

673. Self-Portrait, c. 1627-28
Pen, bistre, brush and India ink 127 × 95 mm Ben. 53
London, British Museum

674 Self-Portrait Leaning Forward, Listening

c. 1628
Etching - 66 × 53 mm
One state only

The edges of the plate are black and rough. Impression with surface tone.

W.B. 9; BB 30-12

Provenance: J.-L. de Beringhen, 1731

675 Self-Portrait Leaning Forward

c. 1628
Etching - 44 × 40 mm
Three states

Third state. The plate, which measured 61-64 × 48-49 mm, has been cut down; the head of the Virgin, which appeared upside down near the top margin, is thus deleted. This etching was in fact executed on the same plate used for *The Flight into Egypt* (W.B. 54, figs. 480, 482).

W.B. 5-III; BB 30-13

This impression, in which there is a zigzag on the right shoulder, has sometimes been catalogued as a fourth state (cf. Rovinski 5) and sometimes as a third precisely because of that zigzag (cf. Bartsch 5 and Blanc 209).

680 Self-Portrait with Curly Hair and White Collar

c. 1630
Signed: *RHL* (monogram)
Etching - 58 × 48 mm
Two states

First state. The edges of the plate, here irregular, were trimmed in the second state.

W.B. 1-I; BB 30-11

681 Self-Portrait in a Cap: Laughing

Signed and dated: *RHL* (in monogram) *1630*
Etching - 50 × 44 mm
Six states

First state. The outline of the scarf on the right has not been etched. The horizontal lines at the bottom right do not reach to the plate margin. Details were reworked in the following states; by the fourth state, the plate had been cut down to only 48 × 43 mm. It was heavily reworked in the last two states.

W.B. 316-I; BB 30-P

674. Self-Portrait Leaning Forward, Listening, W.B. 9,

675. Self-Portrait Leaning Forward, W.B. 5,

676. Self-Portrait with a Broad Nose, W.B. 4,

682 Self-Portrait in a Cloak with a Falling Collar

Signed and dated: *RHL* (monogram) *1631*
(the date is retouched: a zero is visible under the first digit)
Etching - 65 × 54 mm
Five states

Second state. The hair has been made to look thicker with drypoint.

In the fourth state, the plate was reworked with the burin by another hand.

W.B. 15-II; BB 30-Q

Provenance: J.-L. de Beringhen, 1731

676 Self-Portrait with a Broad Nose

c. 1628
Etching - 71 × 59 mm
One state only

Impression with surface tone.

W.B. 4; BB 29-1

A difficulty in the printing of this impression caused the double plate mark on the right edge.

677. Self-Portrait, 1630
Panel 49 × 39 cm G. 45
Aerdenhout, Holland, Collection of Jhr. J.H. Loudon

678. Self-Portrait in a Fur Cap, in an Oval Border, W.B. 12
Amsterdam, Rijksmuseum

679. Self-Portrait Bare-Headed: Bust, Roughly Etched, W.B. 338
Amsterdam, Rijksmuseum

681. Self-Portrait in a Cap: Laughing, W.B. 316, p. 595

680. Self-Portrait with Curly Hair and White Collar: Bust, W.B. 1, p. 595

682. Self-Portrait in a Cloak with a Falling Collar, W.B. 15, p. 595

683. Self-Portrait, 1625-31
Panel 89 × 74 cm G. 38
Boston, Isabella Stewart Gardner Museum

599

685. Self-Portrait, c. 1629
Panel 72.5 × 57.5 cm G. 41
Liverpool, Walker Art Gallery

▲▲ **686. Self-Portrait, c. 1630**
Copper 15 × 12 cm G. 44
Stockholm, Nationalmuseum

687. Self-Portrait with Cap Pulled Forward, W.B. 319, p. 604

690. Self-Portrait in a Fur Cap, W.B. 24, p. 604

688. Self-Portrait with Haggard Look, W.B. 320, p. 604

691. Self-Portrait, Scowling, W.B. 336, p. 604

689. Self-Portrait, Frowning, W.B. 10, p. 604

692. Self-Portrait in a Heavy Fur Cap, W.B. 16, p. 604

693. Self-Portrait Open-Mouthed, as if Shouting, W.B. 13, p. 604

694. Christ on the Cross (detail of fig. 658)

696. Christ before Pilate and the People (detail of fig. 656)

695. Beggar Seated on a Bank, W.B. 174, p. 604

687 Self-Portrait with Cap Pulled Forward

c. 1631
Etching - 55 × 45 mm
Six states

First state. The right shoulder is white. In the second state it was shaded with crosshatching; by the third state, the plate had been cut down to 50 × 42 mm.

W.B. 319-I; BB 31-10 (five states)

688 Self-Portrait with Haggard Look or Self-Portrait in a Cap, Open-Mouthed

Signed and dated: *RHL* (in monogram) *1630*
Etching - 50 × 43 mm
Only one state

Impression with smooth edges.

W.B. 320; BB 30-0

689 Self-Portrait, Frowning

Signed and dated only in the first state:
RHL (monogram) *1630*
Etching - 72 × 60 mm
Three states

Third state. The plate, which measured 75 × 75 mm in the first state, was cut down in the second state, thereby eliminating the monogram and the first two digits in the date. Two parallel marks which appear in the background in the second state have been burnished out, as have the two last digits in the date. The edges are no longer black and rough.

W.B. 10-III; BB 30-M

Provenance: A. de Peters, 1784

690 Self-Portrait in a Fur Cap

Signed and dated: *RHL* (monogram) *1630*
Etching - 62 × 52 mm
Four states

Fourth state. The plate, which measured 92 × 69 mm, was cut down in the second state, eliminating the signature and date at the bottom; they were added at the top left in the third state.

The vest is shaded here by horizontal lines. The first version of this portrait lacked the fur hat: the hair is still visible.

Impression with surface tone.

W.B. 24-IV; BB 30-L

Provenance: J.-L. de Beringhen, 1731

691 Self-Portrait, Scowling

Octagonal Plate
c. 1630
Signed: *RHL* (the monogram is not in Rembrandt's hand)
Etching - 39 × 36 mm
Only one state

W.B. 336; BB. 31-13

Provenance: J.-L. de Beringhen, 1731

692 Self-Portrait in a Heavy Fur Cap

Signed and dated: *RHL* (monogram) *1631*
Etching - 61 × 54 mm (the impression has been cut down)
One state only; the top of the head and the hair can still be made out, suggesting that the portrait was originally etched without the hat.

W.B. 16; BB 31-L

Provenance: A. de Peters, 1784

693 Self-Portrait Open-Mouthed, as if Shouting

Signed and dated: *RHL* (monogram) *1630*
Etching - 81 × 72 mm
Three states

First state. The edges of the plate are black, irregular and rough. They were trimmed and smoothened in the third state. The plate was cut down in the second state, to measure only 73 × 62 mm; one part of the signature was thus eliminated.

Impression with slight surface tone.

W.B. 13-1; BB 13-N

Provenance: A. de Peters, 1784

695 Beggar Seated on a Bank

Signed and dated: *RHL* (in monogram) *1630*
Etching - 116 × 70 mm
One state only

W.B. 174; BB 30-B

Provenance: A. de Peters, 1784

It seems as though Rembrandt had been unable to resist the temptation of producing this "self-portrait as a beggar," which seems to cry out his misfortune. A parallel should be drawn with the *Self-Portrait Open-Mouthed, as if Shouting: Bust* (W.B. 13, fig. 693).

697 Self-Portrait with Long Bushy Hair

c. 1631
Etching - 145 × 177 mm
Six states

First state. The plate was cut down for the next state, to measure only 64 × 60 mm.

It was heavily retouched in the fourth state.

W.B. 8-1; BB 31-9

Provenance: J.-L. de Beringhen, 1731

This impression is extremely rare. It is the only one extant from the whole plate, the four other remaining impressions having been cut down.

697. Self-Portrait with Long Bushy Hair, W.B. 8, p. 604

698, 699, 700. Self-Portrait in a Soft Hat and Embroidered Cloak, W.B. 7-IV, VII, VIII, p. 608

698, 699, 700 Self-Portrait in a Soft Hat and Embroidered Cloak

Signed and dated in the fifth state: *RHL* (monogram) *1631*, and in the tenth state: *Rembrandt f.*
Etching - 149 × 131 mm
Eleven states

Fourth state. As in the preceding states, only the head is etched. The increasing detail work on the brim of the hat which characterizes the preceding states continues to develop : the right side of the hat, which had been irregular, is well defined and shading has been added to that side. The right eyelid and the mouth have each been emphasized with a stroke of drypoint.

This precious impression was certainly completed by Rembrandt. The artist has drawn the top of the bust in black chalk with white highlights. He dated and signed the impression at the bottom in black chalk as well : *Rembrandt f. 1631.* At the top left, another inscription was begun in black chalk : *AET. 27*; the *7* replacing an effaced *3* was then covered with a *4* in brown ink.

The cut-down impression measures 148 × 99 mm.

Provenance: R. S. Holford, 1893. Price 11,135 F.

Sixth state. The sketched outline in the fourth state has been abandoned; only the white collar remains. Rembrandt, shown at half-length from the fifth state, is dressed in a fur cloak. Traces of additional working can be seen on the collar and shoulder; the elbow has been lightened. On the right the border of the cloak is strongly shaded. A supporting wall is indicated in the corner on the lower right. Unique impression.

Provenance: A. de Peters, 1784.

(The White and Boon catalogue wrongly reproduces the seventh state, which is not a unique impression, instead of the sixth state.)

Eighth state. The cloak was adorned with embroideries in the seventh state. The background, which had been white, is now covered with lines at the left and top of the plate. The hint of a wall to lean against in the lower right corner has been erased. The background became white again in the eleventh state, when the signature was also erased.

W.B. 7-IV-VI-VIII; BB 31-K (nine states)

Provenance: A. de Peters, 1784.

701 Sheet of Studies: Head of the Artist; A Beggar Couple; Heads of an Old Man and an Old Woman; Torsos of Beggars, in Profile

c. 1632
Etching - 100 × 105 mm
Two states

Second state. The plate has been cut down from its original 101 × 114 mm; the edges have been evened and smoothed, and the stains due to foul biting have been removed.

W.B. 363-II; BB 32-1

703 Self-Portrait in a Cap and Scarf with the Face Dark

Signed and dated from the second state : *Rembrandt f. 1633*
Etching - 134 × 103 mm
Two states

Second state. The plate, which measured 140 × 115-118 mm in

the first state, has been cut down. Shading has been added to the sleeve, the chest, the light parts on the hair, the back of the cap, and under the right eye. The mustache is lengthened beyond the right cheek.

W.B. 17-II; BB 33-G (three states)

706 Self-Portrait with Raised Sabre

Signed and dated : *Rembrandt f. 1634*
Etching, with some touches of burin - 127 × 110 mm
Two states

First state. The blade of the sabre is continued beyond the double border line on the right. In the second state the plate was cut down to measure only 124 × 102 mm, thus eliminating the second border line, the part of sabre that extended to the right, and also half of the *R* in the signature on the left.

W.B. 18-I; BB 34-A

Provenance: A. de Peters, 1784

707 Self-Portrait Wearing a Soft Cap

c. 1634
Etching - 50 × 44 mm
One state only

W.B. 2; BB 34-1

708, 709 Self-Portrait with Plumed Cap and Lowered Sabre

Signed and dated: *Rembrandt f 1634*
Etching - 197 × 162 mm
Three states

First state. Rembrandt is portrayed from the knees up. The paper was tinted after the impression was made. From the verso of the print, it is clear that the inked part has remained totally impermeable to the preparation that was used.

Provenance: A. de Peters, 1784, who paid 1,800 F.

Second state. The copper has been cut into an oval with four earlike handles, thus reducing the portrait to a bust. The plate measures 131 × 108 mm. The background has been shaded with the burin, and much burin work covers this portrait. In the next state the oval was corrected and the four "handles" were eliminated.

W.B. 23-1, II; BB 34-B

It has been suggested that the four "handles" served to attach the plate to a support.

714 Self-Portrait with Saskia

Signed and dated: *Rembrandt f. 1636*
Etching - 105 × 95 mm
Three states

First state. A comma-shaped slipped stroke on Saskia's forehead, visible above her right eye, was removed in the next state.

W.B. 19-I; BB 36-A

718 Self-Portrait in a Velvet Cap with Plume

Signed and dated: *Rembrandt. f. 1638*
Etching - 134 × 103 mm
One state only

W.B. 20; BB 38-B (three states)

Provenance: Leblond

701. Sheet of Studies: Head of the Artist; A Beggar Couple;
Heads of an Old Man and an Old Woman; Torsos of Beggars, in Profile
W.B. 363, p. 608

702. Self-Portrait, 1632
Panel 63 × 48 cm G. 99
Glasgow, Art Gallery and Museum, Burrel Collection

703. Self-Portrait in a Cap and Scarf with the Face Dark
W.B. 17, p. 608

704. Descent from the Cross, W.B. 81 (detail of fig. 559)

705. Self-Portrait, 1633
Panel 58 × 45 cm G. 129
Paris, Musée du Louvre

706. Self-Portrait with Raised Sabre, W.B. 18, p. 608

707. Self-Portrait Wearing a Soft Cap, W.B. 2, p. 608

708. Self-Portrait (?) with Plumed Cap and Lowered Sabre
W.B. 23-II, p. 608

709. Self-Portrait (?) with Plumed Cap and Lowered Sabre,
W.B. 23-I, p. 608

719 Self-Portrait in a Flat Cap and Embroidered Dress

c. 1642
Signed very faintly: *Rembrandt f.*
Etching - 92 × 62 mm
One state only

W.B. 26; BB 38-1

724 Self-Portrait Leaning on a Stone Sill

Signed and dated: *Rembrandt f 1639*
Etching - 205 × 164 mm
Two states

Second state. The edge of the cap on the right, obscured in the first state by a lock of hair, continues beyond this lock, and the outline of the cap on the same side has been strengthened.

W.B. 21-II; BB 39-E

This portrait can be compared with Raphael's painting of Baltazar Castiglione, now in the Louvre. The portrait of Castiglione was part of the Lucas van Uffelen sale, in Amsterdam, and was bought by the dealer Alfonso Lopez for 3,500 florins on April 9, 1639. A pen sketch by Rembrandt of the Castiglione portrait, now in the Albertina, carries the following notations in the artist's hand: *De Conte batasar de Kastylyone van rafael verkoft voor 3 500 gulden, het gehell caergesoen to Luke van Nuffeelen heeft gegolden f. 59456. Ano 1639.* The portrait by Raphael, whose influence can be seen in Rembrandt's *Self-Portrait Leaning on a Stone Sill*, is thought to have been brought back from Italy by van Uffelen as part of a consignment of paintings.

729, 730, 731 Self-Portrait Drawing at a Window

Signed and dated from the second state: *Rembrandt. f 1648*
Etching, drypoint and burin - 160 × 130 mm
Five states

First state. Vigorous lines of drypoint with strong strokes which shape the tunic characterize this state. The hands and the edges of the paper are white. Earlier, partly erased work is visible below the right hand.

Impression on light Chinese paper.

Provenance: J.-L. de Beringhen, 1731

Second state. The signature and the date are added on a scroll suspended at the top of the window. The left hand is shaded. The shadows in the background and on the tablecloth are reworked with the burin. The modeling of the face is more expressive.

Fourth state. The right hand was shaded in the third state. Through the window a landscape can be seen. Crosshatching covers the risers on the window. The signature is covered with lines. The tunic is heavily reworked with drypoint.

W.B. 22-I, II, IV; BB 48-A

732 Sheet of Studies, with the Head of the Artist, a Beggar Man, Woman and Child

Signed and dated: *RL. 1651*
Etching - 112 × 93 mm
Only one state

W.B. 370; BB 38-F

710. Self-Portrait, c. 1632-39
Panel 67 × 54 cm G. 144
Florence, Uffizi

▲ 711. **Self-Portrait, c. 1632-39**
Panel 55 × 46 cm G. 133
Berlin-Dahlem, Gemäldegalerie

712. **Self-Portrait, 1634**
Panel 80.5 × 66 cm G. 157
Cassel, Gemäldegalerie

713. Self-Portrait, 1634
Panel 57 × 46 cm G. 158
Berlin-Dahlem, Gemäldegalerie

714. Self-Portrait with Saskia, W.B. 19, p. 608

715. Self-Portrait, 1635
Pen and bistre, wash 125 × 137 mm Ben. 432
Berlin-Dahlem, Gemäldegalerie

716. Self-Portrait, 1635
Panel 92 × 72 cm G. 171
Great Britain, Private Collection

717. Self-Portrait, c. 1632-39
Panel 62.5 × 47 cm G. 189
The Hague, Mauritshuis

718. Self-Portrait in a Velvet Cap with Plume
W.B. 20, p. 608

**719. Self-Portrait in a Flat Cap and
Embroidered Dress**, W.B. 26, p. 608

720. Self-Portrait, 1635
Pen and wash 145 × 121 mm Ben. 434
New York, Metropolitan Museum of Art
Lehman Collection

721. Self-Portrait, 1640
Panel 63.5 × 51 cm G. 229
Pasadena, California, Norton Simon Foundation

722. Sheet with Two Studies: A Tree, and the Upper Part of a Head of the Artist Wearing a Velvet Cap, W.B. 372, p. 616

723. Self-Portrait, c. 1637
Red chalk 129 × 119 mm Ben. 437
Washington, D.C., National Gallery of Art, Rosenwald Collection

724. Self-Portrait Leaning on a Stone Sill, W.B. 21, p. 616

725. Self-Portrait, 1640
Canvas 102 × 80 cm G. 238
London, National Gallery

726. Self-Portrait, c. 1640
Panel 64 × 49 cm G. 237
London, Wallace Collection

727. Self-Portrait, 1643
Panel 71 × 57 cm G 240
Lugano, Thyssen-Bornemisza Collection

728. Self-Portrait, c. 1647
Panel 69 × 56 cm G. 262
Karlsruhe, Staatliche Kunsthalle

729, 730, 731. Self-Portrait Drawing at a Window, W.B. 22-I, II, IV, p. 616

732. Sheet of Studies, with the Head of the Artist, a Beggar Man, Woman and Child
W.B. 370, p. 616

733. Self-Portrait, c. 1655
Pen and bistre on brownish paper
203 × 134 mm Ben. 1171
Amsterdam, Rembrandt's House

734. Self-Portrait, 1652
Canvas 112 × 81.5 cm G. 308
Vienna, Kunsthistorisches Museum

735. Self-Portrait, 1654
Canvas 73 × 60 cm G. 310
Cassel, Gemäldegalerie

736. Self-Portrait, 1655
Panel 66 × 53 cm G. 320
Vienna, Kunsthistorisches Museum
737. Self-Portrait, 1657
Panel 49.2 × 41 cm G. 324
Vienna, Kunsthistorisches Museum

738. Self-Portrait, 1657
Canvas 50 × 42.5 cm G. 329
Edinburgh, National Gallery of Scotland, Duke of Sutherland Collection
739. Self-Portrait, 1659
Canvas 84.5 × 66 cm G. 376
Washington, D.C., National Gallery of Art, Andrew W. Mellon Collection

637

740. Self-Portrait, 1658
Canvas 131 × 102 cm G. 343
New York, The Frick Collection

741. Self-Portrait, 1660
Canvas 111 × 85 cm G. 389
Paris, Musée du Louvre

742. Self-Portrait, c. 1659-69
Canvas 114 × 94 cm G. 380
London, Kenwood House, The Iveagh Bequest

743. Self-Portrait, 1658
Pen and bistre 69 × 62 mm Ben. 1176
Rotterdam, Boymans-van Beuningen Museum

744. Self-Portrait, 1660
Pen and bistre 84 × 71 mm Ben. 1177
Vienna, Albertina

745. Self-Portrait, 1660
Canvas 80.3 × 67.3 cm G. 381
New York, Metropolitan Museum of Art,
Bequest of Benjamin Altman

746. Self-Portrait as the Apostle Paul, 1661
Canvas 91 × 77 cm G. 403
Amsterdam, Rijksmuseum

747. Self-Portrait, c. 1669
Canvas 82 × 63 cm G. 419
Cologne, Wallraf-Richartz Museum

748. Self-Portrait, 1669
Canvas 86 × 70.5 cm G. 415
London, National Gallery

749. Self-Portrait, 1669
Canvas 59 × 51 cm G. 420
The Hague, Mauritshuis

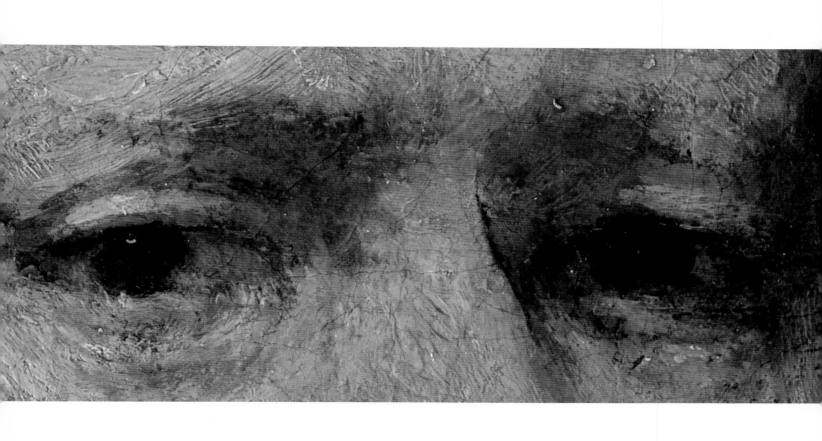

An Historical Note on Rembrandt's Work in the Collection of the Bibliothèque Nationale

The Rembrandt collection in the Department of Prints — the Cabinet des Estampes — of the Bibliothèque Nationale in Paris comprises approximately nine hundred items and is extremely rich in different impressions and states. The holdings were put together at an early date but have been rearranged constantly since.

At the time of its creation in 1667, with Jean-Baptiste Colbert's purchase for Louis XIX of the Marolles collection — "123,000 works of art of over six thousand masters" — the Department held two-thirds of the work of Rembrandt, a contemporary artist. The Beringhen collection and the Peters collection, acquired in 1731 and 1784 respectively, added to these holdings and also provided a selection of impressions and states.

Michel de Marolles

The first collection of Rembrandt's works acquired by the Department of Prints consisted of 224 etchings. This had been assembled by the Abbé Michel de Marolles (1600-1681), one of the first great print collectors known. Born in Touraine, Marolles was appointed commendatory abbot of the Abbey of Villeloin in 1626 in Paris. His protector was Princess Marie, the daughter of Charles de Gonzague, Duc de Nevers, who later became queen of Poland. As early as 1626 Marolles had developed a passionate interest in prints; he commented on this in his memoirs: "I have been fond of these curios ever since my early youth, but I did not cultivate my taste for them until the time I mentioned [1644]; as for my preference for them over and above pictures, which I have also held in high esteem, it was because I found them better suited to my own energies and because prints, from which books are made, serve better than pictures to swell a library."[1]

Marolles had few competitors and was in contact with contemporary artists and art lovers. He made numerous acquisitions, buying in particular the greater part of the collection assembled by Delorme, clerk to the financier Monerot (who died about 1655), and part of the collection of Claude Maugis, abbot of Saint-Ambroise (1600-1658) and counselor to Marie de Médicis. He also acquired various items from the collector Denis Pétau (1583-1652); from G. N. de la Reynie (1625-1709); and from the Abbé Desneux de la Noue (who died before 1657), all contemporaries of Rembrandt. In addition, Marolles owned the finest collection of prints amassed in the seventeenth century. He was the perfect fit for La Bruyère's portrait of the print-lover — may indeed have inspired it — provided the satire is seen merely as illustrating an insensate though laudable taste for all images: "'Would you like to see my prints?' Democède would add, and he would soon spread them out and show them to you; you notice one... but he assures you... that very few impressions have been pulled at all and that this is the only one in France of this drawing, that he paid a great deal for it and that he would not exchange it for better."[2]

Marolles drew up a catalogue of his collection, published in 1666, in which he listed the items he owned.[3] His brief remarks reveal his tastes and those of his period. He betrays no particular admiration for Rembrandt: "RHINBRAND. The work of this Dutch painter and printmaker consists of a large number of items and I have collected as many as 224 in this volume, including portraits and highly interesting caprices."[4] And in quatrains about etchings in his *Livre des peintres et graveurs* Marolles scarcely values Rembrandt more: "But who are the authors of all these fine works? Let us say that the order is as it is, and I can only explain it here as my memory brings the images to mind.... Albert Flamen is praised and Garnier deserves to be. The Dutch artists are: Waterlo, Polembout, Velde, Lives, Rhimbrandt, Visscher, Ostade, Gout; but if I were to continue, I would be worthy of reproach."[5]

The inventory of the collection, drawn up between about 1722 to 1730 by Ladvenant and de La Croix, lists the prints in 105 volumes.[6] Volume 97, entitled "Rhimbrant, Jean Live, Ostade, van Vliet, Gout," begins as follows: "This volume contains 520 mounted items from page 1 up to and including page 144: there are scenes from the Old and New Testament and subjects of Devotion; there are a great number of portraits, scenes from fables, landscapes, caprices, etc."[7] There is no strict arrangement to the inventory. Etchings and different kinds of the subject matter follow one another in no apparent order. De La Croix pointed this out himself to the Abbé Bignon, keeper of the Royal Library, ascribing it to lack of time. Rembrandt's prints, however, can be identified accurately by their titles or their descriptions: "A philosopher working, who perceives mysterious signs in rays of light [W.B. 270, fig. 28].... A naked woman holding a palm leaf [W.B. 192, fig. 24].... A shepherd playing the flageolet to his shepherdess [W.B. 188, fig. 176].... A drug-seller [W.B. 129, fig. 166]" and so on. All these items were mixed in with those that later came to the department. Where there were two copies, some were used for exchange; others were replaced by more beautiful impressions. Since the prints are not marked, it is not always possible, at present, to say for certain which "Rembrandts" belong to the Marolles collection; that some do can be deduced from

750. Detail of fig. 748

Œuvre de Rembrandt.

L'œuvre de Rembrandt de la Bibliothèque du Roi
est composé de ————————————— 800.

    Savoir de l'œuvre de Peters ——— 404.
    de l'ancien œuvre du Roi ——— 272.
    de diverses acquisitions ——— 44
    de hollande ——————— 80.

L'œuvre de Peters, lorsqu'on en fit l'acquisition était
composé de ————————————— 736 pièces.
    dont il faut déduire celles de Bot. &c. 81
        Total ———————————— 655
    parmi les quelles une vingtaine de copies.

L'œuvre ancien du Roi contenait ——— 610. pièces
    a déduire celles dans le goût de Remb — 95
        Total ———————————— 515
    parmi lesquelles une vingtaine de copies

L'œuvre de Bevinghen qui faisait partie de
l'ancien Rembrandt du Roi était composé
de ——————————————— 478 pièces
    parmi lesquelles quelques copies

751. A page from the inventory of prints at the Bibliothèque Nationale

the more precise lists of prints in other collections, which allow one to suppose that the Marolles collection must be the provenance of all those works of unspecified origin; and there are still many more to be discovered.

Marolles is sternly self-critical at the end of his catalogue, accusing himself of having devoted too much energy to his collection: "I regret not having used my time for better things, because I have much else to do which would be more to my taste and in keeping with my profession."[8]

Luckily, Marolles was not the only one to spend his time in this fashion, and the initial Rembrandt holdings were soon swelled by the Beringhen collection.

Jacques-Louis de Beringhen

Jacques-Louis, Marquis de Beringhen (1651-1723), knight of Malta, master of the horse, then standard-bearer of the guardsmen of Bourgogne, bequeathed about a hundred thousand prints to his son François, bishop of Le Puy. This collection was acquired by the Royal Library in 1731 at the initiative of the Abbé Bignon. In a draft letter, the abbé writes: "If this business succeeds, this section of the king's library will be so complete that no other collection in Europe will rank with, or even be mentioned with that of His Majesty."[9] A lengthy exchange of letters was to follow for the acquisition of this collection of more than 800 volumes; they already bore His Majesty's arms and had been bound by the collector himself, which betrays his intentions. As the Abbé Bignon had prophesied, the Department of Prints, till then part of the Royal Library housed in the Hôtel de Nevers, became a new section with its own functions and operation. Jacques-Louis de Beringhen appears to have begun collecting at about the time Marolles stopped. He approached it in a very different spirit. Being an art lover rather than a scholar, he favored the works of the masters of his day. His collection is representative of the art of engraving under Louis XIV and Louis XV and was the largest in Paris; it contained 579 volumes, 5 portfolios and 99 bundles. The inventory is less detailed than Marolles's catalogue except with reference to the Rembrandt prints, which are carefully listed and described. These were kept in volume 27. Altogether, the Beringhen collection included 426 Rembrandt prints and an additional 27 items by Rembrandt's pupils.[10]

Hugues Adrien Joly

It was not until Hugues Adrien Joly was appointed keeper of the Department of Prints in 1750 that a reclassification of all Rembrandt's prints was undertaken. Joly set about amalgamating, by selection, the prints from the Marolles and Beringhen collections, so as to form a single œuvre. One of his notes bears witness to this aim: "This body of work was kept in too small a volume, which came from the collection acquired in 1730 from the Marquis de Beringhen. The large pieces were folded and becoming torn as a result of frequent consultation; I decided to detach the entire contents and remount the prints on double-elephant paper. I also added the prints collected by the Abbé de Marolles... selecting those that were not included in Beringhen's collection or that were finer impressions; the others I exchanged."[11]

By October 12, 1755, Joly had drawn up a full list of the duplicates: "Tally and appraisal of 190 works etched by Rembrandt found to be duplicated in the Marolles collection after comparison with the works of the same master in the collection of the Marquis de Beringhen, with the exception of 43 items which are copies and variants." The appraisal of the pieces shows which of them attained the highest prices at the time: *The Angel Appearing to the Shepherds* [W.B. 44, fig. 472] "4 livres." *The Raising of Lazarus,* large plate (with the cap) [W.B. 73, fig. 504] "6 livres." *Christ Before Pilate, Ecce Homo,* large plate, [W.B. 76, 77, figs. 551, 552, 553], *Christ Crucified Between the Two Thieves: "The Three Crosses"* [W.B. 78, figs. 556 to 558], *The Descent from the Cross,* first plate, companion piece to *Christ Before Pilate* [W.B. 81, figs. 559, 560] "60 livres." *The Death of the Virgin* [W.B. 99, fig. 447] "4 livres." *Lieven Willemsz. van Coppenol, Writing-Master,* small plate [W.B. 282, fig. 268], and *Lieven Willemsz. van Coppenol, Writing-Master,* large plate [W.B. 283, fig. 267] "248 livres." *Jan Uytenbogaert, Preacher of the Remonstrants,* oval plate, [W.B. 279, fig. 265] "6 livres." *Four Illustrations to a Spanish Book,* [W.B. 36, figs 459 to 462] "8 livres." The estimates are much lower for depictions of beggars, genre subjects, and studies of heads.

Hugues Adrien Joly requested an authorization to enter into relations with the dealer Joullain: "Mr. Joly, keeper of the king's prints, takes the liberty of setting forth to Mr. Bignon that, having assembled the very complete œuvre of the celebrated Rembrandt, 189 duplicate pieces have been found and estimated by experts at a sum of 249 livres. If it would please you to give him an order to transfer the duplicates to Mr. Joullain and receive other works in exchange, the collection would be rid of what has become useless to it and little by little would be further enriched."[12] It was Joullain who acquired for Joly the extremely rare impression of *Jan Six* on Chinese paper (W.B. 285-I, fig. 258) at the sale of the Comte de Chabannes, at such a high price, 864 livres, that all collectors were astonished. At that time dealers were extremely influential not only as intermediaries supplying prints, but as connoisseurs of the works of artists. Edmé François Gersaint was a perfect example of those in the profession in the eighteenth century, and it is essential to include him in a discussion of Rembrandt.

Edmé François Gersaint

Gersaint was a Dutch dealer, established in Paris. The Department of Prints possesses Gersaint's first manuscript catalogue of a sale, date 1733, which offered to art lovers etchings by "Vouet, Le Brun, Lafosse, Rubens, Vandeck, Jordans, Reimbrant, etc."

This precious commercial document informs collectors of the provenance of the works: "Catalogue of the drawings, prints and plates brought from Holland and Flanders by Mr. Gersaint and Mr. Jourdan, dealers, pont Nôtre-Dame and quai de Gêvres, the sale of which is to be made to the highest bidder on Monday, November 23, 1733, and the days after at 2 o'clock in the afternoon at the said Mr. Gersaint's, pont Nôtre-Dame." Then follows a list of drawings and prints first by great masters and then by lesser masters. Six prints by Rembrandt are mentioned.[13]

Gersaint was the author of the first catalogue of Rembrandt's etchings (fig. 753), which appeared in 1751 and was consulted throughout the eighteenth century by the artist's many admirers: Mariette, Coypel, Boucher, Paignon Dijonval, the Duc d'Orléans, Le Bas, Julienne, Watelet, Bourlat, Campion de Tersan, etc.

The "Manuscript Remarks Made in 1755" inserted in the catalogue of the sale of one of the most famous collections of the time, that of Amadée de Burgy, praise Gersaint's catalogue and underline the prominent role of the dealer, biographer, and researcher: "The Rembrandt catalogue which Mr. Gersaint prepared on his last visit to Holland, and which Mr. Helle and Mr. Glomy completed, has contributed not a little to enhancing the value of this famous master's prints, spreading knowledge of their beauty, rarity and singularity. It is indeed only since then, as it were, that the said prints have reached such high prices. Quite certainly the catalogue aroused and indeed still arouses a kind of rivalry among collectors and a desire to enjoy the fine things this celebrated artist has brought into being."[14]

Helle and Glomy, Hyver

After Gersaint's death, Helle and Glomy finished and published the catalogue. In the preface they recall the author's character: "No one understood better than he the art of conducting a sale of curios to the advantage of those interested. Of how many prints did he not unveil the worth. To relieve the inevitable dryness of a catalogue, he adorned the book with anecdotes relating both to the prints and to Rembrandt himself."

The two cataloguers then list the chief collections they and Gersaint had consulted, devoting considerable space to the holdings in the Royal Library: "In preparing this catalogue Mr. Gersaint used a very fine collection owned by Mr. Houbraken, the excellent artist from Holland; it had formerly belonged to the burgomaster Six, who was a close friend to Rembrandt and

had been happy to form it as he etched some pieces. Mr. Houbraken made his acquisition at the time of the sale of the burgomaster's collection; we can therefore be certain of the veracity of all the pieces described in this catalogue as by Rembrandt. So that the catalogue should be the more complete, we have carefully visited the collections known in Paris, mainly those of Marolles and Beringhen now in the King's Library. There we found many rare pieces certainly not seen by Mr. Gersaint in Mr. Houbraken's Œuvre collection and also several notable differences." Descriptions of the Silvestres, Jullienne, d'Argenville and Potier collections come next.[15]

A supplement to the catalogue was drawn up in 1756 by Hyver, who describes 341 pieces, together with dubious items or wrong attributions, prints etched after Rembrandt and prints by his pupils. The arrangement is by theme. This remained the only source of reference until the publication of Adam Bartsch's catalogue in 1797.

Pierre-Jean Mariette

When, in 1775, the Rembrandt collection of another very well-known dealer, Pierre-Jean Mariette (1694-1774), was sold, it was classified in the order used by Bartsch. Joly, ever avid for fine impressions, purchased a few of the items. Antoine de Peters, the collector, bought others, which joined the holdings of the Department of Prints not long afterwards.

Pierre-Jean Mariette, a bookseller-publisher, print dealer, art historian and artist, was one of the most famous print lovers of the eighteenth century. He had inherited his father's and his grandfather's collections and had refused all the offers made by the principal courts of Europe, wishing that, on his death, the works he owned become part of the king's collection. This wish was thwarted by the claims of his heirs, however, and the works were dispersed at a series of sales. Rembrandt was represented by 423 original pieces.

Antoine de Peters

Still far from satisfied with his holdings, Joly, on April 13, 1784, bought the extensive Rembrandt holdings in the print collection of Antoine de Peters (1723-1795): 736 engravings for the price of 24,000 livres.

Peters, who was painter to King Christian IV of Denmark and Prince Charles of Lorraine, had specialized in miniatures and the depiction of rather free subjects. His collection of prints had been put up for auction in 1770 and withdrawn for want of a bidder. A long notice, which may have been by Joly, dated April 1784, gives the details of this exceptional acquisition: "In the first days of April of the present year, Mr. Peters, painter of known and esteemed reputation, informed Mr. Joly, keeper of His Majesty's Department of Prints, of his regret at being on the eve of transferring his collection of Rembrandt; in the course of thirty years he

had assembled 728 items and no collection, be it that of the emperor or even of the king of France, counted more than 500 different pieces. Although the emperor already possesses two Rembrandt collections, one bequeathed to the Imperial Library by Prince Eugene and the other brought from the print collection of Prince Charles of Lorraine in Brussels, Mr. Peters was nevertheless offered 20,000 livres for its Rembrandt possessions and the hope of a present without further explanation of its nature; but Mr. Peters regarded the fruit of his

April 13, we had this superb collection brought to Mr. Le Noir's and after admiring it I transferred it to the king's Department of Prints. In recognition of the patriotic behavior of Mr. Peter's display in the assignment of his Rembrandt collection, the Baron de Breteuil and Mr. Le Noir announced prompt payment of this acquisition for the king."[16]

Joly expressed his satisfaction at this addition: "By combining what the king's Department of Prints already

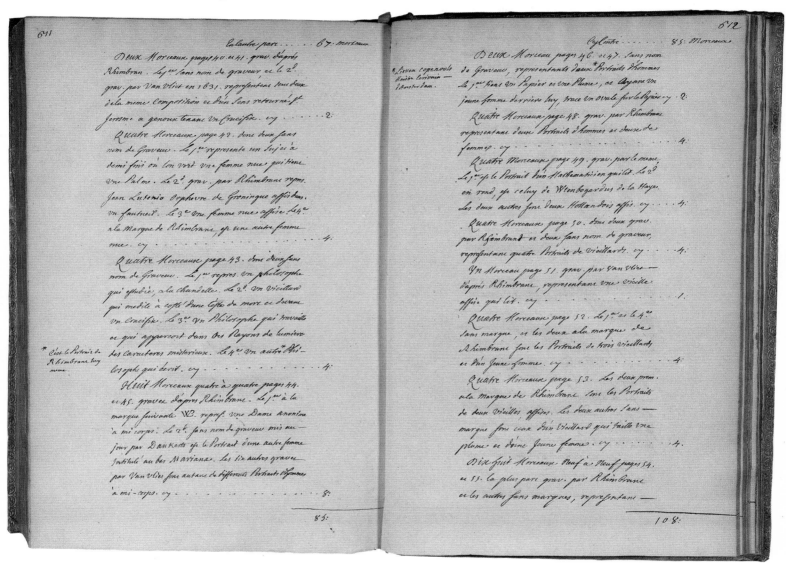

painstaking and costly research as lost for the collection of the king of France; he declared to the said Joly that he would prefer to see it stay in France for a sum of *twenty-four thousand francs*. On considering the report on the worth of this object and the sensitivity of Mr. Peter's feelings, the Baron de Breteuil, minister and secretary of state, and Mr. Le Noir, councillor of state and grand master of His Majesty's Library, authorized the said Joly to acquire the rare and unique collection of Rembrandt for the said sum of twenty-four thousand livres. And on

possesses with what the said Peters has assembled in greater quantity, both in single items and in variants hitherto missing from the king's collection, this will be the finest representation of Rembrandt ever seen; a second beautiful and plentiful collection will be formed with the residue, so as to unburden the present collection and still give great pleasure to the public. There are two ways to appraise the œuvre of this master collected by Peters: 1. By allowing two louis d'or for each piece; 2. By appraising each piece at the present

752. A page from the inventory of the Marolles Collection

price. It is known that the portrait of the burgomaster Jean Six, an advance proof on silk paper, was not bought for the king at its true worth, since the king only paid 50 louis, whereas the late dauphin had another bought for him in Holland by Colins for 150 louis; and that the work called the *Lit à la polonaise* [The Polish Bed], which the heirs estimated to be worth a thousand *écus* and wanted to throw into the fire, was bought from them at their estimated price by Mr. Peters, whose money they distributed to the poor. Finally, it is known that a great many other works by this master are currently purchased at considerable prices, even in Holland, his native country, in England, in Russia, and above all in France."[17]

The diversity of the Rembrandt holdings stemmed not only from the prodigious gathering of all of the master's prints — of those attributed to him, of etchings made from his works, and of copies — but also from a number of falsifications.

Peters had in fact been unable to resist touching up some pieces, with great skill. Thus, for a long time several impressions in his collection were regarded as unique. He excelled at highlighting with India ink washes, surpassing the velvetiness and the blacks of drypoint, or at the use of very light washes, delicately varying the shadows. His skillful retouches with the pen were attributed to Rembrandt's own hand. Sometimes he went even further. Insatiable despite the range and quality of his collection, he changed two impressions into unique first states: *Jupiter and Antiope,* smaller plate (W.B. 204, fig. 215), and *Christ Preaching, "La Petite Tombe"* (W.B. 67, fig. 501). He had scraped the monogram of the first and retouched it in India ink with the brush and, in the second, scraped the spinning top beside the child lying face downwards. All the cataloguers had considered the last state unique until François Couboin, curator at the Department of Prints, revealed the hoax at the exhibition organized at the Bibliothèque Nationale in 1908.

It must be admitted that certain works in which the shading has been accentuated by India ink washes are unusually striking, and could easily be taken for pieces retouched by Rembrandt himself.

Peters was not the only one to seek to augment the states and impressions of Rembrandt's etchings. Copiers and imitators abounded and were well known. Sometimes their reasons were quite honorable. An announcement in *Mercure de France,* dated January 1775 (Vol. 2, p. 175), concerning the etcher, Jacques-Philippe Le Bas (1707-1783), states: *"Descent from the Cross* and companion piece after the prints etched by Reimbrand [sic]: *Ecco Homo, Descent from the Cross.* These two prints, etched by Reimbrand, bear the title *To the Glory of God;* one represents Our Lord shown to the people and the other Our Lord brought down from the cross after his death. We know how much these two pieces are coveted and how much they deserve to be. There is the

fullness of composition, the variety of expression and above all the discernment that alone speaks for the fame of this great painter. These two prints are very rare and therefore worth a very high price. Mr. Le Bas, artist in the king's Department of Prints, whose productions up to now have had the good fortune to please the public, has just had copies made of these two prints. In directing the task, he strove to ensure that the illusion of the originals be preserved wherever possible — the same lightness of execution, the same feeling for forms, and the same means of highlighting an effect. His aim was to grant art lovers the advantage of having, for a moderate sum, pieces that were excessively priced. The originals are up to as much as eight and nine louis, whereas the price of the copies is three livres each. If this experiment is popular and proves successful, Le Bas will give the best of Rembrandt executed in the same manner. The address of Mr. Le Bas, artist to the king, is rue de la Harpe in Paris."

Copies, falsifications, retouches, re-etchings: the most regrettable of these is that of *The Hundred Guilder Print,* which was reworked by William Baillie (1723-1810), captain of the light cavalry and an amateur artist. A note by Joly states the following: "He [Baillie] ressuscitated the famous etching known as *The Hundred Guilder Print;* the plate being worn, an ignorant amateur made so bold as to seek to revive it, with lamentable results. This can be judged by the impression a Russian gentleman gave as a curio in 1750 to Mr. Joly, keeper of the Department of Prints of the king of France. It was in this state that Captain Baillie saved the plate from the hands of a coppersmith who was about to destroy it; he touched it up so cleverly that it is a match for the finest impression ever done by Rembrandt. Lest any like adventure should befall this excellent piece of work, Baillie, after printing a small number of impressions, cut the plate into five pieces which are very pleasing to the eye."[18]

It is obvious, unfortunately, that Baillie's contemporaries fully appreciated this initiative. They bought the impressions by subscription in 1775.[19]

The Rembrandt Collection at the Beginning of the Nineteenth Century

At the beginning of the nineteenth century an archives report lists the various sources of the Rembrandt holdings in the Department of Prints, mentioning individual acquisitions and a collection from Holland in addition to the three large collections (fig. 751).[20] The separate items were "pieces of the highest repute, setting apart the collection of a king from those of private persons. Mr. Bignon, commander of the king's orders and director of the literary treasury of France, was ever alive to the different branches composing that august museum," and was always ready to acquire them.[21] This was the case with the portrait of Jan Six on

Chinese paper (W.B. 285), which Joly included in his "first choice of works with a view to a reserve of prints" in 1790. Joly writes: "Of the immensity of valuable and rare objects kept in the king's rich Department of Prints, which today might be called a world history in action, here are a few of the precious volumes that the President d'Ormesson, grand master of His Majesty's Library, might wish to exhibit before the king. And which the keeper of the said collection has placed in reserve." Then follows an account of the pieces regarded as the finest in the collection with, in fourth position: "The work of Rembrandt, where one wonders whether he surpassed himself more with the burin or the brush; two of his pieces are: *The Hundred Guilder Print; The Portrait of the Burgomaster Jean [sic] Six*. Only 12 impressions are known, [Rembrandt] out of respect for his protector having broken his plate so that the portrait might become rare."[22]

The collection from Holland consisted of the 10,243 etchings and 20 volumes of prints from the Department of Prints in The Hague, which had been deposited with the Department of Prints in Paris in 1812 under Napoleon and returned in 1815.

Several etchings by Rembrandt had been chosen from this collection.[23]

Jan Gijsbert Verstolk van Soelen

But no Rembrandt collection, however rich, can ever be complete in states or in impressions with different effects, and it is always tempting and necessary to continue to extend it. This is what the curators did in the nineteenth century, in particular in 1847 at the sale of the possessions of Baron Jan Gijsbert Verstolk van Soelen (1776-1845), the Dutch diplomat and minister. His Rembrandt collection was among the most beautiful that had been assembled. The 815 impressions came from the collections of the most renowned print lovers: Wilson, Buckingham, Pole Carew, Robert-Dumesnil, Revil, de Claussin and earlier collectors like J. Barnard, P.-J. Mariette, and even, it was said, Houbraken. The prices were the same as those offered for other Dutch masters. A few higher bids were noted for some outstanding items. Fifteen of these entered the collection of the Department,[24] including the three states of the *Negress Lying Down* (W.B. 205, figs. 213, 214).

Donations and Later Acquisitions

The sale of the prints of R. S. Holford (1818-1892), in 1893, included 144 Rembrandts, several of which were very rare. Georges Duplessis, curator in chief at that time, succeeded in obtaining the only impression of the self-portrait of Rembrandt in a soft hat and embroidered cloak retouched with black chalk (W.B. 7-IV, fig. 698). In the twentieth century, a few more items have come to the Bibliothèque Nationale with the great Béjot and Curtis donations in 1933 and 1946, and some individual purchases reflecting, among other things, nineteenth-century taste.

In 1819, the most valuable holdings of the Department of Prints were framed and placed on permanent exhibition in showcases where they could be viewed by visitors.[25] The sole impression of Rembrandt included among them was the first state of *Christ Before Pilate*, large plate (W.B. 77, fig. 551), "one of the largest and most beautiful compositions by Rembrandt," according to the notice. It had just been acquired, together with its companion piece *The Descent from the Cross*, from Duchene for a sum of one thousand francs.

Tastes have changed since and it is doubtless the *Christ Presented to the People* (W.B. 76, figs. 552, 553) that would be shown now.

In 1855 a broader selection grouped eighteen items (New Testament scenes, portraits, landscapes), including the impressions of *"La Petite Tombe"* without the spinning top, forged by Peters (W.B. 67, fig. 501), still considered as unique.[26]

For two centuries Rembrandt's seventeen cataloguers have tirelessly sought to come to grips with his elusive production, which has brought forth such a disparity of opinion over the years. Discoveries and descriptions of states, dating, information about paper and sales have steadily enriched and diversified the descriptions of the prints.

Eight new catalogues have appeared in the twentieth century, a sure sign of the enduring appeal of Rembrandt's work.

The "golden legend" emerges in the preparation and composition of the present collection, one of the finest in existence. The many impressions sought out and assembled in the course of three hundred years reflect the myth attached to Rembrandt's name: beautiful, unique, very rare, retouched by the artist, successives states — and also impressions pulled from worn, reworked or even cut-up plates, falsifications, copies, photomechanical reproductions. The handwritten inventories of the collection drawn up after each important acquisition and each new classification between the eighteenth and the twentieth centuries, are covered with notes, comments, appraisals and anecdotes in the margin. They stand as testimonies to the collectors' passion, the interest each impression aroused, the often surprising evolution in taste. The transformation of titles, subjects, attributions, states — the code of the initiated — is inseparably linked with the works; it forms part of the magic legacy of a visionary world, perpetuated even today. Thus *"La Petite Tombe"*, impression with the white sleeve, impression with the black sleeve (W.B. 67, fig. 501), *The Hundred Guilder Print* (W.B. 74, fig. 512 to 549), *"The Goldweigher"* (W.B. 281, figs. 271, 272), *Christ Driving the Money Changers from the Temple*, state with a large mouth, state with a small mouth (W.B. 69, fig. 508), *Joseph* with a black face (W.B. 37, fig. 497),

The Presentation in the Temple in the Dark Manner
(W.B. 50, fig. 494), etc. — these appellations by art
lovers have sometimes been abandoned as the identifi-
cations of the states have been modified. But the interpretations of the subjects by cataloguers are continuing.
The Woman with the Arrow (W.B. 202, fig. 210) is also
*Cleopatra and Mark Antony, Venus and Love, Venus
Arming Her Son Cupid; The Ship of Fortune* (W.B. 111,
fig. 32) is Rembrandt's critical fortune.

Gisèle Lambert

1. Michel de Marolles, *Mémoires*, Amsterdam, 1755, vol. 1,
   p. 288.
2. G. Duplessis, "Michel de Marolles, abbé de Villeloin,
   amateur d'estampes", *Gazette des Beaux-Arts*, 1869,
   pp. 526-527.
3. Abbé de Marolles, *Catalogue de livres d'estampes et de
   figures en taille-douce*. Paris, 1666, pp. 24-25.
4. Ibid., p. 54.
5. Michel de Marolles, *Le livre des peintres et graveurs*,
   Paris, 1855, pp. 24, 35.
6. "Inventaire de la collection de Marolles", Ye 18 to Ye 18 c
   rés. in fol.
7. Ibid., Ye 18 a rés., pp. 606, 617.
8. F. Lugt, *Les marques de collections de dessins et d'estampes...* Amsterdam, 1921, notice 1855, p. 340.
9. Bibliothèque Nationale, Estampes, Archives, Ye 146 rés.,
   nᵒ 18.
10. "Catalogue de l'œuvre de Rembrandt..." in the compen-
    dium from the collection of the Marquis de Beringhen,
    Ye 22 rés.
11. Bibliothèque Nationale, *Expositions d'œuvres de Rem-
    brandt : Dessins et gravures*, Paris, 1908, p. 13.
12. Bibliothèque Nationale, Estampes, Archives 1750-1779,
    Ye 1 rés., nᵒˢ 157, 158.
13. "Catalogue du fonds de Gersaint", Yd 5 c, pp. 14-15.
14. "Catalogue de la collection d'Amadée de Burgy par Pierre
    Gérard van Bralen, marchant d'estampes", June 6, 1755,
    Yd 31.
15. E.-F. Gersaint, *Catalogue raisonné de toutes les pièces qui
    forment l'œuvre de Rembrandt*, Paris, 1751, pp. 8, 14, 15.
16. Bibliothèque Nationale, Estampes, Archives 1723-1847,
    Ye 1 rés.
17. "Catalogue de l'œuvre de Rembrandt acquis par le Roy du
    sieur Peters", Ye 32 rés.
18. "Table des maîtres dont les œuvres se trouvent réunies au
    Cabinet des Estampes", Ye 47 rés., p. 7.
19. Rembrandt's copperplates were retouched and reprinted
    several times from the eighteenth to the twentieth century,
    until all that remained of the artist's work was the prestige
    of his name.
    Claude-Henri Watelet (1718-1786) bought a certain num-
    ber of impressions, which he mentions in the foreword to
    his *Rymbranesque* written in 1783: "Having had purcha-
    sed in Holland some original plates by Rymbrand, the
    majority altered, effaced or spoilt by heavy and clumsy
    reworking. I ventured to compare one or two with their
    first state by consulting the good impressions that have
    been preserved."

About 78 of these plates were included in the Watelet sale
in 1786. They passed into the possession of Pierre-
François Basan (1723-1797) and then to his son, H.-L.
Basan; both were dealers, and they published a compen-
dium, *Le Recueil Basan*, a copy of which has only just
been acquired by the Department of Prints for the sake of
its historical interest.
Successive editions contain the following addresses:
"Paris, H.-L. Basan, print dealer, rue et maison Serpente,
nᵒ 14"; and later "rue and Hôtel Serpente, nᵒ 14."
In 1810, the plates reappeared in the possession of the
print dealer Auguste Jean, who published a new compen-
dium ("Paris, chez Jean, Marchand d'Estampes, rue Saint
Jean-de-Beauvais, nᵒ 10".) At the sale arranged by his
widow in 1846, they were bought by Auguste Bernard.
His son, Michel Bernard, had prints made for the last time
with Alvin-Beaumont in 1906. In 1938 the plates became
the property of an American collector, Dr. Robert Lee
Humber, who deposited them with the North Carolina
Museum of Art in Raleigh. They remained there until
Robert Lee Humber's descendants, Mrs. John and Marchel
B. Humber, reclaimed them. Four other original plates are
in private collections: the Six collection in Amsterdam
(W.B. 272), the Bruijn, Spiez collection (W.B. 66), the
University of Göttingen Library (W.B. 286), and the
Rosenwald collection in Philadelphia (W.B. 281).
20. Bibliothèque Nationale, Estampes, Archives 1780-1795,
    Ye 1 rés., nᵒ 370. The report was classified in this
    eighteenth century compendium by mistake.
21. Ibid. Archives 1750-1779, Ye 1 rés. nᵒ 157.
22. Ibid. Archives 1780-1795, Ye 1 rés. nᵒ 330.
23. Ibid. Archives 1809-1826, Ye 1 rés. nᵒ 558 (1812), nᵒ 582
    (Oct., Nov. 1815).
24. *Journal du département, 7 avril 1851, acquisition 1518.*
25. *Notice des estampes exposées à la Bibliothèque Royale*,
    Paris 1819.
26. Duchesne J., *Description des estampes exposées à la
    Bibliothèque Impériale*, Paris, 1855.

N.B. Ye: filing code used by the Archives of the Réserve du Cabinet
des Estampes de la Bibliothèque Nationale; Yd: filing code used for
sale catalogues in the Cabinet des Estampes.

753. Title page of the catalogue raisonné by Gersaint

754, 757. Abrégé de la vie de Rembrandt
(pages from the catalogue raisonné by Gersaint)

J.B. G. Sculp. 1750.

REMBRANDT-Van-RHEIN
Peintre et Graveur.

né en 1606, mort a Amsterdam en 1668.

CATALOGUE
RAISONNÉ
DE TOUTES LES PIECES
Qui forment l'Œuvre
DE REMBRANDT,

Composé par feu M. GERSAINT,
& mis au jour, avec les Augmen-
tations nécessaires,

Par les Sieurs HELLE & GLOMY.

Dédié aux Amateurs des beaux Arts.

A PARIS,
Chez HOCHEREAU, l'aîné, Quai de
Conti, vis-à-vis la descente du Pont-
Neuf, au Phénix.

M. DCC. LI.
Avec Approbation & Privilege du Roi.

⸎⸎⸎⸎⸎⸎⸎⸎⸎⸎

ABRÉGÉ
DE LA VIE
DE REMBRANDT.

REMBRANDT, d'une naissance
obscure, a sçu par son génie
en relever la bassesse. Il étoit fils
d'un Meûnier, nommé Herman
Gerriste, surnommé Van-Rhin,
à cause qu'il occupoit un Moulin
situé sur le bord d'un Canal, for-
mé par les eaux du Rhin, entre
les Villages de Leyerdorp, & de
Koukerck, près la Ville de Leyde.
Sa Mere, appellée Cornelie Van-
Suidbroeck, le mit au monde dans
ce même Moulin, le 15. Juin de
l'année 1606, & on lui donna au
Baptême le nom de Rembrandt,
qui est le seul sous lequel ce cé-
lebre Maître soit maintenant con-
nu; on y ajoûte le surnom de Van-
Rhin, à cause de son Pere, qui le
portoit, par la raison que nous ve-
nons de dire.

Rembrandt, ayant donné de bonheur des marques d'un génie vif, cela obligea son Pere à faire tous ses efforts pour lui procurer une éducation différente de celle que son état sembloit lui permettre ; il l'envoya pour cet effet au **Collége de Leyde** pour y faire ses humanités, mais la passion qu'il se sentit pour la Peinture, ne lui permit pas de différer long-tems à s'y livrer. Les Auteurs qui ont écrit sur Rembrandt, varient sur le Maître qui lui donna les premiers principes de l'Art ; les uns attribuent cet honneur à Georges Van-Schooten, & d'autres à Jacques Pinas. M. Houbraken assûre que ce fut Jacques Van-Swanenbourg, chez lequel cet illustre Eleve demeura trois ans, qu'ensuite il entra chez Pierre Lastman, Peintre d'Amsterdam, où il ne resta qu'environ six mois, & qu'enfin il travailla quelque tems chez Jacques Pinas. Quoi qu'il en soit de ces opinions, il est certain que Rembrandt n'a dû

son goût qu'à lui - même.

Jamais on n'a vu de Peintre dont la maniere ait été aussi singuliere dans ses Tableaux, ainsi que dans ses Estampes. On le regarde comme le plus fier Coloriste de toute la Flandre. On sçait que les Maîtres de cette Ecole se sont particulierement attachés à cette partie, mais il semble que Rembrandt l'ait pratiquée d'une façon toute contraire à ses Compatriotes, dont les Ouvrages sont pour l'ordinaire extrêmement fondus & léchés ; pour les siens, on y voit la touche des plus grands Maîtres Vénitiens. Il étoit si certain de l'effet de ses couleurs, qu'il les plaçoit successivement les unes sur les autres, sans les fondre, ce qui rend de près ses Tableaux raboteux, mais d'une certaine distance, produit un effet merveilleux. Cependant il a quelquefois fondu, principalement ses Têtes de Femmes, pour leur donner plus de suavité.

Il semble que la pratique de sa

gravûre tienne de sa peinture ; on n'y voit point ce travail arrangé qui se trouve dans les Estampes des autres Graveurs : son génie libre semble s'y jouer, & ses tailles, quoiqu'elles paroissent tracées au hazard, rendent cependant dans la plus grande vérité les différens effets qui conviennent aux objets qu'il a voulu représenter : ses Estampes par ce moyen deviennent extrêmement piquantes, aussi la plûpart des Artistes, qui quelquefois ne font pas grand cas de nos meilleures Estampes finies avec soin, recherchent avec ardeur celles de Rembrandt : en effet elles sont une source inépuisable d'intelligence du clair obscur, partie dans laquelle il est si difficile de réussir, comme il paroît par le peu de Peintres qui y ont excellé : & quel Peintre eût été Rembrandt, si plus correct dans son dessein, il se fût appliqué à rendre la belle nature, telle qu'elle se voit dans les Antiques, & dans les Ouvra-

ges des grands Maîtres Italiens ! Mais peu soigneux de s'écarter du naturel grossier de son Pays, il a fait ses compositions dans un goût pésant, & très-souvent ignoble ; il affectoit même une singularité qui alloit jusqu'au burlesque dans les Sujets qui en étoient le moins susceptibles ; il s'attachoit sur-tout à donner à ses Figures des habillemens & des coëffures extraordinaires : il avoit à cette fin rassemblé un grand nombre de bonnets Orientaux, d'armes anciennes, & d'étoffes depuis long - tems hors d'usage ; & lorsque ses amis lui reprochoient de négliger l'imitation des belles Antiques, il leur montroit cet assemblage, en leur disant que c'étoit-là ses Antiques. Quand il a voulu introduire du nud dans ses compositions, c'est alors qu'il n'étoit pas supportable ; & quoiqu'il ait donné une grande vérité à ses chairs, les mauvaises attitudes de ses Figures, principalement celles des femmes, jointes à leurs

proportions outrées, en font des objets très-désagréables, & un Amateur ne peut leur donner son approbation, quoique d'un coloris admirable.

La partie la plus brillante de Rembrandt font ses Portraits ; ils feront toujours les délices des Connoisseurs, & il en est peu qui n'effacent ceux des meilleurs Maîtres. On sçait qu'il leur donnoit un relief à tromper, comme il l'éprouva par le Portrait de sa Servante qui fut pris pour elle-même, Rembrandt l'ayant placé à une croisée de sa maison, ainsi que le rapporte M. de Piles dans sa Vie des Peintres.

Le goût dominant de Rembrandt étoit de donner à ses compositions des effets d'une lumiere accidentelle (*), qu'il tiroit ordinairement d'en-haut, ce qui produisoit de fortes ombres, avec des

_____

(*) On appelle en Peinture lumiere accidentelle, celle qui est produite par un flambeau, ou quelque coup de soleil qui passe à travers un nuage, ou dont l'effet est rompu par quelque corps opaque.

jours extrêmément piquans, cependant ses ombres ne sont point tranchantes, comme on les remarque dans le Caravage, le Valentin, & quelques autres Peintres, & les demies-teintes qui les unissent aux clairs, les fondent de maniere que l'objet en paroît d'un relief étonnant. On voit pourtant de lui des Morceaux entierement éclairés, dont l'effet n'est pas moins admirable que dans ses compositions les plus ombrées.

Entre les illustres Amis que les talens de Rembrandt lui avoient acquis, le Bourguemestre Six étoit son plus intime ; il alloit souvent à une maison de Campagne que ce Magistrat avoit aux environs d'Amsterdam, ce qui nous a procuré la plûpart des beaux Paysages de son Oeuvre ; car cet habile Artiste avoit tant d'attachement pour son Art, que négligeant presque tous les divertissemens que l'on prend ordinairement à la Campagne, il n'en connoissoit point de plus

grand que celui que lui procuroit la gravûre : pour se satisfaire, il avoit toujours soin de porter des planches toutes préparées au vernis, sur lesquelles il gravoit directement avec la pointe les vues qui lui faisoient le plus de plaisir ; on trouve même dans son Oeuvre un Paysage qu'il grava en attendant le dîner, comme il est marqué à l'endroit où l'on parle de cette Piece, au N°. 200.

Rembrandt se maria en Hollande à une femme très-entendue dans le débit de ses Ouvrages qu'elle vendoit fort chers. On rapporte à ce sujet une histoire singuliere. Elle engagea son mari à sortir secretement d'Amsterdam, & à s'absenter pendant quelque tems, alors elle fit courir le bruit qu'il étoit mort, & en prit le deuil : l'effet qu'elle se promettoit de ce stratagême, étoit d'engager les Curieux à venir lui demander avec empressement les Ouvrages de Rembrandt, qu'elle leur faisoit alors valoir, en leur

disant qu'il n'étoit plus en état d'en faire d'autres : quelque tems après il reparut. Cette histoire pourroit bien être une fable, imaginée sur la réputation où cette femme étoit d'avoir le talent de bien vendre les Ouvrages de son mari.

Rembrandt a plusieurs fois gravé le Portrait de sa femme, entre autres on le voit dans une petite Piece fort jolie, avec le sien, & dans quelques feuilles de griffonnemens. On prétend en Hollande que c'est à tort que M. de Piles marque dans la Vie de Rembrandt, que ce Maître étoit à Venise en 1635 & 1636, la raison qu'on en donne, est qu'il ne paroît point par les Ouvrages qu'il a fait postérieurement à ces années, qu'il ait rien pris du coloris des grands Maîtres Vénitiens ; raison qui ne semble point convainquante, puisqu'on pourroit de même nier que Rembrandt ait jamais eu une collection nombreuse de Desseins & d'Estampes des grands Maîtres Italiens, ainsi que

le rapporte le même M. de Piles, parce que certainement il n'a point profité de ces sçavantes études ; cependant on ne conteste point en Hollande qu'il n'ait eu effectivement ce Recueil, qui a été dispersé depuis sa mort en divers Cabinets ; au reste la preuve de ce voyage de Rembrandt à Venise, se trouve dans trois Têtes de son Oeuvre énoncées au N°. 266, où se voit écrit de la main de ce Maître, Rembrandt *Venetiis*, 1635. Il est vrai qu'on n'en voit point qui soit marquée de l'année 1636, ainsi il pourroit tout au plus être probable qu'il n'étoit à Venise que dans l'année 1635. Cet excellent Peintre mourut à Amsterdam, selon M. de Piles, en 1668, & selon M. Houbraken, en 1674.

La maniere de graver de Rembrandt approche de celle de Benedette ; mais son originalité consiste en ce qu'on y trouve la pointe séche jointe à l'eau-forte & à la maniere noire, aussi le doit-on regarder com-

me l'inventeur de cette derniere gravûre, qui n'est devenue en usage que depuis Rembrandt.

La plûpart des premieres épreuves ont été tirées sur du papier de la Chine, & c'est principalement dans celles-là que l'on trouve dans plusieurs parties beaucoup de maniere noire. Il paroît que lorsque les planches commençoient à s'user, Rembrandt éclaircissoit ces endroits, & les retouchoit à la pointe séche, ce qui fait la différence que l'on remarque dans plusieurs épreuves de ses compositions ; ainsi la meilleure marque pour connoître les bonnes épreuves de ses Morceaux principaux, comme la Piece de cent florins, la Résurrection du Lazare, & autres, c'est lorsqu'il s'y trouve beaucoup de cette maniere noire.

Pour ne point réfroidir ses compositions, Rembrandt les dessinoit souvent directement sur ses planches, sans faire comme les autres Graveurs des Desseins arrêtés, pour les calquer ensuite, & même

les desseins qu'il traçoit avec la pointe sur ses planches pour ses Estampes au burin, n'étoient que de simples croquis qu'il terminoit ensuite avec soin, comme il paroît par la Piece qui représente un Atelier de Sculpteur, que Rembrandt n'a pas rachevée, où se voit une Statue, qui n'est que tracée à la pointe, & un Homme qui dessine d'après cette Figure, aussi tracé à la pointe, & très-peu arrêté.

Dans le grand nombre de Desseins que Rembrandt a laissé, on n'y trouve guéres que des griffonnemens très-imparfaits, à l'exception de quelques Portraits & Paysages qu'il étoit obligé de dessiner d'après nature. Il ne faisoit apparamment des Desseins que pour développer ses idées, aussi y voit-on souvent le même Sujet retourné de plusieurs manieres différentes ; & comme il les destinoit à l'oubli, il ne s'embarrassoit guéres de les terminer avec soin.

Fin de la Vie de Rembrandt.

C A

De t

Por

N°. 1

pouce
de lar

N
ressem
de fa

A Short History of Rembrandt's Life

Of humble birth, Rembrandt succeeded, thanks to his genius, in rising above his origins. He was the son of a miller named Herman Gerriste, surnamed van Rijn, after the name of his mill on the bank of a canal formed by the waters of the Rhine between the villages of Leyerdorp and Koukerck, near the city of Leiden. His mother, whose name was Cornelia van Suidbrocck, brought him into the world in that very mill on the 15th of June, 1606, and he was baptized with the name of Rembrandt, the only name by which this celebrated master is now known.

Rembrandt having at a very early age shown signs of keen intelligence, his father made every effort to provide him with an education better than his position would seem to allow; for he sent him to the college in Leiden to study the humanities. But Rembrandt did not wish to wait any longer before devoting himself to painting, for which he had a genuine passion.

Rembrandt's biographers do not agree on the name of the master who gave him his first introduction to the painter's art: some say van Schooten had that honor, others say it was Pinas. M. Houbraken claims that it was van Swanenburch, with whom he studied for three years; that he then went to Amsterdam to study under Pieter Lastman, but stayed with him only six months; finally, that he worked for several months with another, named Pinas. Be that as it may be, what is certain is that Rembrandt owed his talent only to himself.

Never has there been a painter with more originality in his paintings and his prints. He is held to be the greatest colorist in all Flanders. The masters of the Flemish school, as we know, are particularly attached to the use of color; but it would appear that Rembrandt practiced that use in an altogether different way from that of his compatriots, whose works were generally speaking extremely mellow and polished. In his paintings we can recognize the touch of the greatest Venetian masters. So sure was he of the effect of his colors that he placed them one on top of the other without blending them; which, seen close at hand, gives his canvases a very rough aspect, but when seen from a certain distance produces a marvelous effect. At times, however, he did blend his colors, particularly in his portraits of women, in order to give his paintings a gentler aspect.

It would seem that his manner of etching is closely related to his manner of painting; you see in his etchings none of that artificial work you find in the prints of other artists. His genius has free play in his etchings; and although his strokes might seem to be placed at random, yet they render with the utmost veracity the several effects which suit the objects he has chosen to represent. It is this technique which makes his etchings bold in the extreme; and accordingly most artists, who sometimes care little for the best of our carefully finished etching,

seek out those of Rembrandt with great zeal; for they are an inexhaustible source for the study of chiaroscuro, a technique in which it is very difficult to succeed, as witness the limited number of painters who have excelled in it. What kind of painter might Rembrandt have been had he been more faithful to his drawings and applied himself to rendering the beauties of nature as we may see them in the works of the ancients and of the greatest Italian masters! Instead, in no way anxious to gloss over the rustic nature of his own country, he produced compositions that were unsubtle and often very ordinary in style; he even went so far in his peculiarity as to bestow a burlesque character on subjects which in themselves were the farthest removed from the burlesque. In particular, he portrayed his figures in extraordinary garb and headgear. To this end, he had amassed a large collection of Oriental turbans, ancient weapons, and long unused fabrics; when his friends reproached him with neglecting the imitation of handsome works of the past, he would show them this accumulation of objects and say that there was the past. But it was when he introduced the nude into his compositions that he became insupportable; and although he rendered his bodies with great truthfulness, his figures — especially the female figures — were shown in such displeasing positions and endowed with such exaggerated proportions that they became highly disagreeable objects such as no art lover can rejoice in, even when their coloring is admirable. His portraits constitute the most brilliant portion of Rembrandt's work; they are always the connoisseurs' delight, and there are but few of them which do not outshine those by the greatest masters. He gave them the most deceptive three-dimensional look, as for instance in the portrait of his servant: Rembrandt stood it in a corner of the house, where it was mistaken for the servant herself, as M. de Piles tells us, in his Vie des Peintres.

Rembrandt's most remarkable feature was to provide his compositions with effects of "accidental lighting,"* which he normally drew from high up, thus producing great masses of shadow and the most vivid areas of light. Yet at the same time, his shadows are not sharp like those we see in Caravaggio, Valentino and other painters; and the half-tones linking them to the light tones blend the whole in such a way that the objects in question stand out in astonishing relief. Nonetheless, Rembrandt's fully lighted works are of an effect no less admirable than his more shaded compositions.

Among the famous friends whom Rembrandt's talents attracted, Burgomaster Six was the closest. Rembrandt often went to the magistrate's country house near Amsterdam, a fact which occasioned most of the handsome landscapes that his work includes; for this talented artist went about his art with such passion that he neglected virtually all of the usual amusements one normally enjoys in the country and there indulged in his greatest pleasure, which was etching. To that end, he always took care to bring with him plates which had already

* What is called "accidental lighting" in painting is that which is produced by a torch or by the sun's rays coming through a cloud, or yet again, that whose effect is deflected by some opaque body.

663

been varnished and on which he etched directly with a needle the views he liked best. Among his works there is even one landscape that he etched while waiting for dinner to be ready.

Rembrandt married in Holland a woman who proved very skillful in finding buyers for his works, at very high prices. There is a singular anecdote about this. She persuaded her husband to leave Amsterdam secretly and remain away for some time; she then started rumors to the effect that he was dead, and wore mourning for him. The purpose of this stratagem was to encourage art lovers to come to her and beg her to sell them some of Rembrandt's work; with which requests she complied, pointing out to them that never would he paint again. Some time afterward, Rembrandt reappeared. This story may be a mere fable, based on his wife's reputed cleverness at selling her husband's work.

On several occasions Rembrandt engraved his wife's portrait; among other places, it is to be seen, along with his own portrait, in one very pretty little work and in several studies. It is said in Holland that M. de Piles mistakenly states, in the Vie de Rembrandt, that the master was in Venice in 1635 and 1636; for it is said that the works he produced after that period do not seem to have been influenced by the way the great Venetian masters used color. This would not appear to be a convincing reason; for it might, in the same way, be denied that Rembrandt ever had a large collection of drawings and prints by the great Italian masters — as the selfsame M. de Piles gives us to understand — on the grounds that he certainly never put such scholarly studies to use. Yet no one in Holland denies that he did indeed possess such a collection, which after his death was dispersed among various other collectors. Moreover, the proof that Rembrandt traveled to Venice can be found in three of his works', where we can see in the upper part, written in the master's own hand, "Rembrandt Venetiis, 1635." It is true that none of them is dated 1636; hence it is probable, at most, that he stayed in Venice only during the year 1635. This excellent painter died in Amsterdam — in 1668, according to M. de Piles, or in 1674, according to M. Houbraken.

Rembrandt's manner in etchings is similar to that of Benedetti, but his originality lies in the fact that he combines drypoint with etching and the "dark manner"; accordingly he must be considered the inventor of the latter method of etching, which came into use only after Rembrandt's time.

Most of the first impressions were printed on Chinese paper, and it is chiefly in these that we frequently find the "dark manner" in several places. It appears that when the plates began to become worn, Rembrandt would lighten the worn portions and retouch them with drypoint, which accounts for the difference that we can observe among several impressions of his compositions. And we can tell which are the good impressions of his

major etchings — The Hundred Guilder Print, The Raising of Lazarus, and others — for they display a good deal of the "dark manner."

So that his compositions would not have to wait, Rembrandt often drew them directly onto the plate, contrary to other etchers' practice, which was to finish their drawings, then transfer them to the plate. Moreover, the drawings that he etched on his plates for works to be produced with the burin were mere sketches, which he then carefully completed, as we can see from the print (which Rembrandt never finished) that shows a sculptor's studio. In that print we note a statue which has been merely outlined with the needle, and also a man who is drawing from that statue, he too is merely outlined, and very incomplete.

Rembrandt left many drawings. They are but very imperfect sketches, with the exception of some few portraits and landscapes that he was obliged to draw from nature. His only purpose in drawing was, it would appear, to develop his ideas; that is why we find several versions of the same subject, in different manners; and, as he did not intend them for posterity, he took no pains to finish them with care.

Edmé François Gersaint
Paris, 1751

758. Turbaned Soldier on Horseback, W.B. 139

758 Turbaned Soldier on Horseback

c. 1632
Signed: *RHL* (monogram in reverse)
Etching - 82 × 58 mm

This is one of the first impressions with rough plate edges.

W.B. 139; BB 32-6

There is a related drawing in Rotterdam (Benesch 151).

759 A Cavalry Fight

c. 1632
Etching - 104 × 78 mm
Two states

Second state. The plate, 108 × 83 mm in the first state, has been reduced. Shading in the background has been burnished out.

W.B. 117-II; BB 32-7 (three states)

Provenance: Citoyen Delamotte, 1801

759. A Cavalry Fight, W.B. 117

760 The Small Lion Hunt (with One Lion)

c. 1629
Etching - 157 × 117 mm
One state only

W.B. 116; BB 29-3

Rembrandt again drew inspiration from a hunting scene by
Antonio Tempesta.

761 The Small Lion Hunt (with Two Lions)

c. 1632
Etching - 155 × 124 mm
One state only

W.B. 115; BB 41-3 (two states)

762 The Large Lion Hunt

Signed and dated: *Rembrandt f. 1641*
Etching - 224 × 300 mm
Two states

First state. The head of the horse in the right foreground, shaded with open parallel lines, was heavily reworked in burin in the second state.

This is one of the three known impressions.

W.B. 114-I; BB 41-D

The subject was derived from a hunting scene engraved by Antonio Tempesta. Rembrandt projects the past into the future and nineteenth-century Orientalism emerges here.

A Brief Chronology

Rembrandt was born in Leiden on **July 15, 1606,** the eighth of the nine children of Herman Gerritszoon van Rijn, a prosperous miller, and Cornelia van Zuytbroeck, a baker's daughter.

For seven years Rembrandt attended the Latin school in Leiden. In **1620** he registered at the University but within a few months he left in order to devote all of his time to painting, becoming the pupil, first, of Jacob van Swanenburgh, then of Pieter Lastman, a renowned Dutch painter of historical subjects.

In **1624** Rembrandt opened his own studio, in his parents' house. His first dated painting, *The Stoning of St. Stephen* (fig. 585), was done the following year.

In **1628,** Rembrandt set up a studio jointly with Jan Lievens (1607-1674), a young prodigy who had also been the pupil of Pieter Lastman. In this year Rembrandt produced his first dated etchings.

On April 23, 1630, Constantin Huygens, secretary to the Staathoeder Frederic Henry, Prince of Orange-Nassau, noted in his diary, "The miller's son and the embroiderer's son are already on an equal footing with the best-known painters and will soon become more famous than they... Lievens has more grandeur and inventiveness than his friend, but the latter excels when it comes to judgment and the ability to express emotions... *Judas Returning the Thirty Pieces of Silver* **(1629)** (fig. 639) may be compared to the finest work produced by the ancient world or by the Italians. An adolescent, the beardless son of a Dutch miller, outshines Protogenes, Apelles and Parrhasios."

In April **1630,** Rembrandt's father died. The following year the painter moved to Amsterdam, setting up his studio in the house of Hendrick van Ulenborch, a dealer in paintings, antiques and objets d'art. Rembrandt's fascination with curios and fine works, so eloquently attested in the list included in the posthumous inventory of his belongings, probably stems from this association.

In **1632** Rembrandt painted his first group portrait, *Doctor Nicolaas Tulp Demonstrating the Anatomy of the Arm* (figs. 14 to 16).

On **July 22, 1634,** Rembrandt married Saskia van Ulenborch, the art dealer's wealthy niece. During this same period, the Staathoeder commissioned Rembrandt to paint three scenes from the Passion and purchased two others from him.

The following year, Rembrandt and Saskia moved into a house in the Nieuwe Doelenstraat (numbers 16-18 on that street today). Their first child, Rombertus, was born in December **1635,** but lived only two months. By now, Rembrandt had many pupils and took a new studio on the Bloemgracht.

During the period from **1636 to 1638,** Rembrandt painted his first landscapes: *Landscape with the Baptism of the Eunuch* (fig. 128), *Landscape with a Stone Bridge* (figs. 120 to 122).
In July **1638,** a daughter, Cornelia, was born; but she died within a month.

In January **1639,** the couple moved into the Binnemanstel (no. 41 Zwanenburgerstraat today). Rembrandt completed the scenes from the Passion that had been commissioned. He was able to view and take careful note of two Italian portraits, Raphael's *Castiglione* and Titian's *Ariosto.* Their influence can be seen in the self-portrait he etched the same year (fig. 724) and the one he painted in **1640** (fig. 725).

In May Rembrandt and Saskia bought a fine mansion in the Sint Anthonies Breestraat. Rembrandt was an avid collector and he filled the house with exotica and works of art. Today, this "Rembrandthuis" is a public museum.
In July **1640,** a second little Cornelia was born but soon died. In September of the same year Rembrandt's mother died.

In **1641,** the first biography of Rembrandt was published; the author was J. Orlers. In September, Titus was born and became the only one of the three children to outlive their mother.

On **June 14, 1642,** Saskia died of tuberculosis, at the age of 30. That same year, Rembrandt completed *The Night Watch* (figs. 373-374). In 1678, Samuel van Hoogstraten was to write of it: "In truth, no matter what criticisms may be made of this work, it will outlive all those that claim to equal it... Alongside this painting, all the others present are no more than playing cards."
After Saskia's death, Rembrandt hired Geertghe Dircx to take care of Titus. She became his mistress.

The years 1643-1646 were ones of intense activity. Nearing 40 during this period, Rembrandt painted *Bathsheba with King David's Letter* (fig. 610), *Saskia (Posthumous Portrait)* (fig. 343), *Christ and the Woman Taken in Adultery* (figs. 644-645), *Girl Leaning on a Windowsill* (fig. 386), *Winter Landscape* (fig. 123), *Susanna Surprised by the Elders* (fig. 609).

In **1648,** Geertghe Dircx, maintaining that Rembrandt had agreed to marry her, sued him for breach

of promise — and lost. Soon afterwards, he succeeded in having her locked up for dissolute conduct.

At the beginning of **1649,** Hendrickje Stoffels came to live with Rembrandt; they were to remain together for many years. This same year, Rembrandt, now 43, etched *The Hundred Guilder Print* (figs. 512 to 549).

Early in **1654,** Rembrandt and Hendrickje were summoned before a church tribunal on charges of living together out of wedlock; they did not appear. In July, Henrickje appeared alone; she was found guilty and denied the right to take communion.
In October, their daughter, Cornelia, was born.

In December **1660,** Rembrandt and his family — Hendrickje, Titus and Cornelia — moved into an unpretentious house on the Rozengracht (situated at no. 184 today). In August **1661,** Hendrickje drew up her will, in favor of Cornelia; it named Rembrandt as guardian and stipulated that he was to enjoy full use of the property.
In the same year, Rembrandt completed *The Conspiracy of Julius Civilis: the Oath* (figs. 36 to 38).

In **1662,** he painted *The Sampling Officials of the Drapers' Guild,* his last major portrait commission (figs. 411 to 413).

On or about about **July 21, 1663,** Hendrickje died.

On **February 10, 1668,** Titus married Magdalena van Loo. He died on September 4.
Toward the same year, Rembrandt painted *The Return of the Prodigal Son* (fig. 619).

In March **1669,** Titia, Titus's posthumous daughter, was born.
1669 is the date usually assigned to the *Simeon with the Christ Child in the Temple* (fig. 667); it may have been Rembrandt's last painting.
On **October 4, 1669,** Rembrandt died, at the age of 63. He was buried in the Westerkerk four days later.

Glossary

Border line. The ink line around the intaglio print. While the dimensions of a print are usually determined by measuring the imprint on the paper left by the edge of the metal plate, a print may be sized by measuring between border lines, when the plate mark is not fully visible.

Burin. A small quadrangular steel rod, with its end cut obliquely. The handle is shaped like a mushroom or pear cut in half. With a burin, an engraver incises the lines of his design into a copperplate. Every stroke of the tool raises a fine ridge of metal, creating a perfectly clean groove. The plate is inked and wiped so that ink remains only in the grooves. In printing, the paper picks up the ink from the grooves.

Burnisher. A polished steel tool with a flattened and rounded blade, used to polish a metal surface, rendering it smooth and shiny. The artist oils the metal plate lightly, then rubs the burnisher back and forth to break down lines, remains of burr, shallow strokes, and to erase all unwanted marks.

Burr. A ridge of metal raised by the burin or the point of the graver when lines are incised in the plate. In an engraving, the burr is removed with the help of a burnisher. In a drypoint, it is preserved; it holds ink and results in velvety blacks and soft lines.

Counterproof. An impression printed by applying a piece of paper to a freshly made, still wet print. It is lighter than the original impression, and the image is reversed. A counterproof has the advantage of showing the image in the same direction as the design in the copperplate, so the artist can see where corrections might be made.

Drypoint. Print taken from an unvarnished copperplate into which a design has been incised with a steel needle. The drypoint needle is sharper than the etching needle. The grooves that it cuts hold less ink than etched lines, since the latter are hollowed out by acid in their entire width. On the edges of the lines in drypoint, the copper forms ridges, or burr, which can become very dense if the strokes cross. The ink accumulates on the burr to create velvety blacks, especially on early impressions. The burr is fragile and wears down quickly during printing. If the artist does not want this very black effect, he can scrape off the burr with a scraper.

Edition. The group of impressions taken from a plate within a limited period of time. Editions can be distinguished by different kinds of paper and inking. Editions should not be confused with states; a state is characterized by work done on the plate itself. The size of Rembrandt's editions is not known.

Engraving. Print taken from a metal plate into which a design has been incised with a burin. Lines are cut, burr is removed, and the plate is inked and wiped. Ink remaining in the incised lines is transferred to the paper during the printing process.

Etching. Print taken from a copperplate prepared with a covering of varnish on which a design has been drawn with a steel needle. The needle removes the varnish, uncovering the copper. The plate is then immersed in nitric acid, which eats into the uncovered copper, leaving intact the areas still covered by varnish. This is called biting. The remaining varnish is then removed, and the plate is ready for inking and printing.
The acid bites the copper more or less deeply according to the length of time the plate is left in it. If the artist wants certain sections bitten more deeply, he brushes a new coat of varnish over areas to be protected, then re-immerses the plate. By rebiting the plate in this manner, lines of varying depth can be obtained.
If, after pulling a trial proof, the artist wants to make changes on the plate, he can work on the image and rebite it, make accents with a drypoint needle or burin, or diminish the blacks by destroying certain lines with a burnisher or scraper. To correct any resulting unevenness in the plate, which would mar the print, the plate may be banged on the reverse side with a hammer and thus straightened.

Flowers of sulphur. Powdered sulphur, used to create a print with a very fine grain. The copperplate is spread with a layer of oil and then dusted with a fairly thick layer of Flowers of sulphur, which eats into the copper. The length of time this substance is left on selected areas of the plate determines the tone of the areas so treated.

Hatching. Closely spaced parallel lines, used to create areas of shading; as distinguished from crosshatching, or intersecting series of such lines.

Impression. A printed sheet pulled from a plate.

Inking, wiping. Application of ink to the plate and its partial removal from the plate. After a plate has been inked, excess ink is removed by wiping first with a stiff muslin cloth and then with the palm of the hand. The wiping can be modified as desired, to leave a light transparent tone on the entire plate, or only in certain areas.

Intaglio. The generic term for all methods of incising grooves in metal plates: engraving, etching, drypoint, etc.

Needle. A steel implement with a point of variable sharpness, solidly fixed into a handle that is easily manipulated, like a crayon. It is used for incising lines into a plate.

Plate. A flat piece of metal on which the artist works his design.

Plate mark. In intaglio printing, the imprint on the paper produced by the edges of the plate. The dimensions of a print are usually determined by measuring the plate mark.

Press. A machine for printing from a plate. In intaglio printing, two rollers of the same diameter are used, between which passes a sliding bed supporting the inked plate and paper.

Scraper. A sharp, three-sided, wedge-shaped steel tool (also called a parer) used to remove ridges or burr from the plate. Burin grooves can be removed with this tool; it is used for all corrections that must be made by rubbing out.

State. The condition of the plate at various stages of the artist's work. Impressions taken from the different states of a plate permit its history and the evolution of the artist's work to be reconstructed. An impression in pure etching is the impression taken from a plate which has as yet undergone only the biting by acid that creates the essential lines of the composition. The plate is usually finished by supplementary work in burin, drypoint, etc.

Stroke. Incision made by the artist in the plate. The artist may create shading by the use of various types of strokes, including simple lines with no intersection (different tonal values are created by varying their thickness and placement); hatching (a series of parallel lines); crosshatching (two series of parallel lines intersecting one another); and *contretaille* (lines of uneven depth that cross one another at right angles or obliquely).

Rembrandt's Materials

Rembrandt sought varied effects when he printed his plates. He often did this himself with two presses for printmaking: one made of an exotic wood; the other, which was his own, of oak. He experimented with the inking of etched copper, with the wiping, with the printing process itself, and especially with the kinds of supports used, with their absorption capacity, tones, textures, suppleness.

He used parchment, vellum Japanese paper, Chinese paper, Indian paper, cartridge paper (oatmeal paper), and, especially, white European paper. Sometimes he prepared the paper himself, dyeing it or glazing it (W.B. 23-I, 78-IV, 40).

To obtain more nuanced shadows, a kind of washing, imprecise blacks on certains parts of the sheet, he would leave a film of ink on his plate (inking effect or surface tone).

Lights and shadows varied according to the background (white, bluish, pearly, gold, gray, reddish, yellowish), the surface (smooth, grainy, uneven), the sheet (stiff or supple, permeable or not). These differences meant that the same plate could give entirely different effects.

Rembrandt usually used European paper, which was easier to find. It was an ordinary white laid paper, made by hand, as were all papers until 1812. It was composed essentially of linen and hemp fibers, and imported from Germany or Switzerland until about 1650. Later it came from France, though high-quality French paper was known as Holland paper. The Japanese paper on which Rembrandt printed a great many etchings came from Nagasaki via Batavia in Java. It was made from plants called *gamfi* or *itsumata*. Dutch etchers used it as early as the seventeenth century, though with certain exceptions it was not used by other European etchers until the nineteenth. Less absorbent than "Holland paper," it allowed very delicate nuances of tone and sumptuous blacks, while avoiding contrasts that were too marked. Rembrandt, as a painter-etcher, as a great colorist of shadow and of light, appreciated all its subtleties (W.B. 104-I, W.B. 197-III, W.B. 199-I and II, W.B. 200).

Chinese paper — an inaccurate designation since it probably did not come from China — was an Oriental paper, thinner and more fragile than that from Japan, which was usually pasted to another paper to make it more resistant. It rendered the whole scale of white to black with even greater subtlety (W.B. 22-I, 74-I, 76-III, 285).

Indian paper, with a strongly yellowish or reddish tint and a very obvious texture, was similar to that used in Indian miniatures (W.B. 76-IV, 199-I, 200).

Vellum, made from the skin of a still-born calf, smoother, more diaphanous, whiter than parchment, absorbs little ink. Contours are vague and imprecise, the passage from diffused light to velvety shadows is a melting one (W.B. 76-IV, 199-I, 200).

Parchment gives the same effects as vellum, but more markedly. Thicker and more rigid, it is particularly sensitive to humidity and yellows with time (W.B. 78-I).

Gisèle Lambert

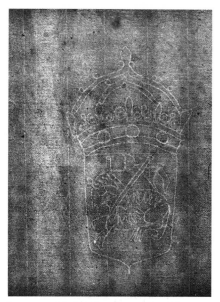

Coat of arms with lamb surmounted by a crown
Near Heawood 2842-2843
Clump of Trees with a Vista, 1652 - W.B. 222-II

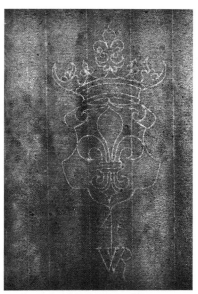

The lily of Strasbourg in an escutcheon surmounted by a crown and terminated by the *4* lorrainer and the letters WR
Near Heawood 1785
The Goldweigher's Field, 1651; (counter-impression) W.B. 234

The cross of Basle; near Heawood 1203
Diana at the Bath, c. 1631 - W.B. 201

The watermarks

Only laid paper, used exclusively until the manufacture of wove paper in 1755, is characterized by the imprint of the metal screen on which it rests in the mold: a sheet held up to the light shows the laid and chain lines, and — if there is one — the watermark. The latter, the trade mark of the paper mill, is a wire device fastened to the screen.

The watermark is useful in researching the provenance, date, and format of the paper, and it supplies certain complementary information to the study of a print. Existing watermark dictionaries still identify very few trade marks of paper used in printmaking. In the absence of other, more specific documents, however, these are valuable for comparative purposes.

Watermarks can be accurately reproduced by means of the beta radiograph, a kind of photograph that uses a source of beta rays. Since the absorption of these rays depends on the thickness of the paper penetrated, traces of ink, writing or printing that the paper bears are practically invisible, unless the ink contains metal salts; on the other hand, irregularities in the paper such as watermarks or laid and chain lines are easily located.

Once the watermark is found, the print is placed between the radioactive source and a photographic film. The radioactive source is a source of carbon 14, which has the appearance of a sheet of extremely flexible plastic. The exposure time, varying between two and a half and three hours, depends on the source used and on the thickness of the paper.

Reproduction of a number of beta radiographs taken during the restoration of certain etchings on exhibition

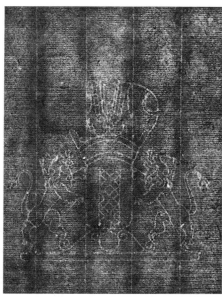

The arms of Amsterdam; near Heawood 419-420
Christ Preaching ("La Petite Tombe"), c. 1652 - W.B. 67

The Raising of Lazarus, 1632 - W.B. 73-IV, VIII

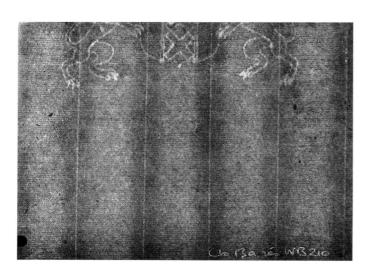

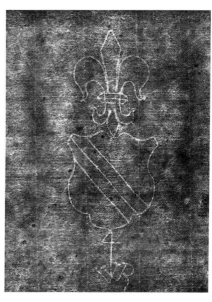

View of Amsterdam from the Northwest, c. 1640 - W.B. 210
(fragment of the arms: lower section)

Escutcheon surmounted by a lily and terminated by the letters
WR; Heawood 141

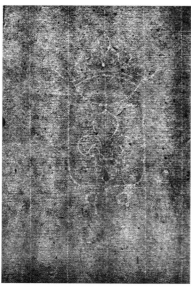

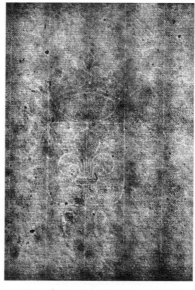

Coat of arms with a lily surmounted by a crown with the
letters PR below; near Heawood 1663
"Ledikant" or "Le lit à la française," 1646 - W.B. 186-IV

The Artist Drawing from the Model, c. 1639 - W.B. 192-II

Coat of arms terminated by a star; near Heawood 482
Self-Portrait in a Cap and Scarf with the Face Dark, 1633
W.B. 17-II

Crowned escutcheon. Heawood 138 reversed
Peter and John at the Gate of the Temple, c. 1629
W.B. 95

Double-headed eagle; near Heawood 1298
Abraham Casting Out Hagar and Ishmael, 1637
W.B. 30

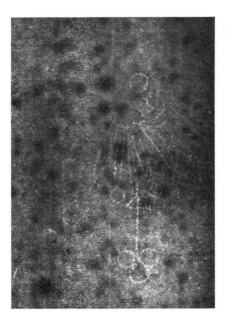

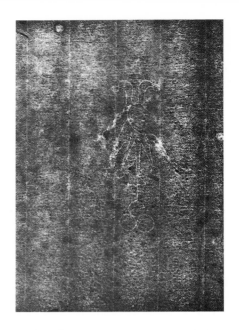

Head of madman; near Heawood 1930
Six's Bridge, 1645 - W.B. 208

The Three Trees, 1643 - W.B. 212

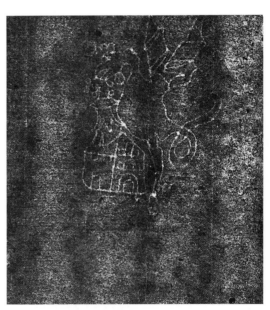

Griffin; near Heawood 842
Self-Portrait with Plumed Cap and Lowered Sabre, 1634
W.B. 23-I

W.B. 23-II (same watermark reversed; the griffin on the right)

I. Selected General Bibliography of Rembrandt

Amsterdam, Catalogue realised by F. Schmidt-Degener, Exhibition 1932

Amsterdam-Rotterdam, Catalogue, Exhibition 1956

R. Avermaete, *Rembrandt et son temps,* Paris, 1952

K. Bauch, *Rembrandt Gemälde,* Berlin 1966

O. Benesch, "Rembrandt and ancient history," *Art Quarterly,* 22, 1959, pp. 309-332

O. Benesch, *Rembrandt,* Geneva, 1957

O. Benesch, *Collected writings,* vol. I, *Rembrandt,* London 1970

W. Bode and C. Hofstede de Groot, *Rembrandt : beschreibendes Verzeichnis Gemälde mit den heliographischen Nachbildungen,* Paris, 1897-1905

P. Bonafoux, *Rembrandt, autoportrait,* Geneva, 1985

A. Bredius, *Rembrandt's Paintings,* London (and Vienna), 1935 (2d. ed., London, 1937; Paris, 1950)

A. Bredius, *Rembrandt, The complete edition of the paintings,* revised by H. Gerson, London, 1969

Ch. M. Briquet, *Les filigranes,* Geneva, 1907

J. Burckhardt, "Rembrandt," lecture of November 6th 1877, reproduced in *Burckhardt Gesamtausgabe,* 14, Stuttgart, 1933, pp. 178-197

J. Bruyn, B. Haak, S. H. Levie, P. J. J. van Thiel, E. van de Wetering, *A corpus of Rembrandt Paintings* (Stichting Foundation, Rembrandt Research Project, The Hague, Boston, London, 1982)

W. A. Churchill, *Watermarks in the Seventeenth and Eighteenth Centuries,* Amsterdam, 1935

K. Clark, *Rembrandt and the Italian Renaissance,* New York, 1966

J. Foucart, P. Lecaldano, *Tout l'œuvre peint de Rembrandt,* Paris, 1971

H. E. van Gelder, *Rembrandt,* Amsterdam, 1948

H. E. van Gelder, "Constantijn Huygens en Rembrandt," *Oud Holland,* 74, 1959, pp. 174-179

H. Gerson, *Seven letters by Rembrandt,* The Hague, 1961. Reports

H. Gerson, *Rembrandt Paintings,* New York, 1968 (French ed. 1969)

B. Haak, *Rembrandt: His Life, His Work, His Time* (American ed.), New York, 1969

C. Hofstede de Groot, *Beschreibendes und kritisches Verzeichnis der Werke der hervorragendsten Hollandischen Maler des XVII Jahrhunderts,* vol. VI, Stuttgart, 1915

R. Hamann, *Rembrandt,* Potsdam, 1948

E. Haverkamp Begemann, *Hercules Seghers,* Rotterdam, 1954

Ed. Heawood, *Watermarks,* Hilversum, 1950

A. M. Hind, *Rembrandt,* Cambridge, 1932

M. Hours, "Rembrandt: Observations et présentations de radiographies...," Bulletin du laboratoire du Musée du Louvre, 6, 1961, pp. 3-43

Cl. de Jonghe, *Inventaire des estampes de Rembrandt...* February 11, 1679, in Oud Holland, VIII, 1980, pp. 180-181

G. Knuttel, *Rembrandt,* Amsterdam, 1956

Leningrad: *Catalogue of paintings, Department of Occidental Art,* Hermitage, Leningrad-Moscow, 1958 (in Russian)

London, National Gallery: N. MacLaren, *The Dutch school,* London, 1960; *Acquisitions,* 1953-1962; *The National Gallery,* June 1962-December, 1964

F. Lugt, *Les Marques de Collections de dessins et d'estampes,* Amsterdam, 1921; Supplement The Hague, 1956

A. Hyatt Mayor, Prints and People: *A Social History of Printed Pictures,* New York, 1971

A. Hyatt Mayor, *Rembrandt and the Bible,* New York, 1979

E. Michel, *Rembrandt: sa vie, son œuvre et son temps,* Paris, 1893

L. Münz, *Rembrandt Harmensz. van Rijn,* New York, 1954

J. E. Muller, *Rembrandt,* Paris, 1968

Munich: E. Brocchhagen, *Holländische Malerei des 17. Jahrhunderts,* Munich, 1967

C. Neumann, *Rembrandt,* Berlin, 1902

F. W. Robinson, "Rembrandt's influence in the 18th century Venise," *Nederlands Kunsthistorisch jaarboek,* 18, 1967, pp. 167-196

J. Rosenberg, S. Slive and E. H. ter Kuile, *Dutch art and architecture 1600-1800,* Harmandsworth 1966, pp. 48-100

J. Rosenberg, *Rembrandt,* Cambridge (Mass.) 1948

H. M. Rotermund, "Rembrandt und die religiosen Laienbewegungen in den Niederlanden seiner Zeit," *Nederlandsch Kunsthistorisch jaarboek,* 4, 1952-53, pp. 104-192

H. M. Rotermund, *Rembrandt's Drawings and Etchings for the Bible,* Pilgrim Press, Philadelphia, 1969

W. Scheidegg, *Rembrandt und seine Werke in der Dresdener Galerie,* Dresden, 1958

F. Schmidt-Degener, *Verzamelde studiën en essays, 2. Rembrandt,* Amsterdam, 1950

J. Smith, *A Catalogue raisonné of the works of the most eminent Dutch, Flemish and French painters,* vol. VII, London, 1836

W. R. Valentiner, *Rembrandt: des Meister Gemälde* (Klassiker der Kunst), Stuttgart, 1921 (2d ed.)

J. Veth, *Rembrandt Leven en Kunst,* Amsterdam, 1906

C. Vosmaer, *Rembrandt: sa vie et ses œuvres,* The Hague, 1877,

A. B. de Vries, *Rembrandt,* Baarn, 1956

W. Weisbach, *Rembrandt,* Berlin, 1926

C. White, "Did Rembrandt ever visit England?" *Apollo,* 76, 1962, pp. 177-184

C. White, *Rembrandt and his world,* London, 1964

C. Wright, *Rembrandt: Self-Portraits,* London, 1982

J. Bruyn, B. Haak, S.H. Levie, P.J.J. van Thiel, E. van de Wetering, *A Corpus of Rembrandt Paintings,* Martinus Nijhoff Publishers, The Hague, Boston, London 1986

II. Some Catalogues of the Etchings in Chronological Order

E. F. Gersaint, Catalogue raisonné de toutes les pièces qui forment l'œuvre de Rembrandt, composé par feu M. Gersaint et mis au jour avec les augmentations nécessaires par les sieurs Helle et Glomy, Paris, 1751

P. Yver, Supplément au catalogue raisonné de M. Gersaint, M. Helle et M. Glomy, Amsterdam, 1756

D. Daulby, A Descriptive Catalogue of the Works of Rembrandt and of his Scholars..., Liverpool, 1796

A. Bartsch, Catalogue raisonné de toutes les estampes qui forment l'œuvre de Rembrandt, Vienna 1797, 2 vol.

J. J. de Claussin, Catalogue raisonné. New edition, Paris, 1824; supplement 1828

Th. Wilson, A Descriptive Catalogue of the Prints of Rembrandt by an Amateur, London, 1836

Ch. H. Middleton-Wake, Descriptive Catalogue of the Etched Work of Rembrandt van Ryn, London, 1878

Ch. Blanc, l'œuvre complet de Rembrandt décrit et commenté. Catalogue raisonné de toutes les estampes..., 2 vol., Paris 1859-61; 3rd ed. 1880

E. Dutuit, Catalogue de l'œuvre gravé de Rembrandt, in his *Manuel de l'Amateur*, V, 1882, and supplement in vol. VI, 1885

D. Rovinski, L'œuvre gravé de Rembrandt, Reproductions des planches dans tous leurs états successifs... Avec un catalogue raisonné. Text 1 vol., repr. 3 vol., Saint-Petersburg, 1890

C. Dodgson, Annotated Chronological Catalogue of Rembrandt's Etchings in P. G. Hamerton, *The Etchings of Rembrandt*, London, 1904

W. von Seidlitz, Kritisches Verzeichniss der Radierungen Rembrandts, zugleich eine Anleitung zu deren Studium, Leipzig, 1895; 2d ed. 1922

H. W. Singer, Rembrandt's Radierungen in 402 Abbildungen. *Klassiker der Kunst,* Stuttgart, 1906; 2d ed. 1910

A. Ch. Coppier, Les eaux-fortes de Rembrandt. L'ensemble de l'œuvre gravé..., catalogue chronologique des eaux-fortes et de leurs états, Paris, 1922

A. M. Hind, A Catalogue of Rembrandt's Etchings, chronologically arranged and completely illustrated. 2 vol., London, 1912; 2d ed. 1923

L. Münz, A Critical Catalogue of Rembrandt's Etchings..., 2 vol., London, 1952

G. Björklund and O. Barnard, Rembrandt's Etchings true and false. A Summary Catalogue, Stockholm, London, New York; 2d revised edition 1968

K. G. Boon and Ch. White, Rembrandt van Rijn, Houstein's Dutch and Flemish etchings, engravings and woodcuts, 2 vol., Amsterdam, 1969

III. Some Catalogues of Etchings and Drawings Exhibitions in Chronological Order

London, British Museum. *Guide to an Exhibition of Drawings and Etchings by Rembrandt, and Etchings by other Masters,* by S. Colvin. London, 1899

Paris, Bibliothèque Nationale. Exposition d'œuvres de Rembrandt. Dessins et gravures. Catalogue written by F. Courboin, J. Guibert, P. A. Lemoisne. Paris, 1908

Amsterdam, Rijksmuseum, Rotterdam, Museum Boymans, Rembrandt, etsen. *Tentoonstelling ter herdenking van de geboorte van Rembrandt* op 15 juli 1606. Amsterdam, 1956

Paris, Bibliothèque Nationale. *Rembrandt graveur.* Catalogue written by Jean Vallery-Radot and Jean Adhémar. Paris, 1956

London, British Museum. *The late etchings of Rembrandt.* Ch. White, London, 1969

Washington, National Gallery of Art. *Rembrandt.* Washington, 1969

Boston, Museum of Fine Arts. New York, Pierpont Morgan Library. *Rembrandt: Experimental Etcher.* Boston, New York, 1969

Paris, Musée du Louvre. *Les plus belles eaux-fortes de Rembrandt.* Paris, 1969-1970

Brussels, Rotterdam, Paris. *Dessins flamands et hollandais du xvii*e *siècle.* Collections of the Hermitage, Leningrad and of the Pouchkine Museum, Moscow, 1972-1973

Boston, Museum of Fine Arts. Saint-Louis, The Saint-Louis Art Museum. *Printmaking in the Age of Rembrandt.* Boston, Saint-Louis, 1981

Amsterdam, Museum het Rembrandthuis. Work in process. *Rembrandt etchings in different states.* Eva Ornstein van Slooten. Amsterdam, 1981

Paris, Musée du Petit Palais. *Rembrandt, Eaux-fortes,* 1986

This volume includes all of Rembrandt's etchings with the followings exceptions: works "attributed" to him or works carried out by pupils, and a few subjects which do not fit in with the theme "The Human Figure and Spirit", such as Sleeping puppy W.B. 158, The Shell W.B. 159, The Bull W.B. 253.

Index of Illustrations

* Not included in the Benesch catalogue. Benesch analyzes it in the
Annual Review of the Museums of Berlin, in an article on the rencently
discovered Rembrandt drawings.

Photographic Credits

Amsterdam, Art Promotion 396; Rembrandt's House 117, 119, 733; Rijksmuseum (Rijksprentenkabinet) 8, 18, 19, 115, 120 to 122, 157, 288, 292, 304, 306, 338, 368, 373, 374, 383, 409, 411 to 413, 489, 578, 583, 588, 606, 622, 669, 671, 672, 678, 679, 746 — **Basel,** Oeffentliche Kunstsammlung 586 — **Berlin-**
Dahlem (Staatliche Museum, Gemäldegalerie, Kupferstichkabinett); 3, 27, 33, 95, 107, 129, 273, 279, 280, 343, 370, 393, 589, 600, 609, 612, 614, 618, 646, 650, 711, 713, 715 — **Brunswick,** Herzog Anton Ulrich Museum 126, 326, 432, 433 — **Brussels,** Musée Royal des Beaux-Arts 369 — **Budapest,** Museum of Fine Arts 93, 283 — **Cambridge,** Fitzwilliam Museum 109 — **Cambridge,** Massachussetts, Fogg Art Museum 91, 624 — **Cassel,** Gemäldegalerie 313, 318, 320, 324, 325, 333, 358, 395, 632, 670, 712, 735 — **Chatsworth,** Derbyshire, Devonshire Collection 99 to 106, 108, 110 to 112, 116, 294, 399, 568, 581, 599 — **Chicago,** Art Institute 314, 380 — **Cincinnati,** Ohio, The Taft Museum 359, 398 — **Cleveland,** Ohio, Museum of Art 319, 345, 621 — **Cologne,** Wallraf - Richartz Museum 747 — **Copenhagen,** Hans Petersen 652 — **Cracow,** Czartoryski Museum 127 — **Darmstadt,** Hessisches Landesmuseum 35 — **Detroit,** Michigan, The Detroit Institute of Art 607, 627 — **Dresden,** Deutsche Fotothek 2, 6, 7, 13, 287, 293, 302, 332, 342, 604, 605 — **Drumlanrig Castle,** Scotland, Collection of the Duke of Buccleuch 402 — **Dublin,** National Gallery of Ireland 633, 634 — **Edinburgh,** National Gallery of Scotland 346, 390 to 392, 738 — **Frankfurt,** Städelsches Kunstinstitut 570, 598, 613 — **Glasgow,** Art Gallery and Museum 9, 420, 702; Hunterian Art Gallery 663 — **Glens Falls,** New York, The Hyde Collection 628 — **Gothenburg,** Konstmuseum 410 — **Haarlem,** Teylers Museum 89, 118, 284, 298, 579 — **Hamburg,** Kunsthalle 572, 640 — **Innsbruck,** TLMF, Fotoarchiv 312 — **Karlsruhe,** Staatliche Kunsthalle 728 — **The Hague,** Royal Library 569; Mauritshuis 11, 14 to 16, 311, 397, 407, 425, 608, 613, 643, 684, 717, 749 — **Lausanne,** André Held 10, 123 to 125, 128, 307, 310, 323, 330, 341, 365, 387, 389, 406, 592, 593, 597, 598, 610, 611, 616, 617, 619, 625, 629, 630, 655, 660, 661, 664, 665, 666, 668, 677, 705, 710, 741 — **Liverpool,** Walker Art Gallery 685 — **London,** British Museum 26, 294A, 305, 571, 573, 574, 582, 673; Courtauld Institute of Art 428; Dulwich Gallery 386, 418; Edward Speelman, Empire House 716; Kenwood House, The Iveagh Bequest 742; National Gallery 12, 340, 344, 354, 401, 414, 415, 421, 601, 635, 644, 656, 662, 725, 748; Buckingham Palace, Royal Collection 321, 355, 371, 372; Photographic Records Limited 379, 381; Victoria and Albert Museum 638; Wallace Collection 130, 363, 364, 404, 726 — **Los Angeles,** California, Los Angeles Museum of Art 651 — **Lugano,** Thyssen-Bornemisza Collection 727 — **Lyons,** Musée des Beaux-Arts 585 — **Madrid,** Prado 5, 339 — **Melbourne,** National Gallery of Victoria 427, 590 — **Montreal,** Museum of Fine Arts 423 — **New York,** Art Resource 352, 353, 648, 683; The Frick Collection 315, 400; The Metropolitan Museum of Art 20, 94, 322, 360, 377, 378, 388, 394, 426, 580, 626, 647, 720, 740, 745; The Pierpont Morgan Library 282; Malcolm Varon 98 — **Nuremberg,** Germanisches Nationalmuseum 591 — **Oeiras,** Portugal, Calouste Gulbenkian Foundation 419 — **Ottawa,** National Gallery of Canada 595, 596, 649 — **Oxford,** Ashmolean Museum 295; Thomas Photos 376 — **Paris,** Bulloz 329, 653; Giraudon 114 — **Pasadena,** California, Norton Simon Foundation 721 — **Prague,** Národuí Gallery 361 — **Rotterdam,** Museum Boymans-van Beuningen 90, 92, 113, 274 to 276, 281, 289 to 291, 296, 297, 300, 301, 303, 367, 382, 403, 576, 584, 620, 743 — **San Diego,** San Diego Museum of Art 316 — **San Francisco,** M. H. de Young Memorial Museum 327 — **Stockholm,** Nationalmuseum 25, 36, 37, 38, 97, 278, 285, 328, 384, 594, 667, 686 — **Stuttgart,** Staatsgalerie 575 — **Tokyo,** Bridgestone Museum of Art 587 — **Toledo,** Ohio, Toledo Museum of Art 317 — **Toronto,** Carlo Catenazzi 417 — **Tours,** Photo Arsicaud 637 — **Vienna,** Albertina 277, 286, 577, 744; Kunsthistorisches Museum 308, 356, 357, 405, 734, 736, 737 — **Villeneuve sur Lot,** Ray Delvert 658 — **Washington,** D.C., National Gallery of Art 331, 362, 366, 385, 416, 424, 429, 431, 615, 641, 654, 723, 739 — **Windsor,** Windsor Castle, Royal Collection 309 — **Woburn Abbey,** Collection of the Duke of Bedford 375.

The black-and-white reproductions of the etchings are from plates made by the photography department of the Bibliothèque Nationale and by Guy Vivien, Paris.

Printed by Mondadori Verona with the collaboration of Mondgraph, Paris

763. **The Abduction of Ganymede** (detail of fig. 7)
764. **Woman Going Downstairs with a Child in Her Arms** (detail of fig. 282).